REVOLUTIONS IN AMERICANS' LIVES

Recent Titles in **Contributions in Family Studies**

A Coat of Many Colors: Jewish Subcommunities in the United States
Abraham D. Lavender, Editor

Passing: The Vision of Death in America
Charles O. Jackson, Editor

Cross-Cultural Perspectives of Mate-Selection and Marriage
George Kurian, Editor

A Social History of American Family Sociology, 1865-1940
Ronald L. Howard, Edited by John Mogey

Women in the Family and in the Economy: An International
Comparative Survey
George Kurian and Ratna Ghosh, Editors

REVOLUTIONS IN AMERICANS' LIVES

A Demographic Perspective on the History of Americans, Their Families, and Their Society

Robert V. Wells

Contributions in Family Studies, Number 6

Greenwood Press
WESTPORT, CONNECTICUT • LONDON, ENGLAND

Library of Congress Cataloging in Publication Data

Wells, Robert V., 1943-
    Revolutions in Americans' lives.

    (Contributions in family studies, ISSN 0147-1023;
no. 6)
    Bibliography: p.
    Includes index.
    1. United States—Population—History. 2. Family—
United States—History. 3. United States—Social conditions. I. Title. II. Series.
HB3505.W4   304.6′0973   81-6949
ISBN 0-313-23019-6   (lib. bdg.)   AACR2

Library of Congress Catalog Card Number: 81-6949
ISBN: 0-313-23019-6
ISSN: 0147-1023

First published in 1982

Greenwood Press
A division of Congressional Information Service, Inc.
88 Post Road West
Westport, Connecticut 06881

Printed in the United States of America

10 9 8 7 6 5 4 3 2 1

CONTENTS

ILLUSTRATIONS

TABLES

PREFACE

For a number of reasons, it is appropriate that this particular work should be published in a series of books on the family. Although this study is, at heart, a demographic history, most of the fundamental events with which we are concerned here, that is, birth, death, marriage, and migration, occur within a family context and can only be fully understood by taking the influence of families into consideration. The individual who experiences these phenomena in isolation is the exception rather than the rule. Similarly, the realities of family life (if not necessarily the ideals) are shaped by demographic limits and change in response to new demographic patterns. For example, until both birth and death rates are relatively low, it is unlikely that many households will contain three generations of a family, whether they want to or not.

In addition, many of the most important recent discoveries made by historians of past populations use methods that rely on the family as the primary unit of investigation. Family reconstitution, a method of analysis akin to genealogy made famous by the French demographer, Louis Henry, is, more than anything else, responsible for the recent surge of interest in demographic history. Henry and his colleagues demonstrated that it was possible to learn far more about the private lives of seventeenth- and eighteenth-century men and women than most historians and demographers realized. This discovery combined with questions about what had happened to families in the first century of European settlement in America to stimulate a great deal of research into patterns of birth, death, marriage, and family life that were once considered beyond the reach of historians.

A second line of historical research of great value has developed from the use of censuses that provide information for separate households. Some of the findings produced by these studies have been closely related to the topics best examined by family reconstitution—namely, childbearing and marriage. Others have provided fascinating insights into residential patterns and the amount and direction of mobility in American society.

The scholars who have produced this work have come from a variety of backgrounds. Some, like myself, began with questions about demographic patterns in the past; others started with an historical interest in family life. But in the end it is difficult, and in fact not very desirable, to be solely a demographic or family historian. Both subject and method make it necessary to draw on and contribute to both lines of inquiry. After almost two decades of exciting new discoveries, it is difficult to imagine anyone wanting to abandon the rich interaction that results from combining the theoretical perspectives and empirical results of history, demography, and family studies.

In spite of the broad interaction among these and other disciplines, the nature of the records that can be used in demographic history means that most of the studies to date have been narrowly confined by subject and place. As a result, we know a suprising amount about childbearing among eighteenth-century American Quakers, the experiences of Italian immigrants who lived in Chicago at the end of the nineteenth century, the effects of yellow fever in New Orleans in 1853, and the willingness of Americans to move over the last three centuries. We know far less about how these various phenomena relate to each other and to the trends and events that have long attracted the attention of historians, even though such knowledge would obviously benefit specialists in demographic and family history, as well as others whose interest in the American past is more general.

This book is intended to remedy that defect by offering a synthesis of American demographic history that is, in turn, used to broaden and even alter our understanding of many of the topics that have attracted the attention of previous students of life in America. The nature of the subject and sources means that family patterns receive as much or more attention as any other aspect of American history. In fact, American families are the principal concern of three chapters, and are regularly mentioned elsewhere. However, the book goes beyond family life to suggest the value of the demographic perspective, not only for studying the history of Americans and their families, but also to gain insights into the politics, economics, and social structures of particular times and places. Thus, the synthetic effort involves both American demographic history and American history on a much broader scale.

Synthetic efforts are especially beneficial when a field is well established with a rich collection of detailed studies or when a field is just opening up and there is need for some suggestions about what the main lines of research and interpretation are and ought to be. Because of the state of the discipline, this work clearly falls in the second category. It is an outline of what we know and what we would like to know; it is *not* a final statement on the subject. It is an invocation rather than a benediction; an artist's sketch to guide further work rather than a finished painting to be hung on the wall for display. I have written it as part of my own education about the importance of population in American history and have decided to share it in the hope that others will find the perspective offered here useful in their own work. No doubt I could have written several different versions of this study in terms of detail and emphasis. Even now a multivolume work would be possible, although it would vary widely in depth of analysis. My choice for a relatively brief overview reflects not only my own needs at present, but also my conclusion that an additional twenty years of scholarship, reacting in part to this kind of study, would make a much fuller project more feasible and more effective.

Some comments about how this book was researched and written are in order, if only because it is not a normal scholarly monograph, or even a survey of an old, established field. There are ample sources for this project, but they vary widely in nature. For some topics it is possible and, in fact, necessary to rely on basic demographic records like censuses or lists of births, marriages, and deaths. But most of this study is based on the work of others. Where previous work exists it ranges in quantity and quality from topics, such as international migration, with a rich and varied literature that has already been subjected to synthesis, to other subjects, such as mortality in early America, that are just beginning to develop enough literature to allow some tentative generalizations. Perhaps the most important thing to keep in mind is that even the works on demographic history asked questions that were, generally, more narrowly defined than those posed here, while the studies of other scholars were produced in response to queries quite different from mine. What is surprising is how closely related studies of medicine, migration, or the family (to name but a few) can be, even though the authors wrote them without reference to, or even knowledge of each others' work. A list of the disciplines that have contributed to my understanding of the story that follows is, by itself, impressive. In addition to the works of historians (some with demographic interests, and some who would be surprised that I found their efforts relevant), I have had occasion to use the findings of actuaries, anthropologists, archeologists, biologists, demographers, economists, geographers, medical men and women, meteorologists, political scientists, psychologists, sociologists (of the family and otherwise), and statisticians. The notes and bibliography provided here refer only to the most important and influential of the more than 1,500 items consulted during the research for this volume. Although references to specific works frequently are intended to acknowledge the source of particular pieces of information or insights, often the citations are to studies which led me to conclusions different from or beyond those of their authors. Thus, what may appear to readers familiar with parts of this literature as misreading on my part is, in fact, only a rereading, from a quite different perspective. Such, I suspect, is the nature of synthesis as opposed to survey or summary. The publisher of this volume has agreed to issue a separate guide to the literature on American demographic history which will present the full range of materials upon which this book is based.

A study that draws on works from a wide variety of disciplines must inevitably transfer concepts developed for one set of needs into a different context. This is particularly perplexing when specialists disagree about the meaning of the terms they use. I have tried to avoid becoming involved in definitional arguments; the result has been to use some terms less precisely than some scholars might prefer, but in most cases the meaning is clear. For example, I have often used *urban area* and *city* interchangeably, even though a case can be made that cities are only a part of a more general urban experience. Likewise, I have referred to both *regions* and *ethnic groups* in exploring the effects of cultural differences among various groups of Americans on our history. Whichever term I have used, I have been concerned with the values and attitudes, shared by groups of people, that shape not only the ways they relate to each other, but also how they respond to their physical and social surroundings, and the ways they organize their lives on the most personal and basic levels. *Race* on the other hand, has been used in a biological sense, most often in reference to differences in life expectancy. Comments on differences between black and white Americans, or between various groups of European immigrants, should always be understood as referring to differences originating in culture rather than race, except where otherwise noted. *Family* is another term with a variety of meanings, several of which will be used and defined in the text.

With rare exceptions, this study is limited to those parts of North America that eventually became part of the United States. However, the political boundaries of a continental nation such as the United States may not be the most appropriate limits for studies of migration, epidemics, sex ratios, or childbearing. Future studies may suggest that broader frameworks, such as North America or the Atlantic basin, or more local studies, of the Mississippi River Valley, or the Pacific coastal regions, are more logical for demographic history. For the moment those possibilities remain unexamined.

With these thoughts in mind, I hope the reader finds this book as challenging, thought-provoking, and enjoyable to read as I found writing it to be. I also hope that at least some readers may be stimulated to pursue further the issues and perspectives presented here.

One of the most pleasant tasks a writer has is to thank all those who have made his burdens lighter. In his book, *Land and Life*, the prominent geographer Carl Sauer quotes William Osler, an important late nineteenth- and early twentieth-century doctor, who in turn was quoting Saint Chrysostom about the need of every scholar to have a time and place for reflection. The saint advised, "Depart from the highway and transport thyself, in some enclosed ground, for it is hard for a tree which stands by the wayside to keep her fruit till it be ripe." To Union College, the Charles Warren Center for Studies in American History, and the John Simon Guggenheim Foundation, I am grateful for the chance to depart from the wayside. Whether the fruit is now ripe is a matter for each who partakes to judge.

Notes and bibliography serve as partial thanks to the many scholars upon whose work I have relied. More specific thanks go to students who have responded to earlier efforts to develop the ideas presented here in class, especially to Bruce Downsbrough, Steven Levy, Olivette Simmons, and Andrew Walsh. Kay Pontius both took the course from which this book evolved and provided valuable research assistance at a later date. Robert Fisher, Robert Gough, Mary Beth Norton, Peter Wood, and the Warren Center fellows of 1974–1975 offered encouragement and advice at various points along the way. Finally my wife, Cathie; my daughters, Lisa and Vanessa; my parents, Ronald and Patricia; and my brother, David, have contributed as much or more to the shaping of this study by direct effect as the scholars who are mentioned in the formal citations.

REVOLUTIONS IN AMERICANS' LIVES

1

RHYTHMS OF LIFE AND
RHYTHMS OF HISTORY

Twentieth-century Americans live in a world unique in human history. During the last two centuries, changes have occurred in the most basic aspects of human existence—birth, death, marriage, and migration—that have profoundly altered the way we live. Perhaps only the shifts associated with the emergence of the first civilizations thousands of years ago have transformed patterns of life to an equal or greater extent. Over the last 200 years, the number of children in an average family has been cut by more than half, and health and life expectancy have improved enough that today children have a better chance to celebrate their sixtieth birthdays than many babies born before 1800 had of living to the age of one! Millions of people migrated to the United States where they joined the already mobile natives to transform the nation from a cluster of thirteen agriculturally oriented states along the Atlantic seaboard to a continental country of forty-eight states inhabited by a majority of city dwellers.

One effect of these changes was a rise in the total population from about 2.5 million in 1770 to over 200 million in 1970. Another was to increase the proportion of people over the age of sixty-five to more than double that found in most groups in the past. As might be expected, new rhythms of life emerged, which in turn required and produced major adjustments in personal behavior and family patterns, and broader social, economic, and political affairs. Some of the changes occurred easily, but others produced anxieties and uncertainties that are still with us. Social and psychological patterns based on demographic realities thousands of years old are not quickly altered.

Historians have long been aware of these revolutions in Americans' lives but have generally dealt with them in part or in passing. This book marks the first systematic effort to place demographic factors in a dominant position rather than on the edges of history. The organization of this study revolves around two basic principles. First, to demonstrate the full impact of these changes, they will be considered first from the perspective of individuals, then of families, and finally of society as a whole. This approach differs from normal demographic analysis that begins with general patterns and only occasionally works down to families or individuals. The fact that general patterns emerge from the actions and decisions of numerous individuals and their families makes it desirable to try to understand the rhythms of life in the past from the perspective of the individuals who lived then.

People's experiences with birth, death, marriage, and migration are central to the way they live out their lives. The most basic rhythms of human existence revolve around how often new relationships are established by birth, marriage, or migration, and how frequently death or movement break old ties. Not only are the day-to-day and year-to-year rhythms of life determined by these factors, but becoming a parent, losing a loved one, marrying, or moving often mark a major change in the life of an individual. Presidents, tariffs, treaties, and congresses can come and go without the profound effect that a single birth or death may have.

To focus exclusively on actual experiences with childbearing, death, marriage, and migration would be to tell only half the story. Most men and women seek to make their lives as coherent and comprehensible as they can. Thus, it is important to ask not only how many children American couples have had at various points in time but also what values they attached to childbearing. Similarly, to fully understand what it meant to be exposed to smallpox, figures on the death rate must be placed in the context of the fears a disfiguring killer could generate when it struck at apparently random intervals. The fact that humans often hold values that are inconsistent with the way they behave only enhances the importance of studying what women and men felt about having children, marrying, moving, and dying.

Obviously, individuals do not exist in isolation. For most persons the family is the most important group of which he or she is a part. The family is where most experiences with birth, death, marriage, and migration occur. Values and attitudes frequently are shaped by parents, children, and other relatives. The most intimate interpersonal contacts and most fundamental rhythms of life develop and occur within the family. Families also serve both as fundamental building blocks of society and as buffers between their individual members and larger social institutions and forces. Therefore, when people married, how many others they lived with, how often family ties were formed or broken, and what individuals might *expect* the future to bring, are among the elements of family life shaped by demographic factors that are an important part of this study. Curiously, as Americans became aware of the dramatic changes in their lives, they often were more concerned for what the new patterns meant for their families than what the implications were for their own personal existence. The debates on the future of families that emerged as a result also require attention.

Whether or not individuals and their families are aware of it, the sum of their separate actions has a profound effect on a nation's history. The most basic patterns and rhythms of individual lives can combine to produce major effects on society as a whole. American governments from the seventeenth century to the present frequently have found their most serious problems rooted in rapid population growth, migrations to new environments in the west and in the cities, and conflicts generated by people with widely differing backgrounds living in close proximity. Economic changes ranging from the choice of crops grown in a particular region to the emergence of industrial society and an overall rise in the standard of living are closely connected to shifting population patterns. Similarly, basic social relations such as the values attached to individual men and women, the interactions among family, church, and state, and the fundamental rhythms of life have been transformed by the demographic revolutions of the past two centuries.

The second organizing principle of this book involves a search for a chronology appropriate to demographic history. Because many of the most spectacular changes in childbearing, death, marriage, and migration occurred between 1770 and 1920, that period of 150 years is the heart of this work. Separate chapters are devoted to basic demographic changes, their effects on family life, and some of the social, economic, and political results. The period before 1770 is treated as a whole, not so much because population patterns were static then (they were not), but because life in the seventeenth and eighteenth centuries was so different from life in the present. Likewise, many of the nineteenth-century changes have continued past 1920, but by that date the structures of contemporary society were becoming clear even though their functions and values were, and are, still uncertain. These chronological divisions are not precise. A case could be made that the dividing line between the first and second periods includes most of the years between 1770 and 1820. Within each period, distinctions must be made regarding when new patterns of migration, birth, or health emerged. Nonetheless, the organization adopted here (three perspectives on demographic patterns in each of three periods) is more appropriate than trying to force a new subject into an old framework.

Although specialists will no doubt recognize the perspectives that help to shape this study, more general readers may not. Therefore, it is only fair to offer some general comments on the theoretical assumptions that are at times explicit but are often implicit below. Specific lines of inquiry can be traced to work done by demographers, students of "modernization," and experts on the family, but all are linked by a common interest in what distinguishes life in contemporary, western society from human experiences in the past or in much of Asia and Africa today.

Demographers have long been interested in some of the changes of concern here. Under the general heading of the "demographic transition," they have noted how both birth and death rates have fallen considerably in urban-industrial societies.[1] Often a period of rapid population growth occurred when a significant gap developed between the birth and death rates. Eventually growth slowed as birth and death rates came into balance at levels much lower than normal throughout much of history. In light of recent rapid population growth throughout much of the rest of the world, the demographic transitions of the past have acquired special interest as demographers have sought to determine if the experience of countries like England, the United States, or Japan can be replicated in India or Brazil.

Any demographic history of the American peoples must include elements of previous work on the demographic transition. But the classical model of the demographers must not dominate, if only because the details of American demographic history do not fit very well.[2] For example, the American population grew rapidly in the eighteenth century (because of an unusually high birth rate), long before a move to an urban-industrial society began. Significant reductions in childbearing occurred long before a major improvement in life expectancy can be observed; the classical model assumes that growth occurred when urbanization caused the death rate to fall before the birth rate. An overreliance on the interest of demographers would eliminate from consideration many other areas of demographic change that are also of consequence. The theory of the demographic transition is concerned primarily with population growth caused by natural increase. Migration (except for rural-urban) receives scant attention.[3] Because the mechanism of growth in this country was complicated by immigration, that subject, and the closely related story of the emergence of a society based on many cultures (cultural pluralism), of necessity become main themes in American demographic history. How individuals and their families contributed and responded to these major shifts in the rhythms of life has rarely been of interest to demographers. But historians should not overlook these matters. Of necessity, a concern for the "demographic transition" broadens into the story of "revolutions in Americans' lives," in order to reflect the complex historical reality of American population patterns.

Just as this book has ties to work on the demographic transition, so too is it rooted in studies of modernization. This term is frequently used to refer to the processes or characteristics which most clearly differentiate the developed nations from the rest of the world today and from life as it was organized in Europe two or three centuries ago. A vast literature has emerged from attempts to define and comprehend the precise meaning of modernization. Much of the writing has focused on institutional arrangements and has only occasional interest for us. But a second line of inquiry has tried to isolate values, attitudes, and behaviors which are indicative of a "modern personality." It is of considerable use here as a means of integrating and explaining a number of changes that have often been studied in isolation.[4]

The best way to define what is meant by "modern personality" is to provide a study in contrasts. The most fundamental definition of the modern personality revolves around the concept of rationality. In particular, modern men and women value efforts to (1) assign individuals their place in society on the basis of talent rather than birth, (2) define social roles narrowly and with a concern for specialization, (3) establish the rule of law in place of arbitrary authority, and (4) promote self-advancement rather than sacrifice to broad social or institutional goals. The goal of all this is to know and control one's world for the purpose of improving the present and *future* condition of one's self and one's immediate family.[5] In contrast, traditional (nonmodern) people hold attitudes that stress their powerlessness and hopelessness in the face of gods, fates, or men who appear ruthless and capricious. In such a context life is to be accepted and survived. The future will bring what may, and if all goes well, it will not be any worse than the present.[6]

This distinction between traditional and modern personalities is an arbitrary one. Few individuals are completely one or the other. Likewise, societies are composed of people at various stages along a continuum from one ideal type to the other. As used here, "modern" does not refer to Americans presently alive, but to anyone who has shared the appropriate configuration of values, attitudes, and behaviors, whenever they lived.

Use of the concept of a modern personality can help us to understand what was happening as revolutions took place in Americans' lives. Many of the demographic changes occurred because individuals wanted to bring more order and control into their lives. The adoption of inoculation against smallpox, decisions by couples to have fewer children, and the flight of young men and women from the old family farm are among the specific demographic actions that can be traced to spreading modern values that led people to believe that epidemic diseases, large families, and limited opportunities at one's place of birth were no longer accidents of life to be automatically accepted.

However useful this concept may be, it should not detract from the main story—the revolutions in Americans' lives. There is no doubt that basic demographic and domestic changes occurred and that they are vitally important. If, as we learn more about the revolutions, some other means of integrating and explaining them appears more satisfactory, then it should be adopted. At present, however, the insights offered by the idea of a modern personality pull together more of the story in a more comprehensible fashion than anything else.

The influence of students of family life on this work also requires mention. Because professional study of the family has emerged only in the twentieth century, it is natural that one of the questions that has most interested experts in this field involves what life in urban-industrial society has meant to families.[7] Numerous monographs, articles, and textbooks have explored this and related questions, with frequent interest in the origins and significance of the nuclear family (two generations living alone) as well as in the "problems" and "crises" faced by families in transition.

From the historian's point of view, these studies are often more interesting for the questions they raise than the answers they provide. Sociological studies have often been static, with little effort made to portray families in the process of adjusting to the new demographic realities. When history has entered the picture, past families either have been described according to what theory said they should be like, or have been judged according to current standards.[8] Thus, while this study certainly reflects the interests of students of the family with regard to who the members of a family are and how they relate to each other and to the world at large, its emphasis is on families responding to the full range of the demographic revolutions rather than just urban-industrial life. The standard of comparison becomes eighteenth- instead of twentieth-century families, not only because of the historical perspective of this work, but also because judgments about current families should be tentative until the demographic transformations are completed and their consequences fully understood. As with the demographic transition, this work (like those on which it is based) often offers specialists on the family as much as it takes from them.

Since the demographic transition, the process of modernization, and urban-industrial families have been observed in many nations besides the United States, it would be logical to ask how the demographic and family patterns of Americans compare to those elsewhere. The endurance of both author and reader would be overtaxed by anything more than an occasional reference to these matters. However, it is desirable to examine the considerable differences that existed with regard to birth, death, marriage, and migrations among various groups within this country. Although the revolutions under study here eventually touched the lives of almost all Americans, they did not affect women and men, young and old, blacks and whites, or farmers and city folk at the same time in the same way. At present, it is sufficient to come to some understanding of the contrasts in the rhythms of life that existed within the American population; the international comparisons must wait.[9]

In order to fully understand why American demographic patterns developed as they did in the seventeenth and eighteenth centuries, it is necessary to briefly examine the consequences of Columbus's establishment of permanent contacts between the Old World and the New, and the ebb and flow of England's population over the two and a half centuries that preceded the settlement of Jamestown in 1607.

Human penetration of the New World began as much as 30,000 years ago when small bands of hunters crossed over from eastern Asia to western America. Although population in the Americas grew slowly for thousands of years (even a 1 percent per year growth rate would have been sufficient to transform an initial party of explorers of three persons into 100 million in about 1,750 years), eventually between 50 and 100 million people inhabited the continents and adjacent islands, living in environments ranging from the arctic to tropical rain forests.[10] Over the centuries, a wide range of cultures emerged, some with highly complex languages, religions, economies, and governments.[11] The greatest concentrations of populations developed in what is now Mexico, in the rest of Central America, and along the Andes Mountains. Elsewhere (including what eventually became the United States) settlement was less dense, though archeological evidence suggests the existence of rather elaborate societies in the central Mississippi River Valley. Perhaps no more than one of every ten of the first Americans lived north of the Rio Grande, but this still included 5 to 10 million people, a rather impressive total in view of the fact that the population of the United States reached 10 million only after 1820.

Of equal importance to the large numbers of people who were living in the Americas by 1492 is the fact that they had been out of touch with the rest of the world for thousands of years. This did not inhibit the attainment of significant cultural accomplishments in the New World, but it did prevent the development of critical protective devices—biological immunities. We tend to think of diseases as relatively constant phenomena, but they too evolve, forcing population changes. This is of major consequence, for it is clear that a number of major killers emerged in Europe, Africa, and Asia only after the first Americans had lost contact. By 1492, many old-world peoples had acquired at least limited defences against diseases like smallpox, measles, or malaria; the Americans had not.

Columbus effectively ended the isolation of the New World, an accomplishment for which he justly deserves acclaim. During the century before 1492, one of the major transportation revolutions in human history had occurred. Taking advantage of new ship-building and navigating techniques, Europeans, especially the Portuguese and Spanish, transformed the world's oceans from barriers into highways. As a result, large quantities of goods could be carried long distances quickly and efficiently; so, too, could disease. Initially, only the patterns of old-world contacts were altered. Columbus changed this when he brought a region isolated for thousands of years into the network. The economic consequences of this worldwide growth of communication have long been understood; the demographic importance has only recently emerged.

Increased speed of communication and the inclusion of the Americans in the worldwide network of exchange had two major demographic consequences. One was that once-isolated diseases began to appear among new groups, often with catastrophic effects. The other was that new foods became available around the world, with results that were more favorable to humanity but slower in developing.[12]

The impact of the exchange of diseases brought on by Columbus's voyages was both immediate and horribly spectacular for the first Americans. In the span of half a century, Indian populations were exposed to smallpox, measles, whooping cough, chicken pox, bubonic plague, typhus, malaria, diphtheria, amoebic dysentery, influenza, and various types of worms. Yellow fever may also have been introduced at that time, though possibly it was present before Columbus. The Indians could offer little resistance to this unintentional germ warfare. Some argue they eventually got their revenge via syphilis, but that disease, which became prevalent in Europe shortly after Columbus's return, may have arrived from other parts of the world.

The results of the contact between Europeans and Indians border on the incredible. In 150 years, the Indian populations may have lost 95 percent of their pre-Columbian totals. On the island of Hispaniola, population declined from a total which may have been as high as 3.7 million in 1496, to 92,300 in 1508. By 1540, only 250 Indians remained alive there.[13] Even if the figure for 1496 is too high, as some scholars suggest, the decline is still awesome.[14] The most optimistic assessments place the loss of life among the Indians on a par with that experienced in Europe during the worst epidemics of the black death.

Elsewhere in America the catastrophe may not have been as great as on Hispaniola, but it was still striking. In west central Mexico, the population may have fallen from 295,000 in 1548 to 38,000 in 1650. All of Mexico may have lost 10 million people, out of a total of 25 to 30 million, in the first ten years after contact was established in 1519.[15] By 1605, the once mighty Aztec empire had only 1 million survivors. It is difficult to envision a situation that could produce more profound human suffering and social dislocation.

Indians who lived at higher altitudes or latitudes where cooler, drier climates prevailed were spared some of the worst effects of the diseases. Others benefitted from delays in contact with Europeans. For these people not only was the chance of contracting disease reduced, but they also were less exposed to death from the warfare, starvation, and forced labor that accompanied European intrusion. Some Indians in North America avoided the worst ravages of contact until the middle of the ninteenth century. In fact, it is the well-documented impact of disease on some of the more isolated Indian tribes in the nineteenth century that gives credence to the scale of catastrophy which appears to have occurred in the sixteenth century.[16]

Although Europeans and Africans, whose presence in America resulted from Spanish efforts to replace the loss of Indian labor, also died rapidly in the new disease environment, they never suffered to the extent that the first Americans did.[17] Since blacks were worked as hard as Indians, it seems safe to attribute their higher rate of survival in large measure to biological resistances and genetic immunities built up in the Old World, which protected them at least partially from some of the worst of the familiar diseases.

In the long run, contact between the Old World and the New also had positive demographic consequences. Just as new diseases were exchanged, so too were new foodstuffs.[18] Europeans and Africans brought with them wheat, oats, barley, bananas, sugar, and strains of domesticated rice, along with a variety of fruits, pigs, cattle, sheep, goats, and horses. In exchange, Indian farmers showed the rest of the world how to grow maize, beans, peanuts, potatoes, sweet potatoes and yams, manioc (cassava or tapioca), pineapples, tomatoes, cocoa, and coffee. This exchange of foods may explain much of the worldwide population expansion that began about 1650 and is still going on today.[19] Diets became better balanced than they had been in the pre-Columbian era. Food supplies increased as land, previously unsuited to local crops, suddenly became productive when new crops with new growing cycles were introduced from elsewhere in the world.

From the broadest perspective, one of the most important aspects of the history of the Americas since Columbus has been the *resettlement* of the territory from Europe, Africa, and Asia, with the economics of the resettlement closely related to the expansion of food supplies for both the colonists and the rest of the world. In this regard the story has been a remarkably successful one, though the initial cost in human life was extraordinary.

Because of their own demographic history, the English, whose North American colonies formed the nucleus of the United States, became interested in the New World only after the first Americans had been decimated by diseases, and the advantages of new food supplies had yet to be realized. To fully understand when and why the English became interested in America, it is necessary to go back well past 1492 to 1348, the year when bubonic plague appeared in England. At that time, England's population was beginning to level off at a minimum of about 3 million people, after several centuries of slow but significant growth. Within thirty years of the appearance of plague, England's inhabitants had been reduced to about 2 million in number.[20]

Dislocation in religion, economics, and politics brought about by plague were further enhanced by continued declines in population that reduced England's inhabitants to no more than 1.5 million shortly before Columbus set sail. This reduction, combined with political instability arising from the dynastic conflicts known as the Wars of the Roses, meant that England was in no condition to join in any extensive effort to explore and colonize the New World.

In the sixteenth century, the situation in England began to improve. The Tudor monarchs gradually restored relative peace and quiet. England began to participate in the economic integration of the world via a variety of newly established trading companies and joint stock ventures. Population began to recover. By 1600, the losses experienced during and after the great plague epidemic had been replaced. Perhaps as many as 3.75 million people lived in England in that year; a century later, in 1700, the total was over 5.5 million, in spite of a renewed outbreak of plague in the middle of the seventeenth century. By 1800, the total population stood at just over 9 million.[21]

Renewed population growth enabled England seriously to consider colonizing ventures. Moreover, many English politicans began to think of colonies as a solution to some of their domestic problems. Just as the sudden loss of numbers had upset social, economic, and political arrangements, so too did the recovery. Between 1550 and 1650, prices for food, clothing, and housing, all items directly influenced by population growth, rose between

400 and 600 percent.[22] By the seventeenth century, England had become a remarkably mobile society, with some communities losing between 50 and 60 percent of their inhabitants in the space of ten years.[23] For people who still accepted the feudal ideals of hierarchy and order as the prime social goals, these changes were profoundly disturbing. One response was the passage of various poor laws between 1590 and 1630 to control wanderers and provide minimal relief. Another was to think of colonies.

After 1590, some English officials began to argue seriously that England was overpopulated, and that colonies were a way to get rid of the surplus. Considering the inflation and unemployment present in England at the time, there was little doubt that individuals could be found who would be willing to leave home for a new chance. Eventually, at the end of the seventeenth century, the English government reversed its position regarding the desirability of emigration on the grounds that population at home contributed to the nation's power. But this occurred only after a series of colonies had been established in the New World.[24]

If demographic events in England helped determine when she began to consider settlements abroad, it was the demography of the New World that influenced the location of her colonies. From the standpoint of the expanding nations of Europe, England got the leftovers. By the time England was able and willing to participate in colonization, Spain and Portugal had claimed all of the regions of the New World with easily exploitable natural and human resources. The early empire builders had no interest in the sparsely populated regions of North America when they had the Aztec and Inca empires to assault. By 1600, as the result of various epidemics, the North Atlantic seacoast tribes numbered even less than at the time of first contact.[25] The Spanish relinquished control of small, depopulated Caribbean islands like Barbados, the Leeward Islands, and Jamaica without much struggle. Until the second half of the eighteenth century, England never acquired territory in the Americas that another European power felt was an important part of its imperial ambitions.

The importance of England's acquisition of territories rendered undesirable by a lack of people is hard to overemphasize. Normal procedure for empire building emphasized seizing control of land and people already present to exploit them. This was the pattern established by Spain and Portugal, France, and Holland in their ventures overseas, and this was the pattern England followed in Ireland, Africa, and India, where large populations existed. But in America, if anything was to be gained out of the territory appropriated by the English Crown, a new imperial form had to be developed, involving extensive migration of English people (and later, others) across the Atlantic from the outset of colonization. The consequences of this were far-reaching.

Notes

1. For examples of works using this theory, *see* H. J. Habakkuk, *Population Growth and Economic Development Since 1750* (New York, 1972); William Petersen, *Population*, 2d ed. (New York, 1969); or E. A. Wrigley, *Population and History* (New York, 1969).

2. For recent critiques, *see* John C. Caldwell, "Toward a Restatement of Demographic Transition Theory," *Population and Development Review* 2 (1976): 321–66; Ansley J. Coale, "The Demographic Transition Reconsidered," *Proceedings of the International Population Conference* (Liège, Belgium, 1973), pp. 53–72; Robert V. Wells, "Family History and Demographic Transition," *Journal of Social History* 9 (1975): 1–19.

3. Wilbur Zelinsky, "The Hypothesis of the Mobility Transition," *Geographical Review* 61 (1971): 219–49.

4. Richard D. Brown, "Modernization and the Modern Personality in Early America, 1600–1865: A Sketch of a Synthesis," *Journal of Interdisciplinary History* 2 (1972): 201–28; Alex Inkeles and David H. Smith, *Becoming Modern: Individual Change in Six Developing Countries* (Cambridge, Mass., 1974); E. A. Wrigley, "The Process of Modernization and the Industrial Revolution in England," *Journal of Interdisciplinary History* 3 (1972): 225–59.

5. Wrigley, "Process of Modernization," 229–33.

6. Laila El-Hamamsy, "Belief Systems and Family Planning in Peasant Societies," in *Are Our Descendents Doomed?*, eds. Harrison Brown and Edward Hutchings, Jr.(New York, 1970), pp. 335–57.

7. William J. Goode, *World Revolution and Family Patterns* (New York, 1963); Talcott Parsons and R. F. Bales, *Family, Socialization and Interaction Process* (Glencoe, Ill., 1955).

8. Bernard Farber, *Guardians of Virtue: Salem Families in 1800* (New York, 1972); Rudy Ray Seward, *The American Family: A Demographic History* (Beverly Hills, Calif., 1978).

9. Students interested in making international comparisons should begin with D. V. Glass and D.E.C. Eversley, eds., *Population in History* (Chicago, 1965); D. V. Glass and Roger Revelle, eds., *Population and Social Change* (New York, 1972); and Ronald D. Lee, ed., *Population Patterns in the Past* (New York, 1977).

10. The size of the population in the Americas before Columbus is a subject of debate at present. Interested readers can start by examining Sherburne F. Cook and Woodrow Borah, *Essays in Population History: Mexico and the Caribbean*, 3 vols. (Berkeley, 1971–1979); William M. Deneven, ed., *The Native Population of the Americas in 1492* (Madison, Wis., 1976); Henry F. Dobyns, "Estimating Aboriginal American Population: An Appraisal of Techniques with a New Hemispheric Estimate," *Current Anthropology* 7 (1966): 395–449.

11. Peter Farb, *Man's Rise to Civilization: The Cultural Ascent of the Indians of North America*, rev. ed. (New York, 1978); Alvin M. Josephy, Jr., *The Indian Heritage of America* (New York, 1968).

12. Alfred W. Crosby, Jr., *The Columbian Exchange: Biological and Cultural Consequences of 1492* (Westport, Conn., 1972).

13. Cook and Borah, *Population History*, 1: 401.

14. Deneven, *Native Population*.

15. Crosby, *Columbian Exchange*, p. 53.

16. Alfred W. Crosby, "Virgin Soil Epidemics as a Factor in the Aboriginal Depopulation in America," *William and Mary Quarterly* 33 (1976): 289–99; Wilbur R. Jacobs, "The Fatal Confrontation: Early Native-White Relations on the Frontiers of Australia, New Guinea, and America—A Comparative Study," *Pacific Historical Review* 40 (1971): 283–309.

17. Philip D. Curtin, "Epidemiology and the Slave Trade," *Political Science Quarterly* 83 (1968): 190–216.

18. Crosby, *Columbian Exchange*, pp. 165–207.

19. William L. Langer, "American Foods and Europe's Population Growth, 1750–1850," *Journal of Social History* 9 (1975): 51–66; United Nations, *The Determinants and Consequences of Population Trends* (New York, 1953), pp. 5–20.

20. Julian Cornwall, "English Population in the Early Sixteenth Century," *Economic History Review* 23 (1970): 32–44; Philip Ziegler, *The Black Death* (New York, 1969), pp. 117–258.

21. Ian Blanchard, "Population Change, Enclosures, and the Early Tudor Economy," *Economic History Review* 23 (1970): 427–45; D.V. Glass, "Population and Population Movements in England and Wales, 1700 to 1850," in *Population in History*, eds. Glass and Eversley, pp. 221–46.

22. E.H. Phelps Brown and S.V. Hopkins, "Wage-Rates and Prices: Evidence for Population Pressure in the Sixteenth Century," *Economica* 24 (1957): 289–306.

23. Peter Laslett and John Harrison, "Clayworth and Cogenhoe," in *Historical Essays presented to David Ogg*, eds. H. E. Bell and R. L. Ollard (London, 1963), pp. 157–84.

24. Mildred Campbell, "'Of People Either too Few or too Many'; The Conflict of Opinion on Population and its Relation to Emigration," in *Conflict in Stuart England: Essays in Honour of Wallace Notestein*, eds. W. A. Aiken and B. D. Hennings (London, 1960), pp. 171–201.

25. Sherburne F. Cook, "The Significance of Disease in the Extinction of the New England Indians," *Human Biology* 45 (1973): 485–508.

PART I

A WORLD OF
UNCERTAINTY:
POPULATION,
FAMILY, AND
SOCIETY
BEFORE
1770

2

THE WORLD WE HAVE ESCAPED

In 1965, Peter Laslett, an English historian, published a book on English society in the seventeenth century, *The World We Have Lost*.[1] His purpose was to demonstrate the profound differences between the seventeenth century and the present. Americans' history is no different, for we, too, have had our lives altered to the extent that it is difficult for the women and men of the twentieth century to comprehend the realities of existence three hundred years ago. However, if we are to fully understand the rhythms that shape our own lives, it is necessary to explore where we have come from and how far the journey. Unlike Laslett, the emphasis here will be not on a world *lost*, but a world *escaped*, for the past was frequently unpleasant and many of the most basic changes over the last two hundred years were actively pursued.

Of the major demographic processes, migration shows the greatest similarity between past and present. For over three hundred years Americans have moved at extraordinary rates, with important consequences for themselves and their society. However, moving alone is not sufficient to create an area of shared experience between seventeenth-century Americans and their successors because the characteristics of the people who moved, their motivations, and destinations have all changed appreciably.

Although the English need to resettle the parts of North America that they acquired in the seventeenth century produced an obvious impulse toward migration, historians have often overlooked the importance of this story. Records do not exist that tell us precisely how many people came to the English colonies before 1776, but it is clear they were many. The best estimates indicate that about 400,000 blacks contributed unwillingly to the realization of England's imperial ambitions in North America, and that eighteenth-century migrations from Europe may have added 300,000 to 600,000 whites.[2] This latter range of figures is rather broad and tells us nothing of the seventeenth-century migrations from England and Europe. Recent work on migration into Virginia and Maryland suggests that as many as 100,000 people may have moved into the Chesapeake before 1700.[3] If an equal number came to New England, the middle colonies, and the Carolinas, then the total for before 1700 is about 200,000.[4] Taking all the estimates together, the number of immigrants to the colonies appears to have been between 900,000 and 1,200,000. It is not necessary to decide finally how accurate these estimates are, since even a sizable reduction in the minimum figure would still lead to the conclusion that a large number of men, women, and children came to the colonies. Considering that the total population of the colonies was only about 250,000 in 1700, and just over 2 million in 1770, the number of immigrants is quite impressive.

The earliest immigrants were overwhelmingly English. Virginia, Plymouth, Massachusetts Bay, Maryland, Connecticut, and Rhode Island were all initially dominated by individuals who came from England. Before New York and Pennsylvania came under English control in the second half of the seventeenth century, a trickle of Dutch and Swedish settlers had moved to those regions. But they were quickly overwhelmed by their English neighbors, setting a precedent for conquest by population growth that was repeated several times over the next two hundred years.

A predominance of English immigrants did not automatically re-create English society in the New World, partly because not all English men and women were equally prone to move, and partly because the various colonies were settled by different kinds of people. Best known are the religious impulses that sent Puritans to New England, Quakers to Pennsylvania, and Anglicans to Virginia. However, a study of lists of passengers to New England in 1620–1638 and to Virginia in 1634–1635 records some striking demographic contrasts.[5] Slightly over six men went to Virginia for every one woman, whereas in New England there were two female immigrants for every three males. Only 5 percent of the Virginia immigrants were under sixteen; many more children migrated to New England with their parents or shortly thereafter. The result was that New Englanders re-created a pattern of stable family life almost from the start. In the Chesapeake, life was characterized in the early years by a lack of family relationships, mostly because women and children were relatively scarce. Most regional differences in the age and sex composition of the population eventually disappeared, but as they did so, new distinctions emerged.

By 1775, almost half the colonists traced their ancestors back to countries other than England. About 30 percent of the settlers came from Scotland, Ireland, Germany, Holland, France, and Portugal; one of every five Americans had African origins.[6] Throughout the seventeenth century, non-English immigrants were few in number. The first black Americans were brought to Virginia and sold into some form of bondage in 1619, the year before the *Mayflower*. Thereafter, a small but steady stream of blacks arrived until about 1680. Likewise, small numbers of Irish and Scots were sent to America as prisoners of war. A few French Protestants and Portuguese Jews also arrived after conditions in their homelands became dangerous.

After 1680, however, the numbers of non-English immigrants surged upwards. English government officials, who were having second thoughts about whether England was overpopulated, welcomed this movement.[7] Over the next century, they actively encouraged foreign immigration by grants of land and citizenship, as a means of peopling the colonies while maintaining the population at home.

Blacks brought to America as slaves comprised the largest stream of immigrants. The legal definition of race slavery by 1660 in most colonies, changes in the slave trade, and a realization that England was unable to supply the labor desired by colonial landowners produced a significant increase in the number of unwilling migrants after 1680. In the eighteenth century alone, perhaps 350,000 blacks were forced to migrate to North America. Most came directly from Africa, and many landed at Charleston, South Carolina, where Sullivan's Island became the "Ellis Island" of black Americans. About 90 percent of all blacks ended up in the colonies south of Pennsylvania.[8]

Four other groups of people contributed significantly to the growth and diversification of the colonial populations. Scots, Scotch-Irish, and Irish arrived throughout much of the eighteenth century. A surge of migration in the decade between 1765 and 1775 may have brought as many as 100,000 Scots and Irish to the New World.[9] Many individuals from a variety of German states crossed the Atlantic between 1720 and 1760. The precise total is uncertain, but records do show that at least 25,393 Germans arrived in Philadelphia alone between 1740 and 1750. During the period 1727 to 1776, no less than 65,000 Germans arrived at that port.[10] Ships' lists indicate that between 1728 and 1748 males outnumbered females among the adults by 140 to 100, a better balance than in early New England. Children were rare, accounting for only two of every nine passengers from the German states.[11]

Some immigrants continued to arrive in the colonies from England. Almost 17,500 convicts were sent to America between 1719 and 1772. Some servants made their way to the Chesapeake. And between December 1772 and April 1776, just as the War of Independence began, about 6,000 persons (of whom 80 percent were men, 12 percent women, and 8 percent children) left England for the ungrateful colonies.[12] Apparently not all English citizens viewed the colonies with the hostility of their leaders. Nevertheless, the major sources of new inhabitants for the colonies in the eighteenth century lay outside England.

The numbers and varied backgrounds of the men, women, and children who helped to resettle North America are so impressive that it is easy to forget that, for many immigrants, those English colonies were only one of several possible destinations. A greater variety of people eventually found their way to England's North American colonies, but the majority of any one group often went elsewhere. The 350,000 Africans who arrived after 1700 account for a significant part of the total number of immigrants who came to the North American colonies. Their numbers are relatively small compared to the 1.4 million blacks transported to the

British island colonies in the Caribbean in the eighteenth century, or the 6 million slaves brought to the New World between
1700 and 1800.[13] The same pattern seems to have been true for
European colonists. In 1731, religious problems forced 18,000
Germans to flee their homeland of Salzburg. Of these, 240
eventually found their way to Georgia. Many of the others
presumably stayed in neighboring German states, though some
may have found refuge in czarist Russia, a popular alternative to
America at that time.[14]

Even the English did not all move to North America. In the
years between 1620 and 1640, when the Puritans were seeking a
place to practice their religion undisturbed, only a quarter of the
approximately 80,000 people who left England went to New
England. The rest chose either the Caribbean islands or Europe.
In 1637, 193 Puritans left Yarmouth for the New World, but 414
others chose the shorter trip to Holland. Almost half (49.3 percent) of the 10,394 servants whose destinations were recorded
when they left England in 1683 and 1684 went to the island
colonies. Virginia and Maryland received almost as many (48.2
percent), but only 162 (1.6 percent) of these individuals set sail
for New England. In the eighteenth century, the balance shifted
more to the islands. Of 3,257 servants who left England between
1720 and 1732, fully 2,013 (61.8 percent) went to the islands,
almost twice as many as to the Chesapeake colonies. Only 32
went to New England.[15]

Motives for moving to America were as varied as the people
who held them, and are of interest if only because the voyage
across the Atlantic offered formidable obstacles to the hardiest
travellers. Sailing vessels were slow, leaky, crowded, and uncomfortable. Immigrants faced possible shipwreck, capture, or ship-
board epidemics. A quick voyage might take most of a month; a
slow one could last almost half a year, during which food and
water became scarce. Individuals and families who could pay
their own way and provide their own food generally suffered the
least. Servants from England and elsewhere in Europe frequently had more crowded conditions and poorer food. Men and
women who either signed an indenture for four to seven years of
labor in exchange for passage to America or promised to

"redeem" their passage or go into bondage shortly after arriving in the colonies put themselves in the hands of ships' captains who were out to cut costs in order to maximize their profits. The worst experiences, of course, were those of the African colonists. For them, the voyage started with capture and sale at home, involved crossing the Atlantic chained in hot, stinking ships, and ended with sale into slavery in an unfamiliar world. At no point did they have any choice in the matter and their treatment reflected that fact.

As many as half the colonists may have come because they had no choice in the matter, a rather startling conclusion in view of the image of America as the land of opportunity, but one which helps explain why so many confronted the terrors of the trip. The black colonists who were imported as slaves are the most obvious unwilling immigrants. Convicts and prisoners of war who helped resettle North America frequently had no more choice in the matter than slaves. Occasionally convicts were given the option of hanging or transportation to America (not all chose the latter!), but in such cases the decision to emigrate hardly seems voluntary. Presumably very few wives and children who crossed the Atlantic had much say in the matter.

The motives of those for whom the move was voluntary fall under the familiar trinity: God, gold, and glory. Many public appeals were made for colonists to go to the New World to carry the Christian faith to the natives. Individual Puritans, Quakers, Catholics, Jews, and Huguenots saw the New World as a place of refuge from persecution, where their own faith could become the established order.

Often economic motives offer the best explanation for a move. Many of those who left England in the seventeenth and eighteenth centuries did so in order to protect their place in society. Faced with inflation and other economic changes, many men chose to sell modest properties in England in the hope that better land and a more secure future were available in the colonies. Others with bleak immediate futures moved with the idea of improving their status. Probably many of those who came as servants fell into this category, as did younger sons and daughters whose hopes for acquired wealth were limited by inheritance laws that strongly favored eldest sons.

The love of adventure seems to have motivated some of the earliest migrants who came before they realized that success in England's colonies required a commitment to agriculture rather than treasure. Once this became clear by 1650, the conquistador spirit among migrants disappeared. Throughout the seventeenth and eighteenth centuries, potential colonists were exposed to propaganda designed to encourage them to move. Some propaganda stressed the virtues of empire to England. Probably more effective was the recruiting done from America. Investors in the colonies offered land, religious toleration, and political power (three items scarce in Europe) to prospective inhabitants. Friends and family members who had gone ahead frequently wrote letters stressing these public attractions, and mentioning personal inducements, too.

Frequently, individuals had multiple reasons for undertaking the unpleasant voyage to the New World. Many Puritans, for example, suffered economic stress and religious persecution. Under such conditions, a move became more logical.[16]

Finally, many colonists were simply the moving kind. For every person who decided to seek his or her fortune in America, many more stayed home even though faced with equally bleak futures. Many colonists had moved earlier in their lives, before setting out to cross the Atlantic. They continued to move once they got to the colonies. Numerous settlers in Georgia, North Carolina, New Jersey, Connecticut, and New Hampshire came from older colonies, including some of the Caribbean islands. In early Windsor, Connecticut, 48 percent of the first inhabitants eventually moved on. To some extent, restlessness could be cured by success in a community. Only 33 percent of the Windsor church members and 23 percent of the people with 300 or more acres left. In contrast, 63 percent of those who failed to be admitted to the church and 53 percent of those who had 50 acres or less left the community.[17]

Thus, moving to America was only one expression of a lifelong restlessness. Perhaps it was nothing more than that, but it is tempting to see this restlessness as an early manifestation of the modern person's efforts to organize and improve his or her life. To the extent that migration involved a voluntary choice based on a rational assessment of the future, America was being settled by people who would not passively await their demographic, economic, or political future.

A frequent and commonplace confrontation with death is one aspect of life before 1800 that sets that period apart from the present. It requires considerable historical empathy to grasp the health conditions of seventeenth- and eighteenth-century Americans, a task made more difficult by our unfamiliarity with and uneasiness about death. Four questions need to be answered if we are to comprehend this basic aspect of life as our ancestors experienced it: (1) What was the actual "experience" with death? (2) What were the causes of death *and health*? (3) What were the emotional and social responses to disease and dying? (4) What options for care did sick persons have?

The records we have regarding health and death in the colonial period are both scattered and imprecise, but they are more than sufficient to demonstrate the striking contrast between then and now. The seventeenth-century English political philosopher Thomas Hobbes once observed that, in his time, life was "nasty, brutish, and short," a judgment few today would question. Although the toll of life was never as great as that resulting from the initial contact between the Old World and the New, the early participants in the process of resettlement also suffered greatly. Migration across the Atlantic required adjustments to new disease environments by both Europeans and Africans, exposing individuals to a process which the colonists euphemistically called "seasoning." Seasoning was most spectacular in the earliest settlements as disease, war, and "starving" times all took their toll. In Jamestown, Virginia, the number of inhabitants in October 1609 was about 500 persons; the following April only 60 survived. Between 1618 and 1624 approximately 6,000 people came to Virginia to bolster the 400 already there. Even given the extremely unlikely assumption that there were no births during this period, it is still a shock to find that fewer than 1,300 remained in 1624. About 300 people had died in a conflict with the Indians in 1622, but that is only a small portion of the total deaths. Meanwhile, in the Plymouth colony, on Cape Cod, about half of the 100 initial settlers died during the first winter of 1620–21, and only 6 or 7 were healthy at any time. Later immigrants may not have suffered as much, but the seasoning process continued after the colonies were successfully established. Between 1635 and 1699, over 80,000 people came to Virginia, yet only about 60,000 inhabitants were counted in 1699.[18] Among white male immigrants in Maryland in the late seventeenth century, 41 percent of those who reached the age of twenty died before they were forty and only 15 percent survived to reach the age of sixty.[19]

How easily black colonists acclimated to North America is uncertain. A blood characteristic, the sickle-cell trait, gave many blacks an advantage over whites where malaria was present.[20] But hard work, poor diet, and exposure to European disease probably offset this. Because black Americans achieved significant population growth by natural increase in the eighteenth century, we can say with confidence that the individuals who lived in North America were generally better off than those who ended up in the Caribbean. There, mortality was extraordinary even in the late eighteenth century. Although over 35,000 blacks arrived in Barbados between 1764 and 1771, the net increase in population was only 5,300.[21]

The process of seasoning continued in the eighteenth century. Between 1700 and 1750, for example, 62 missionaries were sent to the Carolinas. Their efforts were thwarted by the environment, as 43.6 percent died or resigned for reasons of health within five years of arrival. Less than half lasted ten years, and only about 10 percent survived to preach through two decades.[22] Of the first 114 passengers who set sail for Georgia in 1732, 2 died on board ship, 26 perished within a year, and 11 more passed away before three years were up.[23] As late as the 1760s, West Florida was known as a "graveyard for Britons," a title it could have shared with other colonies.[24] In Louisiana, French efforts at settlement proved equally dangerous to the colonists. Between 1718 and 1721, about 900 convicts were sent to Louisiana. Two hundred ten drowned on the way and only 60 survived long enough to be recorded in the 1721 census. Only 5 of the 60 had been in the colony over eighteen months.[25]

The survivors of the seasoning process were a hardy lot. By 1770, life chances in America could be as good as anywhere in the world. Life expectancies at birth of forty-five years or even a little more were not impossible. However, many colonists faced harsher conditions. Epidemics appeared at irregular intervals along the Atlantic seaboard. Although the warmth and moisture of the Carolinas never matched the potential for demographic disaster found in the Caribbean, climatic conditions in the South made it easier for disease to spread there than in New England. Nevertheless, by the middle of the eighteenth century many Americans had adjusted surprisingly well to life and death in the New World.[26]

At the risk of appearing more precise than is actually possible, a fair estimate would be that life expectancy at birth after about 1650 ranged between thirty-five and forty-five years for most whites. Occasionally, groups of individuals born in particularly favorable circumstances in New England seem to have attained life expectancies of fifty years or better. At the other extreme, life expectancy at birth may have been as low as twenty years for the most unfortunate seventeenth-century Southerners.

Figures on life expectancy at birth take on added meaning when we examine what they meant in terms of an individual's chances of surviving from one age to another. From the columns in Table l with life expectancy equal to twenty-five and fifty-five, it is evident that before 1770, more children survived to age forty-five in the best conditions than reached age one under the worst. Under more normal conditions (that is, life expectancy between thirty-five and forty-five), about 60 to 70 percent of the children born would expect to attain the marriageable age of twenty. Of these children, between 29.2 and 43.2 percent could expect to survive to old age, or sixty. In the eighteenth century, these were remarkably good life chances. But the extraordinary uncertainty of living in early America compared to living here today is made clear by examining the figures in the last column, in which life expectancy equals seventy-five. Today almost everyone lives to forty-five; then only a half did which meant that one's propects were very uncertain.

Life expectancy refers only to a person's chances of living or dying. It tells us nothing of whether they will be healthy or frequently ill. As a rule, however, as life expectancy increases, so does the standard of health in the population. This suggests that many eighteenth-century colonists found life not only longer but more enjoyable than did the seventeenth-century settlers.

Table 1 Survival of Children under Varying Life Expectations

Surviving to Age	Life Expectancy at Birth in Years					
	25	35	45	55	65	75
0	1000	1000	1000	1000	1000	1000
1	695	786	854	907	950	985
5	545	672	774	861	932	982
20	458	597	716	823	913	978
45	278	422	566	707	842	955
60	168	292	432	580	733	886

SOURCE: Ansley J. Coale and Paul Demeny, *Regional Model Life Tables and Stable Populations* (Princeton, N.J., 1966), pp. 2–25.

So far, most of our comments have been restricted to Americans of European origin. Black Americans probably had lower life expectancies, but how much lower is not clear. Early nineteenth-century evidence suggests that, on the average, black life expectancy may have been ten to fifteen years less than that of whites *living in the same region*.[27] Significant variations by time and place must have been present for them, too, although the vast majority of black colonists lived in what was generally the worst disease environment—the southern coastal plain.

The picture was even bleaker for the Indians. Continued and increased contact produced continued disasters. In New England, smallpox in 1633 followed an unknown plague in 1617 to produce up to 75 percent losses among some tribes.[28] On Nantucket and Martha's Vineyard, the Indian population shrank from about 6,000 to just over 600 in the century before 1764. In 1738 almost half the Cherokees in the Great Smoky Mountains died from smallpox, making it easier for Europeans to begin infiltrating the southern Appalachian region.[29] Even in the west, where contact was less regular, the first Americans suffered. The Kansa tribe decreased from about 4,800 to about 1,600 between 1700 and 1800, with major losses from smallpox around 1750.[30] The Pimas of modern Arizona declined from 2,400 to 100 in the same century.[31] In New Mexico, in 1780–81, smallpox caused the death of over 5,000 Pueblo Indians.[32] In such conditions, to talk of life expectancy at all seems inappropriate.

If one could have chosen, it would have been better to be born 1) in America, 2) in the north, 3) in the eighteenth century, 4) of white parents, and 5) a male. Under such circumstances, one's life chances, and the better health that usually accompanies longer life expectancy, would have compared favorably with those almost anywhere else in the world before 1800. For others, conditions of health and death were frequently less favorable and less predictable. For all, most matters of life and death were still beyond the influence of conscious human control.

A variety of biological and social factors caused both death and health at a time when direct medical intervention to ward off death was many years in the future. Evidence of what people died of and why they were healthy is rarely as the historian would wish it to be. Where records exist, they reflect the values of the doctors who generated most of them. In order to determine how current doctors would diagnose a problem, it is necessary to sort through the 2,000 disorders eighteenth-century physicians thougt they could distinguish. This is possible in very general terms, but precision can not be attained.

Accidents posed an ever-present threat to the health and lives of the colonists. Journals of colonial doctors record constant attention to drowning, cuts and infections, gunshot wounds, burns, broken bones, and bites by rabid animals. Frequent mention is made of small children "overlayed" and apparently smothered in crowded beds. Some of these children may have succumbed to what we now know as sudden infant death syndrome; but it is possible that accidental and even deliberate smothering occurred.[33]

Most early Americans were victims of other types of assaults on their bodies. Microorganisms of all sorts continuously infected them; few people lived long enough to die of degenerative problems. Epidemic infections received most of the attention, even though endemic diseases regularly killed far more people.[34] Irregular outbreaks of smallpox, diphtheria, or yellow fever made them less familiar and so more terrible than the regular causes of death. Often the proportion of fatal cases was higher for an epidemic disease. In addition, epidemics generated fear by the violent and visual changes they produced. The annual death rate in a normally healthy community could more than triple in the space of two or three months when an epidemic occurred, jumping from a loss of 2 or 3 percent to 10 percent of the population. In 1721, over half the inhabitants of Boston contracted smallpox, and 7.7 percent died.[35] The visual aspect of epidemic diseases must have shaken many people. To see a spouse, parent, or child die of smallpox as pus-filled sores totally covered the body, to watch a loved one perish from yellow fever, whose major symptom gave it the name of the black vomit, or to stand helplessly by while family members choked to death as diphtheria swelled the throat closed can not have been easy, even for individuals much more accustomed to death than we.

The killers that took a steady, yearly toll of lives can be divided into three broad categories. Intestinal disorders flourished in the late summer and early fall because of stagnant water, spoiled food, and warmth to generate germs. Dysentery, known as the bloody flux, and typhoid fever were always present during those months. Warm weather and mosquitos also brought infections of malaria (fever and ague) with its violent physical shaking during the agues, and, less commonly, yellow fever. Once cold weather reduced the populations of insects and germs, conditions of health improved. However, the cold weather was not without its dangers, as lung disorders became a problem. Pneumonia was a threat in winter, as was tuberculosis, the single most important killer of the colonists. Consumption or pulmonary phthisis, the eighteenth-century names for tuberculosis, appear in the records more than any other single diagnosis, reflecting both the widespread presence of the disease and the fact that most doctors knew what heavy coughing and spitting blood meant.

Noah Webster's analysis of the deaths occurring within the Episcopal congregation of New York City between 1786 and 1795 presents a clear illustration of the yearly cycle of mortality. Although the individuals whose deaths are included in Table 2 died shortly after 1770, it is safe to assume that the pattern prevailed before that time. The most dangerous months of the year were August, September, and October, when both intestinal disorders and insect-borne fevers were prevalent. The effects of dysentery and other similar disorders on small children are readily apparent. Surviving the early years of life was a significant achievement. No doubt the yearly pattern of death in

Table 2 Deaths by Age and Season of Year, New York City, 1786-1795

Ages	Jan	Feb	March	April	May	June	July	Aug	Sept	Oct	Nov	Dec	Total
Under 2	66	43	48	58	51	70	173	360	261	139	78	93	1,440
2–5	12	12	14	7	5	11	8	21	18	25	25	14	172
5–10	8	13	8	4	14	7	11	14	15	17	5	16	132*
10–20	7	5	6	5	13	4	7	8	25	12	7	8	107
20–30	23	16	18	16	17	16	20	28	53	26	20	21	274
30–40	14	24	12	16	25	18	29	28	36	36	24	24	286
40–50	40	35	21	32	45	26	30	33	57	53	38	38	448
50–60	11	23	17	16	25	23	18	28	22	23	20	11	237
60–70	5	18	13	4	19	15	12	8	10	11	11	7	133
70–80	6	8	7	4	10	4	7	6	7	6	9	9	83
80–90	1	4	5	6	7	3	3	1	3	2	3	5	43
90–100	--	1	1	1	3	1	2	--	1	4	--	2	16
100+	--	--	--	1	1	--	--	--	--	--	--	--	2
Total	193	202	170**	170	235	198	320	535	508	354	240	248	3,378

SOURCE: Noah Webster, "Number of Deaths, In the Episcopal Church in New-York, in each month for ten years—from January 1, 1786, to December 31, 1795," *Memoirs of the Connecticut Academy of Arts and Sciences*, vol. 1, pt. 1 (New Haven, 1810), pp. 97–98.

* In original table digits were reversed and read 213.
** In original table digits were incorrect and read 160.

Charleston, South Carolina, or Boston differed from that of New York, but everywhere the rhythms of life and death were attuned to the seasons.

If Webster had separated the deaths of the male and female members of the Episcopal congregation, his table could have been used to demonstrate the impact of sex on one's life chances. Women obviously were the only ones to bear children, but tuberculosis, a killer that afflicts women more often than men, often posed more of a danger. Men may have been more vulnerable to accidents. Studies of small groups and separate communities provide examples in which women outlived men on the average, and vice versa. Which was more common is not as important as the observation that sex was one more factor contributing to the uncertainty of life in early America.

Causes of sound health are often as important in determining life expectancy as causes of death. In early America, both social and biological factors combined to produce the relatively good life chances which emerged by the end of the eighteenth century. Natural quarantines resulting from small, scattered populations hindered the spread of most epidemics. Port cities often had outbreaks of disease that did not spread far inland. The seasoning process also helped to the extent that natural selection worked to preserve only those individuals who were best-suited to the new disease environment. Diets were reasonably good in America because land was accessible and because of the food exchanges between Europeans, Africans, and the first Americans. There is no record, except in the earliest of years, of famines similar to those that hit parts of Europe in the late seventeenth century. When food had to be imported as a result of temporary shortages, it was readily available because of good water transportation and frequent surpluses in neighboring colonies. In fact, food exports were a central part of the economic life of the Middle Colonies.

Considering the importance of smallpox in human history, it is significant that inoculation against that disease was both accepted and successful before 1800. Table 3 shows the advantage inoculation had over natural infection in terms of survival, and indicates that Boston residents recognized that advantage by 1752, only thirty years after Cotton Mather and Dr. Zabdiel

Table 3 Use of Smallpox Inoculation in Eighteenth-Century Boston

Year of Epidemic	Persons Infected Naturally			Persons Infected by Inoculation		
	Number Infected	Number Dying	Proportion Dying (as in original)*	Number Infected	Number Dying	Proportion Dying (as in original)*
1721	5759	884	1 in 7	247	6	1 in 42
1730	3600	488	1 in 7	400	12	1 in 33
1752	5544	514	1 in 11	2109	31	1 in 70
1764	669	124	1 in 5	4977	46	1 in 108
1776	304	29	1 in 10	4988	28	1 in 178
1778	122	42	1 in 3	2121	19	1 in 112
1792	232	33	1 in 7	9152	165	1 in 55

SOURCE: Massachusetts Historical Society, *Collections*, 1st Series, vol. 3 (1794), p. 292.

*Refers to the form, which is not in use today, and to the fact that the ratios are in some cases wrong (although not by much).

Boylston introduced the technique in America, and in spite of opposition from other doctors and newspaper editors.

Although it may seem strange, lack of medical care probably worked to the colonists' advantage. Doctors knew little of use to heal people, and many did actual damage via purging and bleeding. Hospitals frequently spread more infections than they cured. Under such conditions no care was better than even the best.

Finally, the very prevalence and virulence of disease may have changed. The late eighteenth century simply may have had fewer epidemics because of climatic changes, mutations of germs, or other reasons. The last outbreaks of bubonic plague occurred early in the century, and cholera only emerged as a major killer after 1830. A simple change such as the introduction of cattle raising in Virginia in the middle of the seventeenth century may have benefitted residents of the Chesapeake not only by diet but also because, given the choice, malarial mosquitoes will bite cows rather than people.

In spite of the relatively good health of Americans in the eighteenth century, their lives were still much more like those of their contemporaries than ours. The move toward independence from the worst ravages of disease did not begin until almost a century after independence from the British empire.

Values and attitudes were as important as physical manifestations in determining the total experience of early Americans with regard to health and death. Just as diseases evolve biologically over time, the definition of diseases in particular and illness in general is subject to changing social and emotional responses. One thing which distinguishes the colonial period from the present is that illness tended to be defined in terms of visual symptoms. People did not often think about their health in terms of organic disorders or microorganisms. As a result, illnesses with common symptoms, like fever, tended to be lumped together; and the more spectacular disorders received most of the attention.

In general, illness was a private problem. When people got sick, they or their families expected to manage the cure or the death. Public actions rarely went beyond establishing quarantines and pesthouses in times of epidemic. Individuals without a family to offer care found themselves together with other social outcasts in a general institution that isolated the sick, poor, insane, and criminal from the rest of society. Special, "modern" institutions designed to treat each of these groups separately came later. Occasionally, when they occurred at the height of a political struggle, epidemics became caught up dramatically in politics. In Marblehead, Massachusetts, in 1773–74 and Norfolk, Virginia, in 1768–69, responses to outbreaks of smallpox became entangled in ongoing conflicts about how those communities were going to react to the growing crisis with Great Britain.[36] But such intense and overt politicization of medical matters was exceptional; usually the links between health and politics were more subtle and obscure.

The necessity for individuals and families to adjust to ever-present threats of death is closely related to the tremendous importance religion played in the lives of Americans in the seventeenth and eighteenth centuries. The Christian emphasis on life after death made a life on earth that was "nasty, brutish, and short" much more bearable. Death became not an end, but a beginning; it offered release from earthly trials, while religion offered the prospect of salvation. Pain and suffering made a person worthy for the delights of heaven. In New England, the early Puritans refused to accept the full comfort of Christianity by insisting that only a select few would go to heaven. Hell promised more of the same, or worse, for most people. As death approached, many adult Puritans became anxious wondering what their fate might be. Most parents, however, found comfort in the fact that when their children died they escaped a life of pain. By the late seventeenth century, the rigors of Puritan theology were softened by preachers who taught that heaven was open to all who led a good life. New Englanders increasingly accepted the comforts religion provided their Quaker and Anglican sisters and brothers, and refused to add psychic misery to their already significant physical woes.[37]

Efforts to reduce the anxieties associated with illness and death produced two important responses in the eighteenth century. In both instances, the actions taken were clearly designed to help people control their lives, and so may be seen as early manifestations of modern behavior. Throughout the eighteenth century, doctors searched continuously for methods of improving health care. Their understanding of biology and chemistry prevented them from making much headway, but that is less important than that they made the effort. Occasionally, new practices like smallpox inoculation were introduced. Equally important, data like those in Table 3 were collected and printed.[38] This was one of the first attempts to statistically demonstrate the advantage of one form of response to disease over another. Although the lesson was not widely understood at the time, it does mark a beginning of the shift of medicine from philosophy to an empirical science.

After 1760, the desire to control the results of death, although death itself was not yet controllable, led New England and Middle Colony clergymen concerned about the future of their families to explore the possibility of some sort of life (death) insurance.[39] Only a few people contributed to life insurance schemes, but interest in them did lead to the collection and publication of large numbers of tables of deaths (of which Table 2 is a fine example), known as bills of mortality. These statistics were collected as part of an effort to achieve a better understanding of patterns of death in America. After 1810, interest in bills of mortality waned in the absence of improvements in medical care. But the underlying attitude that death could be studied and controlled remained.

In general, it was better not to get sick at all in the period before 1770. But that was not a matter of choice. So the question arises: What could people do to help themselves once they became ill? The answer involves medical history from the perspective of the consumer rather than the vendor of health care.

Because most Americans lived on isolated farms, they often had to choose what was in fact the best option for medical care at the time—that is, to do little, or nothing at all. Given the quality of professional medical care, it was safer to rely on the natural healing processes of the body than to be exposed to a doctor. Do-it-yourself medical guide books were available in the eighteenth century, but there is no way to tell how often they were consulted. Probably most people relied on instinct or folk wisdom.

Local folk healers provided a second option for those whose illnesses drove them to seek aid. Midwives, clergymen, teachers, or other individuals in a community frequently practiced medicine on the side out of personal interest and as a service to their neighbors.[40] Some may have acquired skills in setting bones and soothing burns. Herbal medicines helped on occasion, and valuable knowledge of plant healing was exchanged between Indians, Africans, and Europeans during these years. But the greatest benefit may well have been the psychological lift from having someone come to help.

Professional medical attention was the least attractive possibility. Apothecaries, surgeons, and physicians (mostly medical philosophers) all vied for business in the colonies. In the absence of scientific knowledge, or even much scientific method, doctors argued a series of fundamental questions with more passion than fact. What was the origin of illness? How was illness to be cured? Should specific structures of the body be treated, or the whole person? What was ill-health and what was a normal condition? Was sickness the result of moral failings, and hence deserved, or was it accidental, and treatable? Most medical men were trained to answer these questions through acceptance of a philosophical system rather than by experiment and observation. Under such conditions, admitting to a mistake on one point threatened a whole theory of medicine, making progress through exchange of ideas slow.

The idea of a body in balance, or homeostasis, as the definition of health was widely shared. But there was little agreement on how the balance was disturbed or how it could be restored. Unfortunately, many doctors followed the lead of Benjamin Rush in assuming that the fundamental cause of illness was excessive bodily fluids. To restore the balance it was deemed wise to bleed, or purge through vomiting or bowel movements. Such heroic medicine must frequently have done more damage than good, if only because doctors thought the body had more blood than it does, and so occasionally bled patients to death. Efforts to require a license to practice medicine were successfully introduced in several colonies in the 1760s and may have eliminated some of the worst abuses. But, for the patient, it might have been better to prohibit all doctors from practicing rather than establish a monopoly for some.

The colonists' experiences with marriage and childbearing also distinguish them from both twentieth-century Americans and their contemporaries in the Old World. Childbearing was unusually common, by any standard. Marriage patterns in the colonies took on distinct shapes as Old World customs were altered by new social forces.

As in most societies, marriage and childbearing were closely related in America before 1770, at least for the white population. At most, only 1 to 3 percent of all births occurred outside of marriage, and frequently the couple involved formed a stable union not long after the birth. By the end of the eighteenth century, a third of all brides may have been pregnant at the time of their wedding (up from about 8 percent before 1680), but this did not seriously affect the rate of illegitimacy.[41] Marriage in colonial America was for most women and men a license to reproduce. But what exactly did that mean and how did one get "licensed?"

For colonists of European origin, marriage meant several things, in addition to a license to reproduce.[42] First, it meant that the proposed union met minimal social standards, for whether a couple purchased a license from a colonial governor or posted banns at their church, their marriage was subject to public scrutiny. Marrying close relatives or more than one spouse was strictly forbidden. A promise to wed was generally considered legally binding, unless during the period of surveillance one of the partners was discovered to be already married or an indentured servant. The choice of a spouse was frequently a matter of importance to the whole family since an appropriate union could form or strengthen valuable economic and social ties. Hence, parental consent was often required. On the frontier, marriage practices may have fallen short of legal ideals. The absence of ministers or appropriate government officials made it impossible for some to have their unions recognized by the proper persons. But in terms of childbearing and social acceptance there is little to distinguish these unions from those which were legally correct..

For black Americans, most of what the law and white society had to say about marriage was irrelevant. Slavery defined their status, and slaves could not legally wed. In spite of this, most black colonists formed family units which were as stable as possible under the conditions of slavery. Most childbearing took place within these "marriages" which were recognized and frequently sanctioned by the black community, if not by the white.

Four aspects of marriage important because of their direct effect on childbearing are: the age at which men and women first marry; the proportion of children born who marry; the length of time a marriage lasts; and how often widows and widowers remarry.

White male colonists generally followed customary patterns of marriage brought over from Europe.[43] Over 90 percent of men who lived to a marriageable age (normally twenty-five to twenty-seven on average) took wives. But life expectancy was such that no more than a half to two-thirds of boys born survived to marry. For white women the pattern was somewhat different. A woman in the colonies could expect to marry perhaps as much as five years younger than her counterpart in Europe. In regions where immigration brought in an extra supply of men, women frequently married at twenty or even younger, though few married before sixteen or seventeen. Over nine of every ten potential wives found a husband. Females who arrived as servants were generally prevented from marrying early, but those free of labor contracts could and did marry young. When immigration began to drop off, the age at which women married for the first time climbed gradually toward the European standard of twenty-three or older and the gap between the ages of husband and wife narrowed. This happened in New England and parts of the Middle Colonies over the course of the eighteenth century. Where immigration continued to provide extra men in Pennsylvania and the South the change was probably delayed, although it is likely to have occurred to some extent, especially among women of long-established families who did not mix with the newly arrived, non-English immigrants. The age at which black women formed their unions seems to have been slightly younger than that of white New Englanders, though it may not have differed greatly from Southern white women.[44] Little can be said about the age at which a black man might marry, except that his chances of marrying at all depended upon whether his owner preferred an all-male labor force or allowed a minimum of family life for his slaves.

Once a man and woman married, how long might they expect to live together? Since divorce was rare in early America, the answer to this question is directly related to life expectancy.[45] Although husbands and wives may have deserted each other frequently, the high level of childbearing in the colonies argues against this. Among Quakers of the Middle Colonies, who seem to have had relatively favorable life chances, an average marriage lasted just over thirty years. This average does obscure a relatively wide variety of experiences, as just over one of every ten of these unions lasted less than ten years, and about one of every seven marriages remained intact over fifty years. It seems unlikely that many colonial couples could expect longer marriages than these Quakers; most could look forward to fewer years together.[46] In one New England community the average marriage lasted just under twenty-four years.[47] In the South, especially when mortality was unusually high in the seventeenth century, long marriages must have been rare.[48]

Before 1800, remarriage was most common when first marriages ended early and widows or widowers had a number of small children on their hands. Migration also influenced the chances of remarrying by raising or lowering the number of potential partners. Since widowers preferred to take single women as second or third wives if they had a choice, many more widows than widowers remained alone unless they lived where women were scarce or had property from a previous union. Wealthy widows had no particular incentive to marry unless they found a congenial partner. Although evidence is currently lacking, it is probable that aging widows were far more common in New England than in the South.

Marriage in early America was a license to reproduce, and the colonists made use of that privilege. The best estimates for the birthrate in the eighteenth century indicate that about 50 children were born every year for each 1,000 people in the population. This is much the same as in the most rapidly growing parts of the world today and contrasts sharply with the birthrate in the United States today of under 15 per 1,000. On average, a newly married colonial couple might expect to have between six and eight children by the time childbearing was finished. In eighteenth-century England and France the average number of children born to each couple was generally between four and five.[49]

The high number of children average colonial couples might expect was in reality subject to considerable variation. Probably no more than one out of every eight or ten couples had the "average" number of children. Many had less, many had more. In groups where the average family included between seven and eight children, no more than 2 percent of all couples would be childless, and perhaps 6 percent more would have only one or two offspring. Around one of every five families would have three to five children. Half the couples would have six to nine. Marriages producing ten or more children were not as common, but about one of every four unions had families that large. Couples with fifteen or more children were more unusual than those with none at all.[50]

When mortality was high, the average family size was undoubtedly somewhat lower because of broken marriages and sterility caused by sickness. But by the middle of the eighteenth century, relatively large families appear to have been common throughout the colonies for both blacks and whites.

The question of why colonial families were so large has intrigued people from the eighteenth century to the present. One possible explanation is that American wives gave birth more rapidly than European women. However, this does not seem to have been the case, since couples on both sides of the Atlantic could expect an additional child every twenty-four to thirty months so long as the wife was young enough to bear children. In an essay written in 1751, Benjamin Franklin explained the difference between European and American families as the result of earlier marriages made possible by more accessible land. This argument has considerable merit. But we must also remember that health conditions in the New World were often better than in the Old, and so combined with early marriages to ensure that couples remained together longer and attained a greater proportion of their childbearing potential.

By and large, childbearing before 1770 was subject only to the natural limits imposed by health and death once a marriage was formed. However, around 1770, a change of major significance appeared in American childbearing patterns, as small numbers of parents began to make deliberate efforts to limit the size of their families. How and why they did this is not certain. Some knowledge of birth control techniques such as withdrawal by the husband during intercourse and prolonged nursing of infants by the wife was present at the time. The uncertainties of the Revolutionary era may have encouraged some people to make use of these techniques. Whatever the reasons, it is certain that some women, especially those who married young, ceased childbearing at younger ages than before and that the time between births increased. Both these patterns offer clear indications of efforts to control childbearing. The practice did not become widespread until after 1800, but at least a few Americans were modern enough in the late eighteenth century to see unlimited fertility as an undesirable aspect of their lives which could be controlled.[51] Efforts to limit the size of the family suggest the emergence of attitudes about marriage and children quite different from the values held by individuals who accept children as gifts from God.

Notes

1. Peter Laslett, *The World We Have Lost* (New York, 1965).

2. Philip D. Curtin, *The Atlantic Slave Trade: A Census* (Madison, Wis., 1969), p. 268; James Potter, "The Growth of Population in America, 1700–1870," in *Population in History*, eds. D. V. Glass and D.E.C. Eversley (Chicago, 1965), pp. 645–46.

3. W. F. Craven, *White, Red, and Black: The Seventeenth-Century Virginian* (Charlottesville, Va., 1971); Edmund S. Morgan, *American Slavery-American Freedom: The Ordeal of Colonial Virginia* (New York, 1975), pp. 395–432.

4. A. P. Newton, "The Great Emigration, 1618–1648," in *The Cambridge History of the British Empire*, 8 vols., eds. J. H. Rose, et al. (Cambridge, England, 1929), 1: 136–82; Abbot E. Smith, *Colonists in Bondage: White Servitude and Convict Labor in America 1607–1776* (Chapel Hill, N.C., 1947).

5. Herbert Moller, "Sex Composition and Correlated Culture Patterns of Colonial America," *William and Mary Quarterly* 2 (1945): 113–53.

6. *Report of the American Historical Association, 1931* (Washington, 1932), part 4, "Report of the Committee on Linguistic and National Stocks in the United States"; Potter, "Growth of Population," p. 641.

7. Mildred Campbell, "'Of People Either too Few or too Many'; The Conflict of Opinion on Population and its Relation to Emigration," in *Conflict in Stuart England: Essays in Honour of Wallace Notestein*, eds. W. A. Aiken and B. D. Henning (London, 1960), pp. 171–201.

8. Lester Cappon, ed., *Atlas of Early American History: The Revolutionary Era, 1760–1790* (Princeton, N.J., 1976), p. 25; W. Robert Higgins, "Charleston: Terminus and Entrepot of the Colonial Slave Trade," in *The African Diaspora*, eds. M. L. Kilson and R. I. Rotberg (Cambridge,

Mass., 1976), pp. 114–31; Peter H. Wood, *Black Majority: Negroes in Colonial South Carolina from 1670 through the Stono Rebellion* (New York, 1974), p. xiv.

9. George R. Mellor, "Emigration from the British Isles to the New World, 1765–1775," *History* n.s. 40 (1955): 68–83.

10. Smith, *Colonists in Bondage,* pp. 320–21.

11. Moller, "Sex Composition and Correlated Culture Patterns," p. 121.

12. Mildred Campbell, "English Emigration on the Eve of the American Revolution," *American Historical Review* 61 (1955): 1–20; Smith, *Colonists in Bondage,* pp. 307–37.

13. Curtin, *Slave Trade,* p. 268.

14. Walther F. Kirchner, "Emigration to Russia," *American Historical Review* 55 (1950): 552–66; Felix F. Stauss, "A Brief Survey of Protestantism in Archepiscopal Salzburg and the Emigration of 1732," *Georgia Historical Quarterly* 43 (1959): 29–59.

15. T. H. Breen and Stephen Foster, "Moving to the New World: The Character of Early Massachusetts Immigration," *William and Mary Quarterly* 30 (1973): 206; Newton, "Great Emigration," pp. 136–82; Smith, *Colonists in Bondage,* pp. 307–37.

16. Breen and Foster, "Moving to the New World," pp. 189–222.

17. Linda Auwers Bissell, "From One Generation to Another: Mobility in Seventeenth Century Windsor, Connecticut," *William and Mary Quarterly* 31 (1974): 55–78.

18. Carville V. Earle, "Environment, Disease, and Mortality in Early Virginia," in *The Chesapeake in the Seventeenth Century: Essays on Anglo-American Society & Politics,* eds. Thad W. Tate and David L. Ammerman (New York, 1979), pp. 96–125; Morgan, *American Slavery-American Freedom,* pp. 395–432.

19. Lorena S. Walsh and Russell R. Menard, "Death in the Chesapeake: Two Life Tables for Men in Early Colonial Maryland," *Maryland Historical Magazine* 69 (1974): 211–27.

20. Wood, *Black Majority,* pp. 63–91.

21. Robert V. Wells, *The Population of the British Colonies in America before 1776: A Survey of Census Data* (Princeton, N.J., 1975), p. 281.

22. John Duffy, "Eighteenth Century Carolina Health Conditions," *Journal of Southern History* 18 (1952): 289–302.

23. This is my analysis of data in E. Merton Coulter, ed., "A List of the First Shipload of Georgia Settlers," *Georgia Historical Quarterly* 31 (1947): 282–88.

24. Robert R. Rea, "'Graveyard for Britons,' West Florida, 1763–1781," *Florida Historical Quarterly* 47 (1968–1969): 345–64.

25. James D. Hardy, Jr., "The Transportation of Convicts to Colonial Louisiana," *Louisiana History* 7 (1966): 207–20.

26. Maris A. Vinovskis, "Mortality Rates and Trends in Massachusetts before 1860," *Journal of Economic History* 32 (1972): 184–213.

27. Richard Dunn, "A Tale of Two Plantations: Slave Life at Mesopotamia in Jamaica and Mount Airy in Virginia, 1799 to 1828," *William and Mary Quarterly* 34 (1977): 32–65.

28. Sherburne F. Cook, "The Significance of Disease in the Extinction of the New England Indians," *Human Biology* 45 (1973): 485–508.

29. John Duffy, "Small Pox and the Indians in the American Colonies," *Bulletin of the History of Medicine* 25 (1951): 324–41.

30. William E. Unrau, "The Depopulation of the Dhegia-Siouan Kansa Prior to Removal," *New Mexico Historical Review* 48 (1973): 313–28.

31. Henry F. Dobyns, "Indian Extinction in the Middle Santa Cruz River Valley, Arizona," *New Mexico Historical Review* 38 (1963): 163–81.

32. Marc Simmons, "New Mexico's Small Pox Epidemic of 1780–1781," *New Mexico Historical Review* 41 (1966): 319–26.

33. Todd L. Savitt, "Smothering and Overlaying of Virginia Slave Children: A Suggested Explanation," *Bulletin of the History of Medicine* 49 (1975): 400–404.

34. John Duffy, *Epidemics in Colonial America* (Baton Rouge, 1953); Richard H. Shryock, *Medicine and Society in America 1660–1860* (New York, 1960).

35. *See* Table 3, page 36.

36. George A. Billias, "Pox and Politics in Marblehead, 1773–1774," *Essex Institute Historical Collections* 92 (1956): 43–58; Patrick Henderson, "Smallpox and Patriotism: the Norfolk Riots, 1768–1769," *Virginia Magazine of History and Biography* 73 (1965): 413–24.

37. David E. Stannard, *The Puritan Way of Death: A Study in Religion, Culture, and Social Change* (New York, 1977).

38. For example, *see* the bills of mortality published in the *Massachusetts Historical Society Collections* 1 (1792): 116, and 4 (1795): 19.

39. Walter H. Stowe, "The Corporation for the Relief of Widows and Children of Clergymen," *Historical Magazine of the Protestant Episcopal Church* 3 (1934): 19–33; Edward Wigglesworth, "Observations on the Longevity of the inhabitants of *Ipswich* and *Hingham,* and Proposals for ascertaining the Value of Estates held for Life, and the Reversion of them," *American Academy of Arts and Sciences, Memoirs* 1 (1785): 565–67.

40. Theodore Diller, "Pioneer Medicine in Western Pennsylvania, Pt. 2," *Annals of Medical History* 8 (1926): 292–324.

41. Daniel S. Smith and Michael S. Hindus, "Premarital Pregnancy in America, 1640–1971: An Overview and Interpretation," *Journal of Interdisciplinary History* 5 (1975):537–70; Robert V. Wells, "Illegitimacy and Bridal Pregnancy in Colonial America," in *Bastardy and its Comparative History*, eds. Peter Laslett, et al. (London, 1980), pp. 349–61.

42. The only general history of marriage patterns remains George E. Howard, *A History of Matrimonial Institutions*, 3 vols. (Chicago, 1904).

43. Robert V. Wells, "Quaker Marriage Patterns in a Colonial Perspective," *William and Mary Quarterly* 29 (1972): 415–42.

44. Dunn, "Two Plantations," p. 58.

45. Nancy F. Cott, "Divorce and the Changing Status of Women in Eighteenth-Century Massachusetts," *William and Mary Quarterly* 33 (1976): 586–614.

46. Wells, "Quaker Marriage Patterns," pp. 421–23.

47. Alexander Keyssar, "Widowhood in Eighteenth-Century Massachusetts: A Problem in the History of the Family," *Perspectives in American History* 8 (1974): 83–119.

48. Lorena S. Walsh, "'Till Death Us Do Part': Marriage and Family in Seventeenth-Century Maryland," in Tate and Ammerman, *Chesapeake in the Seventeenth Century*, pp. 126–52; Darrett B. and Anita H. Rutman, "'Now-Wives and Sons-in-Law': Parental Death in a Seventeenth-Century Virginia County," ibid., pp. 153–82.

49. Wells, "Quaker Marriage Patterns," pp. 438–41.

50. Frederick S. Crum, "The Decadence of the Native American Stock. A Statistical Study of Genealogical Records," *American Statistical Association Journal* 14 (1916–1917): 215–22.

51. Robert V. Wells, "Family Size and Fertility Control in Eighteenth-Century America: A Study of Quaker Families," *Population Studies* 25 (1971): 73–82.

3

THE LOCUS OF LIFE: FAMILIES IN EARLY AMERICA

The nineteenth-century revolutions in Americans' lives altered family patterns as fully as they changed individuals' experiences. Before 1800, family members changed frequently under conditions of high fertility and mortality, but the roles of individuals in the family, and of families in society, were clearly understood. Today, family membership is much more stable, while expectations about individual and family relationships are increasingly open to question. Because of their central importance to the lives of most people, such changes in the family become an important part of any history of the American people.

It is easier to demonstrate the importance of the family than to define exactly what it is. We all use the word "family" regularly, without indicating which of its various meanings we intend. At least four separate uses of the term are common today, and to these must be added a fifth definition that would have been familiar in early America. First, "family" can be used to refer to reproductive units. Parents consider their offspring, living and dead, present or absent, as family. Likewise, children talk about their parents, sisters, and brothers as family. A second use of the term encompasses the people with whom one lives. It is more precise to refer to residential units as households, but often we use family instead. In its third and broadest sense, family refers to kinship ties of blood and marriage by which we determine all those people to whom we consider ourselves related. The fourth definition of family is a restricted version of the third, in which one is related to a person but has nothing to do with him or her. Therefore, a more practical definition of kin refers to the family of assistance. By this I mean those individuals to whom one turns in time of trouble for aid and comfort, expecting that help will be forthcoming.

Although all four of these perspectives on the "family" aid our understanding of family life in early America, few of the colonists would have drawn such fine distinctions. To them, a family was composed of a group of men, women, and children who lived together under the control of a common head and engaged in joint economic activity. Slaves and servants as well as parents and children were all part of the family. Kin to whom one turned for help were also considered part of the family. In small, rural settlements dominated by only a few kinship networks, the lines between family and community must often have blurred.

One of the most important results of the remarkable variety of patterns of birth, death, marriage, and migration in early America was considerable unpredictability with regard to individual experiences of family life.

Although couples who lived in eighteenth-century America produced an average of six to eight children, individual experience varied widely. For women who had to bear and rear large numbers of children, and for men who had to feed, clothe, and provide land for heirs, families of six, eight, or ten must have proved a considerable burden. More than one-fourth of all colonial couples were spared these burdens, but their smaller families, which often were the direct result of illness or death, may have led to anxieties about who would care for them when they got old.

From the parents' point of view, families often were large, but from the child's perspective they were even larger. A study of early American families, with an average of 7.4 children, offers the following insights into how children experienced family life.[1] Although only 35.9 percent of the parents had nine or more children, 50.7 percent of the children lived in families that large. At the other end of the spectrum, one of every ten couples had three children or less, yet these families included only 2.6 percent of the children. The number of children living in families with at least twelve offspring was the same as those who lived with four or fewer siblings, even though the number of parents who produced no more than five children outnumbered their more prolific counterparts four to one. Almost 60 percent of the children born to some Middle Colony Quaker couples lived with at least seven brothers and sisters, even though only 35.9 percent of the parents had eight or more children.[2] Of these Quakers, thirty-six couples had one child, or none at all, and only one couple had fourteen children. But the number of children who lived in the one large family was the same as the number who lived with the thirty-six couples with one or no children.

The total number of children an average couple might eventually have sheds little light on how people actually lived at any given time. This is particularly true when births added children into a family for almost twenty years, while death, marriage, and migration regularly removed individuals. Therefore, a look at household size and composition will show what family patterns were present in a whole community at any given time.

Immigration, childbearing, and slavery stand out as the three most important demographic influences on colonial households. Whenever immigrants contributed heavily to the population, the average number of whites per household frequently was between three and four persons. This pattern is evident in early Virginia, in the Spanish settlement around Saint Augustine in 1786, in Louisiana throughout much of the eighteenth century, among immigrants to Georgia in 1732, and in Germantown, Pennsylvania, in the middle of the eighteenth century.[3]

As communities stabilized and natural increase replaced immigration as the source of population growth, household size rose to an average of five to seven white persons in most of England's North American colonies. In communities dominated by immigrants, a quarter to a third of all households might have only one white person (generally a young male), but in places like New York or Rhode Island in the eighteenth century the comparable figure was 5 percent or less. As might be expected, the proportion of large households also rose in more settled regions where older couples with children were common. In these communities about half the household members were children, and roughly half the households contained five to nine white members. In parts of New York between 1712 and 1714, 10 percent of the households contained between five and nine white members.

The third major factor determining the size of a household was slavery. As blacks were imported into the southern colonies in the eighteenth century, the average household size increased. By 1790, the average number of persons in an American family ranged from 5.7 in what later became Maine to 9.5 in South Carolina, and 9.1 in Maryland.[4] The difference was the presence of slaves in the South. In the non-English colonies of Florida and Louisiana, families frequently averaged nine or more persons whenever slavery was a common practice.[5]

To understand how slavery affected the family life of black and white colonists it is necessary to remember that most white households contained few if any slaves, and that most black Americans lived under the control of relatively few white heads of families. In one South Carolina parish, in 1726, fully 38.1 percent of the slaves lived on plantations with fifty or more slaves.[6] These plantations accounted for only 6.5 percent of the white households. Similarly, in Rhode Island in 1774, 63.7 percent of all blacks lived in only 5 percent of the white households.[7] The concentration of black colonists in relatively few white households undoubtedly made it easier for them to establish a semblance of family life within the system of slavery, fostering the emergence of families within families. The vast majority of white colonists had little daily contact with their black counterparts in the intimate setting of familiy activity.

The sex, age, and cultural origins of the household head also influenced living arrangements.[8] On average, women had smaller households than men. Since the proportion of households headed by women varied significantly from one place to another, this obviously had an effect on local family patterns. In early eighteenth-century New York, households in the Hudson River Valley averaged 6.7 persons and were headed by women 4.5 percent of the time; in New York City, the average size was 5.4 and 16.7 percent of households were headed by women. Information on nonwhites in Rhode Island and on the non-Dutch in early Albany County indicates that households headed by a member of a minority group tended to be smaller than those of the dominant cultural group.

The age of the household head also helped determine who lived in a family. The numbers of both children and slaves in white households frequently rose as the head grew older. In the case of children, after the head of the household was about forty numbers declined steadily as marriages occurred. Ownership of slaves also reached a peak when the household head was about forty, but there was little subsequent decline except for those householders who survived to seventy. Where young immigrants were common, as in parts of Louisiana in the 1760s, the small average household size of 3.3 persons was closely related to the relative youth of the population.[9] In more mature settlements with older populations, household patterns took on more normal appearances.

Figures on the average size of households understate the amount of variation among early American families. A short list of households in New York in 1698 shows that each of ten families with two or three members was significantly different from the others. In Lousiana, the average household size of a group of immigrants increased from 3.3 to 3.4 between 1766 and 1769. This appears to be a remarkably stable situation until we realize that only four of the fifty-two families traceable over this period remained unchanged in both size and membership over a three-year span.[10]

What did living in such households mean to its members? Although there is little available evidence with which to answer this question, two suggestions seem plausible. First, a sense of uncertainty and change must have been generated by the remarkable variations in and among colonial households. Second, a sense of one's self as distinct from others must have been hard to develop and preserve. Most people lived in crowded quarters. In New York and Rhode Island in the eighteenth century, fully 70 percent of whites lived in only half of all households. Between 11 and 13 percent of whites lived in the largest 5 percent of all households.

Crowding was further enhanced by small, poorly built houses in which privacy was rare. An unusual list from Germantown, Pennsylvania in 1798 shows that just over half (51.1 percent) of the houses had less than 500 square feet of floor space. In 1975, about the same proportion of American dwellings had over 1,100 square feet of room.[11] Since an average household in Germantown contained about five persons, this meant that in half the families each person had a space of less than ten feet square in which to live. This is remarkably little space even for a community like Germantown, which by 1798 was relatively prosperous and had had over a century to improve its housing.

Much as successful communities had to accommodate a wide variety of living arrangements, individual families and their members had to adjust to repeated changes as each separate family (in the reproductive sense) went through a "life cycle" of growth and decline. The family cycle in early America had at least six separate stages, each with its own special meaning for those involved.[12] The formation of a family via marriage was the first stage. For most women this occurred between the ages of twenty and twenty-two; their husbands were four or five years older. Within a year and a half of marriage the second stage began with the arrival of the first child. If their experience held to the average a couple could expect an additional child every twenty-four to thirty months for most of the next two decades. The end of childbearing did not bring an end to childrearing. This third stage of the family cycle also started with the first birth, but did not end until all the children had left home. On average, almost forty years passed between the birth of the first child and the departure of the last. Since marriages lasted an average of only thirty years under the most favorable conditions, this meant that few colonial families experienced what is now a common stage of the family cycle, that is, the empty nest with both partners living and all children gone. A surviving spouse might expect to live ten to fifteen years as a widow or widower, but all but the last three or four years were occupied with the last children. The end of the family came with the death of the surviving partner, often almost half a century after the union was formed.

The numbers of colonial couples whose family cycle approximately followed the average experience must have been fairly low because of frequent variations from average figures for family size and life expectancy.[13] However, the average experience must have been important in determining what people would expect of family life. To young men and women marrying for the first time, several things would have been obvious. They could anticipate spending most of the rest of their lives raising children, and bearing them too in the case of the women. Few couples anticipated much time when they would be free of the burdens of child care to enjoy each other's mature companionship. A more realistic expectation was that either husband or wife would be required to hold the family together alone for some considerable period of time. Wives and husbands shared this worry equally, for marriages were ended by the death of a husband about as often as by the death of a wife. It is often assumed that parents who have large families do so in order to have someone to take care of them in their old age. No doubt such motives were present in early America, even though few parents lived many years after their children were all grown, and so were not dependent for long. Three generations living under one roof was an unusual occurrance.

For children, the family cycle had its own particular meanings. Much of the psychological impact of family life on a child depended on when he or she was born. Today there are important differences between the experiences of first- and second-born children.[14] In the seventeenth and eighteenth centuries, firstborns had parents who were young and vigorous, whereas an eighth or tenth child frequently had parents who were old, worn, and distracted by the demands for attention from other children. If twentieth-century patterns existed in the past, then children whose mothers had already borne several babies could expect a lifetime of poorer health than their older brothers and sisters.

For all children, but especially the younger ones, the chances of losing one or both parents while still young were high. Broken homes were common in early America, even though divorce was unusual. On the other hand, before 1800 it was rare for grown children to have their aged parents in their homes. Even when parents survived a long time, only one child was expected to support them, leaving all the other sisters and brothers free of that duty.

From the demographic perspective, adaptability and emotional strength were the traits most needed to survive the uncertainties of life in a colonial family. For adults and children, frequent adjustments to new family arrangements were necessary in response to repeated additions to and subtractions from the family through birth, marriage, migration and death.

The contrast between the uncertainty associated with the demographic side of family life and the clarity with which family roles were defined is striking. Perhaps it was necessary to emphasize what was expected of family members in order to provide stability that might not develop through long contact between individuals. Perhaps this merely reflects long-practiced social conventions. Whatever the reason, relationships both within a family and between families and society were well defined.

To put the values that the colonists attached to family life in proper prospective, it is necessary to keep three points in mind. First, values express what people think ought to be happening, but do not always reflect reality. Second, early Americans from all the colonies were remarkably consistent in the values they expressed in their letters, diaries, wills, legal codes, divorce proceedings, children's literature, newspapers, magazines, court cases regarding illegitimacy, sermons, church records, or advice manuals for young husbands or young wives. Finally, much of what follows was produced by white Americans as standards for other white Americans. Aside from the master-servant relationship, white colonists were not overly concerned with defining appropriate family behavior for their black counterparts. Black Americans had their own ideas of family life, but they can only be inferred from records kept by white planters. Hence, how much they differed from white values is uncertain.

Before exploring how families fit into the broader society of which they were a part, it is necessary to understand how a family was expected to function as a self-contained unit. A survey of the various roles in which family members were cast is a good place to begin.

Age defined some of the most obvious family relationships. Throughout most of the seventeenth and eighteenth centuries, young children were expected to be subordinate to their parents. Family life centered on adult concerns and interests; children were expected to honor and obey their parents. Expressions of

individuality by a child were frowned on. Children owed a duty to
their family, even to the point of sacrificing individual advantage
to the needs of the family. In fact, the idea of childhood as a
distinct stage of personal development was unusual. Most colonists saw children as small adults with an innate tendency for
wickedness. As such, they had to be controlled so they would not
bring harm to themselves or others, but at about the age of seven
they were expected to become responsible for their own
behavior.

Adults controlled children in a variety of ways. Close supervision with rapid, and often harsh, physical punishment was common. Religion provided psychological weapons for use against
rebellious young spirits. Children's stories were full of dreadful
things that happened to disobedient or cruel boys and girls.[15] As
children grew older, some families followed the practice of putting their children out to service, not only to learn a trade as
apprentices, but also because parents expected other adults
would exercise discipline untempered by affection.[16] As children
matured and approached marriageable age, financial coercion
was possible. Both sons and daughters risked the loss of property
settlements at the time of marriage if they challenged their
parents' authority. In some instances, parents attempted to
maintain authority over their children by economic means even
when the "children" were thirty or forty years old.[17]

As children grew, they gradually acquired the status of adults
as part of the normal process of aging. Although the assumption
of the full range of adult responsibilities was often spread over a
decade or more, by the age of thirty most men and women were
in charge of their own lives and those of a number of dependents.
For colonists who attained the age of sixty, the remainder of their
lives frequently involved a slow return to dependency.

Although the reversion to dependency based on old age did not
last long in early America, many parents worried about whether
and how well their children would care for them when they
needed help. Aging parents did not rely on love or a sense of
obligation on the part of their children to ensure care. Instead,
wills were carefully drawn, describing the amount of food and
space to be provided if a child was to inherit the family property.
In one instance, a child was threatened with disinheritance if

aging parents were not allowed to walk through the house to get outdoors.

The impression conveyed by parent-child relationships is one in which love was missing as a major part of family life. The emphasis on discipline and control worked against expressions of affection. The development of strong emotional ties between parents and children, or between sisters and brothers, may have been hindered by large families in crowded quarters facing the ever-present prospect of epidemic disease. But love still existed. Parents clearly suffered when their children died and nothing could be done to prevent or relieve their pain. Putting one's children out to service reflected, at least in part, a fear that too much love at home might prevent discipline needed for the child's own good. Wills were carefully written to protect children from possible abuse by stepparents; no one wanted to count on a Prince finding a glass slipper to rescue real Cinderellas. Many parents made diligent efforts to provide estates for their children, though pride may have been as important here as affection. In the end, however, the child was expected to be subordinate to the family's interests rather than the family to the the child's.

Sex defined a second major set of roles in colonial families. The difference between husband and wife is most obvious.[18] According to law, the woman merged with her husband when they married, and he was responsible for making all family decisions. Occasionally, wealthy widows or daughters with sympathetic fathers might have some independence preserved by a prenuptial contract. But such women were rare. More often, women exercised authority in a family only when necessity required that their husbands grant them some control. Men who travelled or who were particularly incompetent often found their wives to be helpful in business matters. Some even had their wives represent them in court. Undoubtedly some women acquired significant control within their families by threats, pleas, or other forms of bargaining, but such actions only emphasized the wife's subordinate role by law.

Women and men had different spheres of responsibility in early American families. Women frequently had control over the house, garden, and barnyard. Field work and any economic activity involving the community at large generally were handled by husbands. One spouse knew little about the details of the other's domain unless problems arose.[19]

The most burdensome task a woman faced before 1800 must have been the bearing and rearing of large numbers of children. Fathers paid considerable attention to acquiring property for sons and, to a lesser extent, daughters, and to handling major discipline problems. But these concerns seem relatively minor compared to the burden of seven or eight pregnancies and the demands of caring for several small children while running the domestic end of the farm. No wonder colonial women often looked upon pregnancy with resignation rather than enthusiasm.

Sex roles have some basis in biology, but most differences are taught by one generation to the next. In the seventeenth and eighteenth centuries, sons were reared with the understanding that they would eventually become heads of families. A certain amount of independent action was encouraged, and schooling was provided in some communities. For daughters, the future meant a switch in subordination from their parents to a husband. In the words of the old folk song known as "The Wagoner's Lad," daughters were "Controlled by their family until they are wives, Then slaves to their husbands the rest of their lives." Under such circumstances, a girl's education consisted of learning domestic skills and little else.

A third set of roles existed in some colonial families. This was the relationship between master and servant or slave. Both white servants and black slaves were under almost complete control of the head of the household. Servants did have some legal rights if they knew the laws and had access to court, but slaves had no protection from possible abuse beyond physical resistance unless some other white cared to interfere. Female servants were so frequently subject to sexual abuse by masters that laws were eventually passed requiring the removal of a woman from the household of a master who allowed her to become pregnant.[20] Black women never enjoyed such protection. For servants, the passage of time brought an eventual end to their bondage, and in some instances they received personal and real property with their freedom.

Slaves had no hope for change in the future. Perhaps the worst position for a slave was to live alone in a white household under constant supervision. On large plantations, where blacks had separate quarters, they were able to develop family lives of their own, at least partially removed from the whites'. However, black families constantly feared the sale of a member, and many day-to-day decisions could be changed by a master. Sex roles that were carefully observed by white owners in their own immediate family were ignored when it came to black women. Female slaves labored in the fields alongside the men. In spite of this, black Americans perpetuated strong family ties and developed extensive networks of kin whenever they could. Consistent with extensive subordination in other family roles, many white colonists referred to slaves and servants as family members. Whether servants or slaves felt they were part of the family, or even wanted to be, is another matter.[21]

Fully as important as relationships within a family was the way in which it functioned as a whole. The success or failure of a family often depended upon how well it performed a variety of economic activities. Alliances of property through marriage were a concern among the wealthier classes; more mundane economic considerations affected all families. The acquisition and allocation of food, clothing, and housing were central concerns. The common economic goals of the family determined the daily and yearly rhythms of life. For women, the daily cycle of feeding and caring for family, and often animals as well, overlapped with a seasonal cycle involving the harvesting of crops, spinning and weaving, making soap, planting the garden, and other similar chores. For men, the daily cycle may not have been as monotonous since they could pick and choose among the tasks required to maintain and improve a farm. The passage of a year, however, brought periods of intense labor at planting and harvest times followed by times when the work was less demanding. Bad weather enforced idleness or indoor work.

In the seventeenth and eighteenth centuries, families expected to provide for the welfare of their members. Old age, sickness, or the loss of parents were the responsibility of the family, not society. When individuals had no kin available to offer aid, most communities placed them in families rather than creating separate institutional asylums. Whenever possible, families provided funds for the purchase of land or other capital goods; banks were almost nonexistent. Merchants preferred to trade with their kin rather than with some unknown businessman.

In early America, strong family ties seem to have gone hand in hand with strong family tensions. In times of crisis and change, families rallied around the individuals involved. Births, deaths, marriages, and migrations all involved transitions made easier by the aid and comfort of kin. Personal problems often resulted in extensive consultation within the circle of kin, including those who had to be reached by mail. On the other hand, the emphasis on control and authority, crowded houses, and continual efforts to eliminate expressions of individuality introduced considerable tensions into family life. Long winters of enforced companionship must have been hard on many people. The Salem witch hunts and other expressions of hostility among neighbors have been explained as efforts to redirect aggressive tendencies within families to more distant victims.[22] Similarly, a need among young women and servants to release emotional tensions built up by intense family interactions may explain their special responsiveness to religious revivals.[23] Even the political rhetoric of the move for independence from England used the imagery of family conflict, suggesting that many colonists quickly understood the analogy.[24]

Strong families were as important to early American society as a whole as they were to their individual members. In seventeenth-century New England, some communities resorted to fines or threats of expulsion to force single persons under the control of a household head.[25] This may not have been a common practice, but in early eighteenth-century New York and in Rhode Island in 1774, no more than 1 percent of people lived alone.[26]

One of the most important services families provided society was to introduce new members into the world at large. Education was the responsibility of families throughout most of the colonial period. The vast majority of children learned the skills they needed to function in society in their homes or their neighbors'. The few boys and fewer girls who went to school generally had their ways paid by their families. Families provided land or capital to start the next generation on the road to economic success, a process that produced considerable scrambling after worldly goods by fathers of large numbers of children. Access to political office often was determined by parentage, as well as the minimum requirement of being male. Churches came to depend on "birthright" membership in which the regular succession of parents and children replaced the theologically purer, but more unpredictable, conversion experience as the source of support.[27]

Families were so vital to the smooth functioning of society that most colonies provided them with strong legal support. The authority adult white males exercised over their subordinates was ensconced in law codes as well as in customs. If necessary, patriarchs could turn to the state for help in punishing rebellious children, wives, or slaves. Anyone who interfered with the smooth exercise of family power was vulnerable to strong civil penalties.

In return for this support, heads of families were expected to act as police. Few communities had any professional law enforcement officers. Instead, householders were expected to control those under them, and when that was not sufficient, sheriffs, constables, and even night patrols were selected from the available heads of families.

The state and families interacted in other ways as well. Young men seeking office for the first time generally relied on family ties for assistance. Among prominent families, the line between colonial affairs and family interests occasionally became indistinct. Speaker John Robinson's inability to distinguish between the Virginia treasury and his family's fortune, or James Otis's attacks on Thomas Hutchinson for failure to grant his father an office are well-known examples.[28] Voting privileges in early America were not universally granted to all adults, but few seriously questioned this as long as most households had at least one voting member. The family rather than the individual was the basic political unit.

In many colonial communities religion was as important as politics. Churches relied heavily on families for support and vice versa. Churches gave public recognition to the transitions marked by birth, death, and marriage. Many families entered these important events in church registers, even when records kept by civil authorities were available. The Quakers even became involved in migration by granting departing members certificates testifying to their worthiness to aid their acceptance in a new community. The involvement of churches in these basic family experiences went beyond record keeping to include granting of approval of the change by a larger community. Quakers insisted that a couple who wished to marry receive the approval of the whole meeting as well as of their parents. Other sects required that banns be posted announcing an intention to wed, so that anyone knowing of a reason to oppose the union might have a chance to come forth. By keeping track of bastardy and births which occurred "too soon" after a marriage, churches helped to define the difference between appropriate family activity and socially dangerous behavior.

The patriarchal imagery of the Judeo-Christian tradition permeated the teachings of virtually all religious groups in the colonies. Adult males were expected to be in control; women, children, and servants were taught to know their place and accept it on pain of angering the heavenly Father. Some early slave owners questioned the desirability of converting Africans to Christianity, on the grounds that only pagans should be slaves. But as race replaced religion as grounds for slavery, and the benefits of the message of subordination and heavenly rather than earthly rewards became clear to slave owners, black colonists received carefully censored and slanted religious instruction.

Churches received as well as gave support to families. The Puritan congregations of seventeenth-century New England changed significantly after church leaders realized that not enough of the younger generations were experiencing conversion to keep up membership. The solution to the problem was the Half-Way Covenant, a device by which a modified form of "birthright" membership was created.[29] To many, this destroyed the integrity of Puritan theology by substituting family for faith as the prime religious test. Supporters of the change may have comforted themselves with the fact that membership based on birth was common to many religious sects in America, and in Europe as well. Even the religious revivals that periodically swept across the colonies seem to have owed at least some of their success to family life. The enthusiastic response by young women and servants to the messages of dramatic preachers can be seen as emotional reactions to anything that would offer release from their normally dull and oppressed family life.

In addition to encouraging approved family relationships, religious and civil authorities tried to stamp out unacceptable behavior. In particular, they devoted considerable attention to the problems of bastardy and sexual activity outside of marriage. Over the course of the seventeenth and eighteenth centuries, both bastardy and bridal pregnancy became more common. Although neither ever threatened the colonial social order, the way in which guilty parties were treated changed as new attitudes emerged about which kinds of births were to be valued and which were to be punished.[30] In the seventeenth century, almost all sexual activity outside of marriage was lumped under the sin of fornication and was jointly controlled by church and state. In the eighteenth century, churches punished adultery and premarital sex when they discovered it, but they were not always ardent in pursuit of sexual sinners. The civil authorities abandoned any serious efforts at moral correction and contented themselves with ensuring that bastards had someone to pay for their upkeep. Illegitimate children no longer were punished for the behavior of their parents.

White legal and religious codes showed virtually no interest in the status of black children beyond the fact that they inherited their parents' status as slaves. What little we know of black families before 1800 indicates that they, too, followed a pattern of stable, monogamous unions whenever possible, but of custom and preference rather than because the law required it. White Americans may have expressed little concern about sexual behavior among their black neighbors, but they demonstrated considerable anxiety about the prospect of interracial sex. Men and women who engaged in sexual activity with a member of a different race were punished severely. Any children were either enslaved or put out as servants until the age of twenty-five. Mulatto babies were described as "spurious issue" and "abominable mixtures" in the law codes.

In general, most colonists showed remarkable conformity to accepted standards of behavior. In spite of the obvious physical pleasures of sexual activity, most unmarried colonists seem to have refrained from such behavior, at least until they had decided to marry. Most "sinners" accepted the efforts of society to punish them as examples for others, although a few resisted public humiliation. One New England man felt that the fact that his judges were the woman's relatives had prevented his receiving a fair trial in a bastardy suit. A more common objection, however, came from men, accused of fathering bastards, who felt, sometimes with reason, that civil authorities were more interested in ensuring financial support for the child than in finding the true father.

Bits and pieces of evidence suggest that major shifts of power within families began to occur in the second half of the eighteenth century. However, because of the gradual pace of change and the political struggle with Great Britain and its aftermath which preoccupied American attention until after 1800, few persons noticed the first signs that family life was changing.

In retrospect, we can point to a variety of new family relationships that began to emerge at the end of the eighteenth century. Increased illegitimacy and bridal pregnancy between 1700 and 1800 and more tolerant reactions to extramarital sexual activity are among the changes that point to a weakening of the strict social control that early American families had exerted. Although major reforms in divorce did not occur for another century, the years between 1775 and 1800 saw new laws passed making it easier to obtain a divorce, and the laws were used. Parental control over children declined.[31] Children began to wander farther from home; marriage became more a matter of individual attraction and less an economic alliance; and parents recognized the individuality of their offspring by giving them distinct names that often had no particular family ties. Gradually childhood came to be seen as a time of innocence; love for children was expressed by open affection as well as by discipline.[32] Women's roles expanded slightly during and after the struggle with England, though they still had far to go before male dominance would be significantly reduced.[33] Finally, a few parents began deliberately to reduce the size of their family, having decided for some new but uncertain reason that unlimited numbers of children were neither necessary nor desirable.[34]

Perhaps all these changes were unrelated except in time. More likely, the end of the eighteenth century saw some early manifestations of the modern personality. For some eighteenth-century

Americans, new ideas about individual dignity and worth, a belief that the future could be directed, and faith in human progress began to undermine the old order of hierarchy, control, and passive acceptance of one's place within the family.[35]

Notes

1. Frederick S. Crum, "The Decadence of the Native American Stock: A Statistical Study of Genealogical Records," *American Statistical Association Journal* 14 (1916–1917): 215–22. Here, and in some notes below, the citation is to data reworked by the author for the purposes of this book.

2. Robert V. Wells, "Family Size and Fertility Control in Eighteenth-Century America: A Study of Quaker Families," *Population Studies* 24 (1971): 75.

3. E. Merton Coulter, ed., "A List of the First Shipload of Georgia Settlers," *Georgia Historical Quarterly* 31 (1947): 282–88; Bruce Downsbrough, "Household Size and Composition in French Louisiana, 1721–1732" (seminar paper, Union College, 1974), based on data in Charles R. Maduell, Jr., *The Census Tables for the French Colony of Louisiana from 1699 through 1732* (Baltimore, 1972); Irene Hecht, "The Virginia Muster of 1624/5 as a Source for Demographic History," *William and Mary Quarterly* 30 (1973): 65–92; Joseph B. Lockey, "The St. Augustine Census of 1786," *Florida Historical Quarterly* 18 (1939–1940): 11–31; Andrew S. Walsh and Robert V. Wells, "Population Dynamics in the Eighteenth-Century Mississippi River Valley: Acadians in Louisiana," *Journal of Social History* 11 (1978): 521–45; Stephanie G. Wolf, *Urban Village: Population, Community, and Family Structure in Germantown, Pennsylvania, 1683–1800* (Princeton, N.J., 1976), pp. 40–41.

4. Philip J. Greven, Jr., "The Average Size of Families and Households in the Province of Massachusetts in 1764 and in the United States in 1790: An Overview," in *Household and Family in Past Time*, ed. Peter Laslett (Cambridge, England, 1972), pp. 545–60.

5. Downsbrough, "Household Size"; Lockey, "St. Augustine."

6. Peter H. Wood, *Black Majority: Negroes in Colonial South Carolina from 1670 through the Stono Rebellion* (New York, 1974), pp. 155–66.

7. Robert V. Wells, *The Population of the British Colonies in America before 1776: A Survey of Census Data* (Princeton, N.J., 1975), p. 311.

8. Ibid., pp. 297–333.

9. Walsh and Wells, "Population Dynamics," pp. 526–29.

10. Ibid., pp. 530–33; Wells, *Population of the British Colonies*, pp. 131–33.

11. U.S. Department of Housing and Urban Development, *Statistical Yearbook, 1975* (Washington, 1975), p. 174; Wolf, *Urban Village*, p. 35.

12. Robert V. Wells, "Demographic Change and the Life Cycle of American Families," *Journal of Interdisciplinary History* 2 (1971): 273–82.

13. Peter R. Uhlenberg, "A Study of Cohort Life Cycles: Cohorts of Native Born Massachusetts Women, 1830–1920," *Population Studies* 23 (1969): 407–20.

14. John A. Clausen and Suzanne R. Clausen, "The Effects of Family Size on Parents and Children," in *Psychological Perspectives on Population*, ed. James T. Fawcett (New York, 1973), pp. 185–208; Lucille Forer, *The Birth Order Factor* (New York, 1976).

15. Joseph E. Illick, "Child-Rearing in Seventeenth-Century England and America," in *The History of Childhood*, ed. Lloyd deMause (New York, 1974), pp. 303–50; John F. Walzer, "A Period of Ambivalence: Eighteenth-Century American Childhood," in ibid., pp. 351–82.

16. Edmund S. Morgan, *The Puritan Family: Religion and Domestic Relations in Seventeenth Century New England* (New York, 1966), pp. 65–86.

17. John Demos, *A Little Commonwealth: Family Life in Plymouth Colony* (New York, 1970); Philip J. Greven, Jr., *Four Generations: Population, Land, and Family in Colonial Andover, Massachusetts* (Ithaca, N.Y., 1970).

18. In addition to Demos, *Little Commonwealth*, and Morgan, *Puritan Family*, see Mary S. Benson, *Women in Eighteenth-Century America: A Study of Opinion and Social Usage* (New York, 1935); Richard B. Morris, *Studies in the History of American Law, with Special Reference to the Seventeenth and Eighteenth Centuries* (New York, 1930), chap. 3, "Women's Rights in Early American Law"; Mary Beth Norton, *Liberty's Daughters: The Revolutionary Experience of American Women, 1750–1800* (Boston, 1980).

19. Mary Beth Norton, "Eighteenth-Century American Women in Peace and War: the Case of the Loyalists," *William and Mary Quarterly* 33 (1976): 386–409.

20. W. W. Hening, ed., *The Statutes at Large Being a Collection of All the Laws of Virginia (1619–1792)*, 13 vols. (Richmond, 1809–1823), vol. 2, p. 167.

21. Herbert Gutman, *The Black Family in Slavery & Freedom, 1750–1920* (New York, 1976); Alan Kulikoff, "The Beginnings of the Afro–American Family in Maryland," in *Law, Society, and Politics in Early Maryland*, eds. Aubrey C. Land, et al. (Baltimore, 1976).

22. John Demos, "Underlying Themes in the Witchcraft of Seventeenth-Century New England," *American Historical Review* 75 (1970): 1311-311-26.

23. Cedric B. Cowing, "Sex and Preaching in the Great Awakening," *American Quarterly* 20 (1968): 624–44; Philip J. Greven, Jr., "Youth, Maturity, and Religious Conversion: A Note on the Ages of Converts in Andover, Massachusetts, 1711–1749," *Essex Institute Historical Collections* 108 (1972): 119–34; Gerald F. Moran, "Conditions of Religious Conversion in the First Society of Norwich, Connecticut, 1718–1744," *Journal of Social History* 5 (1972): 331–43.

24. Edwin G. Burrows and Michael Wallace, "The American Revolution: The Ideology and Psychology of National Liberation," *Perspectives in American History* 6 (1972): 167–306.

25. Alice M. Earle, *Customs and Fashions in Old New England* (New York, 1893), pp. 36–37; J. H. Trumbull and C. J. Hoadly, eds., *The Public Records of the Colony of Connecticut*, 15 vols. (Hartford, 1850), vol. 1, p. 8.

26. This is a slightly different perspective on data presented in Wells, *Population of the British Colonies*, p. 304.

27. For example, *see* Bernard Bailyn, *Education in the Forming of American Society* (Chapel Hill, N. C., 1960); Robert G. Pope, *The Half-Way Covenant: Church Membership in Puritan New England* (Princeton, N.J., 1969); Thomas L. Purvis, "'High-born, Long-Recorded Families': Social Origins of New Jersey Assemblymen, 1703 to 1776," *William and Mary Quarterly* 37 (1980): 592–615; Philip L. White, *The Beekmans of New York in Politics and Commerce, 1647–1877* (New York, 1956).

28. Charles S. Sydnor, *American Revolutionaries in the Making: Political Practices in Washington's Virginia* (New York, 1962), p. 94; John J. Waters, Jr., *The Otis Family in Provincial and Revolutionary Massachusetts* (New York, 1975), pp. 76–109.

29. Pope, *Half-Way Covenant*.

30. Robert V. Wells, "Illegitimacy and Bridal Pregnancy in Colonial America," in *Bastardy and its Comparative History*, eds. Peter Laslett, et al. (London, 1980), pp. 349–61.

31. Daniel Scott Smith, "Parental Power and Marriage Patterns: An Analysis of Historical Trends in Hingham, Massachusetts," *Journal of Marriage and the Family* 35 (1973): 406–18.

32. Bernard Wishy, *The Child and the Republic: The Dawn of Modern American Child Nurture* (Philadelphia, 1968).

33. Nancy F. Cott, *The Bonds of Womanhood: "Woman's Sphere" in New England, 1780-1835* (New Haven, 1977); Norton, *Liberty's Daughters*.

34. Wells, "Family Size and Fertility Control."

35. For a more extended presentation of this argument, *see* Robert V. Wells, "Family History and the Demographic Transition," *Journal of Social History* 9 (1975): 1–19.

4

POPULATION AND THE EMERGENCE OF AMERICAN SOCIETY

The demographic factors that so profoundly shaped the lives of Americans, either as individuals or within their families, also affected the economy, politics, and society. Although the connections were not always apparent, the private actions of people and families often combined to produce far-reaching public consequences. In the eighteenth century, some Americans already understood the importance for their society of large families and immigration. The results of rapid population growth and the presence of many cultures were easy to see. They were less aware of the implications of the general age and sex composition of the population. But early Americans did not need to recognize the significance or even the existence of particular demographic or family patterns in order for those patterns to have a major influence at the time, and to merit attention now.

The most dominant force shaping early American society was migration. A common image of the resettlement of America includes weary Pilgrims confronting "a hideous and desolate wilderness," after a long ocean voyage. This picture is more romantic than accurate. The only people to move into a wilderness in North America were the migrants who came from west to east long before Columbus. Everyone else encountered an environment already shaped by human activity. From New England to New Jersey and south along the coastal plain, the first Europeans encountered open land which was the result of Indian agriculture.[1] The best springs and river fords had been located by the first Americans; trails had been worn, fields had been cleared, and choice spots for towns had been occupied. In some areas, disease had eliminated the first settlers before the English arrived. Elsewhere competition soon emerged for the best locations for agriculture and trade. Regardless of exactly when the changeover came, the land was not "virgin" but was recently "widowed," and rarely had long to wait for a new spouse.[2]

The efforts surrounding the establishment of the first permanent English colony in Virginia reflect an initial uncertainty about how the New World could best be exploited. Since the English government did not wish to be directly involved in the costly process of resettling North America, grants of land and government were made to companies and individuals (proprietors) to see what they could accomplish. The colonists who landed at Jamestown in 1607 came as employees of the Virginia Company rather than as individuals seeking to establish a new life in the New World. Hostility quickly emerged between English investors and their employees in America over policies that served the interests of one group but not the other. The resulting turmoil was no doubt enhanced by the fact that Virginia was dominated by young, single males; family life was missing.[3]

Beginning in 1618, the Virginia Company introduced a series of reforms aimed at recruiting more, and different, colonists. With these reforms, English efforts at colonization took a major step, from considering colonists as employees temporarily assigned to North America to recognizing the need for residents with strong family ties and strong motives to live permanently in America. First, the company offered fifty acres of land, known as a "headright," to every man, woman, and child who came to the colony at their own or their family's expense. A husband and wife, with two children, who paid their own way to Virginia could claim 200 acres of land. Second, the colonists were offered greater control over their own affairs via a legislative assembly which became known as the Virginia House of Burgesses.

If these reforms had been restricted to Virginia, their importance would be relatively minor. However, many other colonies adopted similar measures, and some added forms of religious freedom as well, as part of the effort to resettle the land. As a result, adult white males came to consider access to wealth, religious toleration, and participation in local politics as rights rather than privileges. Efforts to maintain and expand these rights remain a part of American life even today. New England colonists aggressively pursued these advantages. Elsewhere, they were offered to prospective settlers by investors in need of a stable labor force in the New World. Occasionally the offer was made reluctantly, as by the Carolina proprietors who found their theoretical preferences for a colony modeled on medieval practices compromised by a need to recruit inhabitants, and wrecked by the people who accepted their terms.

In 1619, a year after the Virginia reforms, the need for settlers led to another step which has had equally lasting impact on American society. The first black colonists arrived in Virginia and were sold into bondage. It took more than a generation for the system of slavery to be legally refined and linked to race. The major influx of black settlers only came in the eighteenth century. But after the mid seventeenth century neither Europeans nor Africans in America would ever be able to anticipate completely re-creating the Old World in the New. Race slavery and cultural pluralism prevented that.

Even without the eventual large-scale adoption of slavery in the southern colonies, regional differences emerged to distinguish social organization in one part of England's empire from the style of life in another. The young males who made up the overwhelming majority of the first immigrants to the Chesapeake settled on scattered farms, away from the authority and control that town life brings, creating a society that was both exploitive and volatile. The relatively short life expectancy there in the seventeenth century furthered the aura of instability.[4] In contrast, New England settlers shared and enforced values that emphasized the development of strong family and community ties. Immigrants were welcomed only if they were willing to accept the standards of the community.[5] If not, they were expected to move on. Rhode Island, Connecticut, Long Island, and New Jersey all received Puritans and others who could not live comfortably in Massachusetts Bay. Nonetheless, even these "rebels" chose to live in towns in which family life played a major role. The stability which resulted could only have been aided by the better life chances in the northern colonies.[6]

The arrival of non-English settlers after 1660 and their uneven distribution in England's colonies increased rather than decreased regional differences. By 1770, there were colonial societies in America, but little that could be called American society.[7] Variations in landholding patterns, language, housing, religion, agricultural techniques and crops, demographic patterns, and seasonal cycles produced distinct social arrangements, each with its own rhythm of life.[8] At the time, shrewd observers already recognized that Massachusetts and South Carolina colonies were different, and that those in between did not resemble either very much.

Although most New Englanders in 1770 could trace their ancestors in America back through several generations, those colonies had remained most completely English. New York was rapidly becoming a section of sections, a vision of America's future. New England Puritans lived on Long Island; by 1700, New York City was a place of many cultures; the Hudson Valley was dominated by English and Dutch landlords and their tenants; and around Albany the Dutch influence prevailed, giving way to Iroquois settlements to the north and west.[9] Pennsylvania never entirely lost the early influence of the English Quakers, but by 1770, Germans, Scotch-Irish, and a small group of Welsh were challenging the Quakers and each other for demographic and social control of the region.[10]

In the South, two, if not three, sections existed by 1770.[11] Along the coast, whites of English background lived side by side with the vast majority of black Americans. In some counties whites dominated; in others blacks held the numerical majority. Although the white planters often wished otherwise, this society, based as it was on race slavery, was definitely *not* English. The society that emerged in the South Carolina low country probably deserves to be distinguished from that of the Chesapeake because of a greater emphasis on slavery, the urban influence of Charleston, and the lasting impact of early immigrants from Barbados and France. The southern interior, running northeast to southwest along the Great Valley, was quite different. Blacks were rare, as were English. Instead, other Europeans,

such as Scots, Scotch-Irish, and Germans interacted with Cherokees, Creeks, and other Indians to produce unique social
arrangements.

Anyone who left the colonies controlled by England to travel in
those regions of the future United States colonized by Spain and
France would have encountered additional contrasts. The earliest successful efforts by Europeans to settle in what later became
the United States occurred in Saint Augustine, Florida, in 1565
and in New Mexico in 1598. These efforts were aimed largely at
securing the northern frontier of the Spanish empire and so had
the distinct quality of military outposts rather than agricultural
villages. The Spanish eventually established small military and
missionary outposts in what would become Texas and Arizona,
and in 1769 they gained a foothold in California. These settlements remained small and were frequently dominated by males
in the absence of self-sustaining family life. Saint Augustine
probably did not acquire 1,000 people until about 1700, and may
never have had many over 3,000 inhabitants. Compared to the
100,000 residents of Mexico City or the 50,000 in Havana or
Lima in the 1760s, Saint Augustine was clearly on the edge of the
Spanish empire.[12]

The French settlements in North America that eventually
were incorporated into the United States were also small and
isolated. Although serious efforts to encourage French colonists
to move to the Mississippi Valley began in 1718, upper Louisiana
around Saint Louis had only about 3,500 Europeans and Africans
as late as 1796, a figure which more than tripled in the next eight
years as the Americans began a demographic invasion which led
to the Louisiana Purchase in 1803. Closer to New Orleans the
population was three to four times larger, but not enough to
establish permanent French control over the territory.[13]

The eventual incorporation of these French and Spanish settlements into the United States can be explained by the extraordinary success that the English had in resettling their part of
America. Nonetheless, the influence of both Spanish and French
preferences regarding religion, architecture, farm layouts, and
town plans is still visible in parts of the United States.

West of the Appalachians, European pressure was evident
before the English colonies declared independence, but beyond

the Mississippi, Indian tribes remained in control of their own fates in the seventeenth and eighteenth centuries. Geographers have recently discovered that Indians were pushing the cultivated areas of the northern plains steadily northward in the late eighteenth and early nineteenth centuries.[14] In what is now the southwestern United States, the first Americans reacted to continued Spanish encroachment from the south by voluntarily altering their places of residence to better-protected areas, by active and successful military action (especially in the Pueblo Rebellion of 1680), and by a partial accommodation to Spanish civilization. The Indians indoubtedly were strongly influenced by European contact (before the Spanish, sheep and horses were unknown), but unlike the eastern tribes, they never were overwhelmed by European populations during this period. In fact, many of the tribes in the southwest were as fully occupied in adjusting to the expansion of the Plains Indians as they were in holding off the Spanish. In the nineteenth century, however, continued expansion from the English settlements overwhelmed even these people.[15]

The fact that settlers were recruited by English investors as laborers leads naturally to questions about the economic results of immigration. From an Indian perspective, the need for labor may not have been as obvious as it was to the Europeans. The first Americans were using the land efficiently to provide for themselves and for whatever trading they desired. Many Indian tribes had cleared forests from large tracts of land, where they raised crops native to American soils by long-established techniques. The English, however, interpreted a non-European use of the land as a nonuse of the land rather than an alternative relationship with the environment. They felt free to encroach on land that was not free for the taking. Thus, one of the most significant economic results of immigration was the transformation of the land utilization of the North Atlantic seaboard, from an Indian to a European form. Agriculture became more intensive, new crops were planted, and permanent rights of private property were established. Population density increased.

The arrival of non-English immigrants reinforced the economic changes brought about by the English settlers. More labor was provided, often unwilling, to bring more land into use in the traditional European pattern. New groups of people brought with them new crops and techniques. Africans had the knowledge and skills to make rice a major part of the Carolina economy in the eighteenth century.[16] Mennonite farmers from Germany who settled in Pennsylvania had long been famous for their attention to soil fertilization, barn building, and animal care, procedures many farmers of English origin took lightly.[17]

The influx of immigrants offset some of the economic benefits to the empire gained by new laborers by generating political frictions. The means used to recruit settlers encouraged political expectations among white male colonists that contrast sharply with the English perception of Americans as subservient dependents. Of equal importance was the fact that by 1770 only about half the colonists had any natural political loyalty toward England. Of these, many were of families who had lived in America for several generations, and so had no firsthand knowledge of the mother country. Ironically, over the course of the eighteenth century many legal and political institutions in the colonies became increasingly Anglicized, even as the population moved in the opposite direction. There is no evidence of widespread hostility toward the British empire on the part of the immigrants, but there is no evidence of great affection either.

Rapid movement of people within the colonies created additional problems for English officials. Because of conflicts with France and Spain during the eighteenth century, the English found it desirable to maintain friendly relations with Indian tribes like the Iroquois or Cherokee that were still large enough to alter the imperial balance of power. The continual encroachment by the colonists on Indian lands made English diplomacy more difficult, and presented the English with a serious dilemma since efforts to keep the colonists from moving west conflicted with expectations raised by the seventeenth-century recruitment devices.

In the quarter century before independence, the English began to worry about whether the colonists were escaping the control of the empire. As early as 1751, Benjamin Franklin pointed out that England would have to accommodate the growth of the colonies or face the consequences. His warnings became more pointed in 1765, in the midst of the Stamp Act Crisis, when he wrote to one English lord that because of population growth

America would soon "be able to shake off any shackles that may be imposed on her, and perhaps place them on the imposer."[18] Several years before, officials in London had debated whether the American population should be restricted to territory near the port cities where military garrisons might provide some control, or whether the colonies could be kept weak by encouraging expansion in such a way as to enhance existing differences.[19] By the 1770s, the worst fears of the English were realized. In 1773 Lord Dartmouth, the English minister in charge of colonial affairs, expressed concern about future relationships with the Cherokees (and within the empire, too) when he doubted "whether that dangerous spirit of unlicensed emigration into the Interior parts of America can be effectively restrained by any authority whatever." Two years later, the governor of Virginia observed that "the established Authority of any government in America, and the policy of Government at home, are both insufficient to restrain the Americans and they do and will remove as their avidity and restlessness incite them."[20]

Imperial officials were not the only ones to face political problems arising from migration patterns. Americans of all sorts found questions of who should exercise power and for what purposes complicated by fluid, ever changing societies. For the first Americans, one issue of power was clearly drawn. Could they keep their land, or at least share it with the newcomers, or would they be forced to give it up? The impact of disease coupled with an aggressive assertion that the land was available to be taken made the answer to that question inevitable. In other matters, the Europeans were less successful in establishing their authority. Indians frequently resisted missionary activity in the seventeenth century. One Huron showed an understanding of the link between European culture and Indian catastrophe when he asked, "What profit can there come to us from lending ear to the Gospel since death and faith nearly always march in company." In New England, overtures from Christian Indians to share their faith with their unconverted kin met with sharp refusal. The non-Christians bluntly observed, "We are well as we are, and desire not to be troubled with these new wise sayings."[21] In the long run, the preservation of independent action among the Indians depended upon their ability to withdraw from intimate contact with the newcomers.

The arrival of large numbers of Africans in the late seventeenth and eighteenth centuries had important political consequences. Slavery itself is a major political system involving the establishment and use of arbitrary power. Thus black Americans found themselves caught up in one American political system in which they were the subjects and from which they had almost no chance of escape. At the same time, they were excluded from participation in the political system by which the white colonists governed themselves. Obviously the white colonists provided links between the two systems, for as the number of slaves rose and fears of rebellion and resistance increased, whites made use of local and imperial governments to control the movement and actions of enslaved persons.

Even politics in which only the white colonists were involved were significantly influenced by migration patterns. In colonies where indentured servants were common, social control was a serious problem. Bacon's Rebellion in Virginia in 1676 may have been led by a member of the ruling elite, but many of its supporters were servants. [22] In the eighteenth century, Virginia and Maryland resisted attempts by England to send convicts as indentured servants, on the grounds that they would create trouble in America.[23] Conflict between various religious and ethnic groups was a part of American politics long before the great nineteenth-century migrations. In New York, colonists of English and Dutch background opposed each other from Leisler's Rebellion in 1688–1689 to the time of the War of Independence.[24] Pennsylvania Quakers found themselves in an ongoing three-cornered political contest with settlers of German and Scotch-Irish background.[25] In the South, English inhabitants along the seacoast denied full access to colonial politics to Germans, Irish, Scots, and Scotch-Irish who lived inland. In the 1760s, and 1770s, violence erupted in the interiors of North and South Carolina in the form of the regulator movements in protest over political abuses.[26] Even in New England, where internal migration was not complicated by cultural conflicts, newly settled regions expressed resentment over the fact that power often did not shift as fast as population.

The men who dominated colonial governments were richer and older than the average colonist. This has been correctly attributed to an eighteenth-century habit of deferring to one's "betters." But it may also be related to the rapid population turnover, from both death and migration, which left only a few men in most communities with the experience, income, and knowledge of local affairs to govern in traditionally accepted ways. Survival may well have been as important as deference in determining political leadership, at least on the local level.[27]

Migration was not the only important demographic factor shaping early American society. Rapid changes in the size of the population also deserve attention. The dislocation and destruction of pre-Columbian societies that resulted from rapid decrease in numbers has already been explored. Of interest now is the extraordinary rate of growth of the newcomers. Once the initial period of high mortality and uneven immigration was over, population growth in the colonies stabilized at just under 3 percent per year on average. Newer regions tended to exceed this average; older settlements often fell somewhat below it. But as a whole, the English colonists in North America doubled their numbers about every twenty-five years after 1700. This rate of increase would be labeled explosive today, when only a few nations exceed the figure sustained for over a century in early America.

Then, as now, rapid growth was a mixed blessing. In the realm of politics, growth probably was more beneficial than harmful. In the early years of resettlement, both colonists and imperial officials worried about the security of the colonies against foreign and internal threats. By 1700, much of this concern had disappeared, for it was apparent that the colonies were not only surviving, but thriving. After 1750, the English began to worry that continued growth of the colonial population might generate a move toward independence. Some of these fears were justified. Colonists like Benjamin Franklin, Yale President Ezra Stiles, and Harvard Professor of Divinity Edward Wigglesworth began to interpret population growth as evidence of American power and virtue. To these men, growth was the result of a superior way of life in America. When political arguments with England after 1760 began to stress English corruption and American virtue, demographic evidence strengthened the colonists' convictions that their analysis was correct.[28]

Increased numbers also meant that voters had more and possibly better choices for leaders to fill the limited number of colonial offices. Competition among leading colonial families for political preference may well have encouraged greater attention to provincial interests to attract votes. Efforts on the part of English officials to give patronage to residents of the mother country instead of the colonists meet with resistance. Representative assemblies in most colonies became increasingly important, not only because they gained power within the structures of government, but also because they offered ambitious colonists one of the most accessible routes to office.[29]

The doubling of the population every quarter century both helped and hindered the development of higher standards of living among the colonists. In the early years, increased size meant more complex and specialized economic arrangements were possible. Markets became larger for local merchants and imperial traders. The total amount of trade between England and America increased dramatically between 1700 and 1775, just as the mother country desired.

However, growth in the total economic output of a society does not necessarily mean a better life for individuals or their families. Unless economic growth exceeds the rate of population increase, the well-being of most people either remains the same or declines. What little is known about this subject suggests that economic improvement for most colonists was slight throughout the eighteenth century. The growth of trade with England significantly exceeded population increase only in the Middle Colonies after 1750.[30] Over the course of the eighteenth century, an ever larger proportion of the population appeared on tax lists as owning no property. Wills written at the time indicate the same thing. Large numbers of poor people emerged as population grew and pressure on land and other ecomonic resources increased.[31]

Poverty is not necessarily the result of rapid population growth; it may reflect the fact that not all families had equal access to the goods of society, or, as was common in the South, slaves and planters did not claim equal portions of a family's wealth. In the northern colonies, large families put pressure on available land in all but the most recently settled communities; likewise, opportunities arising from offices and positions of privilege did not keep pace with the numbers of aspirants. Steady migration to newer settlements within the colonies was at least partially the result of expectations of prosperity among members of younger generations that could not be realized in older, more densely settled communities.

The contrast between general economic growth and individual advancement was most striking in those regions where bound labor was a major factor in the growth of the economy. Indentured servants had reasonable expectations of sharing in colonial prosperity only in the seventeenth century or in the newest settlements.[32] Slaves, of course, could never expect to benefit from their labors.

The age and sex composition of the colonial population also deserve attention. In recent years, it has been common to refer to the youthful nature of the American population as the median age dipped from over thirty in 1960 to about twenty-eight in 1970. In the history of the American peoples, this is still a very old population—in the eighteenth century the median age was about sixteen. Four different age and sex pyramids are presented in Chart 1 to help show how important these factors were in early America. Those for Virginia in 1625 and the United States in 1900 and 1970 are constructed directly from census data. Since none of the fifty-seven censuses taken in the North American colonies in the eighteenth century have a comparable breakdown by age, the remaining pyramid is a representative age composition for about 1770. Although this age-sex pyramid closely approximates several eighteenth-century colonial populations with high rates of natural increase, no single colony may ever have had an age composition exactly like it, partly because of fluctuations in birth and death rates, and partly because of the continued, though much reduced, influence of migration. Of interest here are the changes between 1625 and 1770; the shifts between the eighteenth and twentieth centuries will be considered later.

The economic consequences of moving from a population composed like that of Virginia in 1625, to the more normal pattern found in the colonies in 1770, are significant. In early Virginia, the overwhelming majority of the population was males between

CHART 1 AGE AND SEX COMPOSITION OVER 350 YEARS

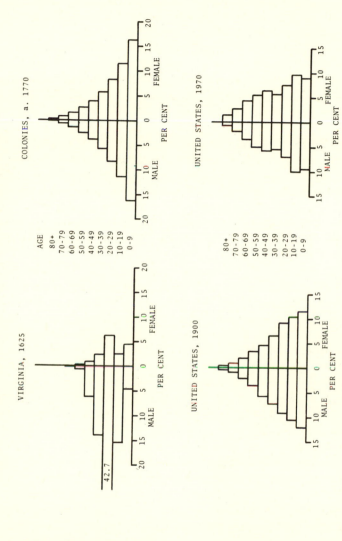

SOURCES: Bureau of Census, *Abstract of the Twelfth Census of the United States, 1900* (Washington, 1902), p. 11; idem, *1970 Census of Population* (Washington, 1973), vol. 1, pt. 1, pp. 263–65; Coale and Demeny, *Regional Model Life Tables*, p. 42; Wells, *Population of the British Colonies,* pp. 92, 115–20, 163, 260–69.

the ages of ten and thirty-nine. Children, women, and old people were rare. Such a population clearly had tremendous labor potential. Assuming that persons under sixteen or over sixty were unable to produce more than they consumed, 83.8 percent of the Virginians were in the productive years of life. There were five producers for every one person dependent upon the labor of others. By 1770, a striking change had occurred. Although the proportion of persons over sixty was still rather low (between 4 and 6 percent in general), the majority of the population was under twenty, about a third were under ten. Only 47.4 percent were in the productive years of life so each individual producer had 1.1 persons dependent upon him or her for support. This factor, primarily the result of high fertility, may well have been as important as rapid growth in curtailing improvements in per capita income. When the proportion of consumers is high, saving for investment for future economic growth becomes difficult. In addition, low life expectancy meant that many young consumers died before they returned anything to the economy, let alone their families.

Historians of early America have spent considerable time debating how democratic (that is, open to widespread participation) colonial politics were. A look at the age-sex pyramid of 1770 suggests that the answer should clearly be "not very." Roles derived from race slavery removed at least one-third of all Chesapeake inhabitants, and over half of all colonists who lived along the Carolina coast from political activity. In New York slightly over one out of ten residents was eliminated from politics on grounds of race. Since age and sex also affected eligibility for office, it becomes clear that all the colonies were governed by a very small minority.

To the extent that males between the ages of forty and fifty-nine provided the leadership for early America, only 6.5 percent of the total population were available to guide the communities. By including men in their thirties, an additional 5.8 percent were available, but this still left almost nine of every ten colonists ineligible for office for reasons of age or sex alone. The fact that early Virginia, with its preponderance of young males, was far more volatile than the eighteenth-century colonies is a measure of how well age and sex roles were learned and enforced. Too many individuals expecting to be politically active were dangerous both in theory and practice in the seventeenth century. The automatic exclusion of most of the colonists from the political process meant that demands on government were minimal. The white men who controlled affairs wanted support for their authority over their families, and occasionally, access to office for financial gain. Beyond this government was expected to do little, and it fulfilled those expectations.

The ways in which age and sex composition affected social structure are not as obvious, but they are nonetheless important. The youthful nature of the colonial population reinforced an already strong cultural emphasis on family life. With half or more of the population in need of some adult supervision or care, it is safe to say that early America was family-centered, even though it was not child-centered. Although the age-sex pyramid for 1770 reflects an even balance between males and females, that was not always the case. When immigration was high, males were in the majority, though not often as much so as in early Virginia. In older communities which began to lose residents through emigration, women comprised a larger part of the population. In the decade before independence, only 91 men resided in Massachusetts and Rhode Island for every 100 women.[33] Such changes not only affected marriage chances, especially among women, but by implication, they must have influenced family life and sex roles as well. No matter how strong the emphasis on forming a family, if demographic realities prevent it then some social adjustments must be made to accommodate the persons who differ from the standard. Historians have suggested that women play an important part in the establishment and enforcement of sexual standards and in supporting religion as well. Thus, newer settlements where males predominate are likely to have looser standards of sexual behavior and less religious influence than are older communities in which women are well represented.[34]

The decision to use 1770 as an approximate end for the first period of America's demographic history makes one last question obvious. Were the American Revolution and the demographic changes of concern here related, or was it a chronological accident that the two occurred simultaneously?[35]

Several demographic patterns already considered in other contexts helped make independence an option to be seriously considered by the colonial leaders when they failed politically to resolve their controversies over the nature of the imperial connections. From the seventeenth century on, efforts to recruit settlers led Americans to *expect* significant control over land, religion, and local politics. The colonists naturally reacted strongly against actions by the English that appeared to threaten what the Americans thought of as their rights. In the eighteenth century, many people who had little natural affection for an English empire arrived in the colonies. By 1750, both English and American observers were aware of rapid growth in the size and strength of the American population. For the former this produced anxiety, for the latter, a sense of confidence in the future. Controlling the geographic spread of the population became a source of some concern to the British, and an additional irritation to the colonists.

Contrasts between the numerical majority of colonies in the Americas that remained loyal to Great Britain, and the rebellious regions, illustrate how population trends made war and independence possibilities that could seriously be considered in parts of England's empire but not in others. All of the future United States had relatively large numbers of people who were physically close enough to aid each other, and who, with the exception of a few southern, coastal regions, were not seriously threatened by an internal or external enemy. The loyal colonies generally had fewer people, were isolated from other settlements that might offer support, and often depended upon Great Britain for military security. White Virginians could contemplate a rebellion against England; the 13,000 white Jamaicans who lived in the midst of almost 200,000 black slaves could not, no matter how much they might sympathize with the North American view of empire.

With rare exceptions, the American revolution in politics had no apparent effect on the revolutions in Americans' lives. Patterns of birth, death, and marriage either remained the same or changed in response to more subtle and complex forces. Independence, and the later European conflicts surrounding the

French Revolution slowed transatlantic migrations. The speed and direction of internal migration was also influenced by imperial policies and their eventual removal. However, both the geographic expansion of America and the development of a pluralistic society were well established by 1750. Perhaps the evolution of these patterns in the nineteenth century would have differed in detail if the United States had remained within England's empire. In general, however, the realities of American demography that plagued the imperial officials continued to confront the American government in the late eighteenth and nineteenth centuries. The reactions of American politicians to these problems will be considered in the context of the demographic revolutions.

Perhaps the best way to examine possible interactions between demographic change and the American Revolution is not to ask whether one caused the other. Instead, both can be seen as early manifestations of the modern personality in American history. The revolution in the political arena gave expression to a stress on individual worth and dignity, to a resentment of arbitrary power, and to a belief that one's future could be changed for the better. On a personal and family level, efforts to limit births and deaths, to recognize the need for divorce, to see children as worthy of love and development, and to move to communities with more opportunity reflect the same values.

Although people who hold such modern values are not unique to America, they may have been more common there in 1800 than elsewhere. Certainly those people who responded to the enticements offered to recruit settlers were behaving in a modern fashion. Many individuals did improve themselves and their families by moving to the New World, a lesson which was not lost on themselves or their neighbors. Several scholars have discovered a tremendous stress on the individual's capacities in eighteenth-century Pennsylvania.[36] Where people of different cultures mixed, old standards by which individuals might be judged and assigned to a certain place in society broke down. For many males, at least, personal ability as indicated by economic success or the power to persuade one's neighbors at a town meeting replaced accidents of birth, religious tests, and other assigned measures of worth as the means of telling who the important people were.

Obviously much of late eighteenth-century society remained traditional in its orientation. Race, sex, and age all too often automatically defined a person as inferior. Families still expected subordination from individual members . Frequent births and deaths were seen as inevitable and unchanging rhythms of life. But in the nineteenth century, more and more persons began to apply modern attitudes and actions to more of their life. By 1920, a series of revolutions in the lives of Americans had occurred, transforming not only how, but for what, we live.

Notes

1. Gordon M. Day, "The Indian as an Ecological Factor in the Northeastern Forest," *Ecology* 34 (1953): 329–46; Erhard Rostlund, "The Myth of a Natural Prairie Belt in Alabama: An Interpretation of Historical Records," *Annals of the Association of American Geographers* 47 (1957): 392–411; Peter O. Wacker, *Land and People: A Cultural Geography of Preindustrial New Jersey: Origins and Settlement Patterns* (New Brunswick, N.J., 1975), pp. 57–119.

2. Francis Jennings, *The Invasion of America: Indians, Colonialism, and the Cant of Conquest* (Chapel Hill, N.C., 1975).

3. Sigmund Diamond, "From Organization to Society: Virginia in the Seventeenth Century," *American Journal of Sociology* 63 (1958): 457–75; Edmund S. Morgan, *American Slavery-American Freedom: the Ordeal of Colonial Virginia* (New York, 1975), pp. 1–292.

4. Herbert Moller, "Sex Composition and Correlated Culture Patterns of Colonial America," *William and Mary Quarterly* 2 (1945): 113–53; Morgan, *American Slavery-American Freedom,* pp. 1–292; John C. Rainbolt, "The Absence of Towns in Seventeenth-Century Virginia," *Journal of Southern History* 35 (1969): 343–60.

5. Kenneth Lockridge, *A New England Town: The First Hundred Years* (New York, 1970); Sumner C. Powell, *Puritan Village: the Formation of a New England Town* (Middletown, Conn., 1963).

6. An interesting perspective on this issue is added by Richard Dunn, *Sugar and Slaves: the Rise of the Planter Class in the English West Indies, 1624–1713* (Chapel Hill, N.C., 1972), pp. 263–341.

7. Lester Cappon, ed., *Atlas of Early American History: the Revolutionary Era 1760–1790* (Princeton, N.J., 1976), pp. 24–25.

8. James T. Lemon, *The Best Poor Man's Country: A Geographical Study of Early Southeastern Pennsylvania* (Baltimore, 1972); Richard H. Shryock, "British versus German Traditions in Colonial Agriculture," *Mississippi Valley Historical Review* 26 (1939): 39–54. Glenn T. Trewartha, "Types of Rural Settlement in Colonial America," *Geographical Review* 36 (1946): 568–96; Wilbur Zelinsky, *The Cultural Geography of the United States* (Englewood Cliffs, N.J., 1973).

9. Thomas J. Archdeacon, *New York City, 1664–1790: Conquest and Change* (Ithaca, N.Y., 1976); Patricia Bonomi, *A Factious People: Politics and Society in Colonial New York* (New York, 1971); Alice P. Kenny, "Dutch Patroons in Colonial Albany," *New York History* 42 (1961): 331–50.

10. Wayland F. Dunaway, "Pennsylvania as an Early Distributing Center of Population," *Pennsylvania Magazine of History and Biography* 55 (1931): 134–69; Owen Ireland, "The Ethnic-Religious Dimensions of Pennsylvania Politics, 1778–1779," *William and Mary Quarterly* 30 (1973): 423–48.

11. Carl Bridenbaugh, *Myths and Realities: Societies of the Colonial South* (Baton Rouge, La., 1952).

12. Theodore G. Corbett, "Migration to a Spanish Imperial Frontier in the Seventeenth and Eighteenth Centuries: St. Augustine," *Hispanic American Historical Review* 54 (1974): 414–30; Theodore G. Corbett, "Population Structure in Hispanic St. Augustine, 1629–1763," *Florida Historical Quarterly* 54 (1976): 263–84.

13. Jonas Viles, "Population and the Extent of Settlement in Missouri Before 1804," *Missouri Historical Review* 5 (1911): 189–213; Jacqueline Voorhies, comp., *Some Late Eighteenth-Century Louisianians: Census Records of the Colony, 1758–1796* (Lafayette, La., 1973).

14. D. W. Moodie and Barry Kaye, "The Northern Limit of Indian Agriculture in North America," *Geographical Review* 59 (1969): 513–29.

15. Elliot G. McIntire, "Changing Patterns of Hopi Indian Settlement," *Annals of the Association of American Geographers* 61 (1971): 510–21; Donald W. Meinig, *Southwest: Three Peoples in Geographical Change, 1600–1970* (New York, 1971), pp. 3–37; Albert H. Schroder, "Shifting for Survival in the Spanish Southwest," *New Mexico Historical Review* 43 (1968): 291–310.

16. Peter H. Wood, *Black Majority: Negroes in Colonial South Carolina from 1670 through the Stono Rebellion* (New York, 1974), pp. 35–62.

17. Shryock, "British versus German Agriculture," 39–54.

18. Quoted in John C. Parish, "The Emergence of the Idea of Manifest Destiny," in his book, *The Persistence of the Westward Movement and Other Essays* (Berkeley, 1943), pp. 56–57.

19. "Hints Respecting the Settlement of our American Provinces," 9 February 1763, and "Some Thoughts on the Settlement and Govern-

ment of our Colonies in North America," 10 March 1763, in British Museum, Additional Manuscripts, #38335, 14–33, 68–77.

20. Quoted in Parish, "Idea of Manifest Destiny," p. 52.

21. Both quotes are from James P. Rhonda, "'We Are Well as We Are': An Indian Critique of Seventeenth-Century Christian Missions," *William and Mary Quarterly* 34 (1977): 66–82.

22. Morgan, *American Slavery-American Freedom*, pp. 250–70.

23. Abbot E. Smith, *Colonists in Bondage: White Servitude and Convict Labor in America 1607–1776* (Chapel Hill, N.C., 1947), pp. 104–33.

24. Bonomi, *Factious People.*

25. Ireland, "Pennsylvania Politics."

26. Charles Woodmason, *The Carolina Backcountry on the Eve of the Revolution*, ed. Richard Hooker (Chapel Hill, N.C., 1953).

27. John J. Waters, Jr., "Patrimony, Succession, and Social Stability: Guilford, Connecticut in the Eighteenth Century," *Perspectives in American History* 10 (1976): 131–60.

28. Robert V. Wells, *The Population of the British Colonies in America before 1776: A Survey of Census Data* (Princeton, N.J., 1975), pp. 23–32, 283–85.

29. David W. Jordan, "Political Stability and the Emergence of a Native Elite in Maryland," in *The Chesapeake in the Seventeenth Century: Essays on Anglo-American Society & Politics*, eds. Thad W. Tate and David L. Ammerman (Chapel Hill, N.C., 1979), pp. 243–73; Carole Shammas, "English-Born and Creole Elites in Turn-of-the-Century Virginia," in ibid., pp. 274–96.

30. James A. Henretta, *The Evolution of American Society, 1700–1815: An Interdisciplinary Analysis* (Lexington, Mass., 1973), pp. 5–81, 138–46.

31. Ibid., pp. 83–117; Gary B. Nash, *Class and Society in Early America* (Englewood Cliffs, N.J., 1970).

32. Lois Green Carr and Russell R. Menard, "Immigration and Opportunity: The Freedman in Early Colonial Maryland," in Tate and Ammerman, eds., *Chesapeake in the Seventeenth Century*, pp. 206–42; Catherine S. Crary, "The Humble Immigrant and the American Dream: Some Case Histories, 1746-1776," *Mississippi Valley Historical Review* 46 (1959): 46–66.

33. Wells, *Population of the British Colonies*, p. 272.

34. Moller, "Sex Composition," pp. 129–53; Wells, *Population of the British Colonies*, pp. 293–96.

35. The following discussion draws heavily on Robert V. Wells, "Population and the American Revolution," in *The American Revolution: Changing Perspectives*, eds. W. M. Fowler and W. Coyle (Boston, 1979), pp. 107–22.

36. Lemon, *Best Poor Man's Country;* Stephanie G. Wolf, *Urban Village: Population, Community, and Family Structure in Germantown, Pennsylvania 1683–1800* (Princeton, N.J., 1976).

PART II

1770 TO 1920: A WORLD TRANSFORMED

5

THE AGE OF DEMOGRAPHIC REVOLUTION

The emergence of the contemporary world, which occurred as the result of major transformations in the way Americans experienced and thought about birth, death, marriage, and migration between 1770 and 1920, was often a slow, uneven, and painful process. As individuals and families redefined and reorganized their lives, sometimes willingly and sometimes not, they found it necessary not only to adopt new standards of behavior but also new ways of thinking about what they wanted from life and why. Many of the decisions that were necessary to produce these changes were made within the privacy of the family, or even alone, and so are not always accessible today. But by the middle of the nineteenth century, the shifts were already visible enough to generate public discussion about whether they should be encouraged, opposed, or left alone. Much debate eventually focused on the future of the family, as the most fundamental institution of society—that will receive considerable attention in the next chapter. Before examining what Americans thought about the revolutions in their lives, it is necessary to consider the revolutions themselves.

Although American experiences with and expectations about birth, death, marriage, and migration all changed dramatically between 1770 and 1920, the shifts did not all begin at the same time, nor did they progress at the same rate. Husbands and wives began to adopt new patterns of childbearing almost a century before they and their children achieved any significant improvement in health. In between, migrants both to and within the United States profoundly altered their lives and those of their neighbors by moving to environments that differed as markedly from eighteenth-century destinations as the migrants themselves did from their earlier counterparts. The contrast between life in 1770 and 1920 may be stark and simple, but the processes by which the demographic revolutions occurred were complex.

The extent to which American couples began to limit their childbearing in the nineteenth century is well established by now. Genealogical materials and evidence from federal and state censuses point to a steady reduction in births in white American families throughout most of the period between 1770 and 1920. A survey of the childbearing experience of over 12,000 wives shows the decline clearly.[1] Women who married in the seventeenth century averaged 7.4 children. Those who married in the late eighteenth century and had some of their children after 1800 averaged 6.4 children. Women married between 1800 and 1849 had 4.9 children, while those married between 1870 and 1879 averaged only 2.8. Among late eighteenth-century wives only 12.8 percent had 2 or less children, while 19.3 percent had at least 10. Women married in the 1870s offer a striking contrast, for among that group just over half had no more than 2 babies, and less than 1 in 200 had as many as 10 children.

Studies based on census data show a similar pattern for the white population in general. These works differ with regard both to specific measures of fertility used and details of the decline, but are remarkably consistent in the overall pattern.[2] From a birthrate of fifty per thousand, or a little higher, in 1800, white American fertility declined until the number of births for every thousand persons was only twenty-five each year by 1920. If, for the sake of convenience, fertility in 1800 is established as equal to 100 percent, then by 1820 childbearing had fallen to 95 percent. By midcentury, fertility was only 75 percent of its previous level. The decline continued until 1900, when the birthrate stood at about 50 percent of what it had been a century before. In 1920 it was only 45 percent of what it had been in 1800. When fertility temporarily stopped falling in 1933, it was equal to about 30 percent of the level at the start of the nineteenth century. Clearly a revolution had occurred.

As might be expected, some groups began to limit their child-bearing before others. However, by 1920 almost every easily identifiable group in the United States had begun to practice some sort of birth control. The question was *when* rather than *if* the change would occur. Black Americans began to practice family limitation relatively late. Black couples in 1800 had children at about the same rate as (or a little higher than) their white neighbors. The turmoil of the Civil War and emancipation may have produced a slight decline in black fertility after 1860, but the significant fall occurred only after 1880. Once blacks began to limit their fertility, they did so rapidly. It took a century for white Americans to cut their childbearing in half; black Americans accomplished the same task in forty to sixty years. Since 1880, trends in white and black childbearing have been almost the same. The level of black fertility has remained above that of whites, primarily because of economic and educational differences, but whenever a change has occurred in the general trend of childbearing for one group, the other has followed within a year or two.[3]

White Americans also differed as to when they adopted birth control. Couples living in the northeastern part of the country began to limit their families first. The practice then spread south and west throughout much of the nineteenth century. By 1820, childbearing in the upper South was about the same as in New England in 1800; couples in Michigan and Wisconsin reduced their fertility to the same level by 1850. In 1850, only Arkansas and Oregon had fertility rates above those found in New York, New Jersey, and Pennsylvania in 1800.[4] Birthrates seem to have fallen first in cities in the nineteenth century, but after 1850, rapid declines in rural family sizes and the influx of immigrants with relatively high birthrates reduced differences between town and country.[5]

Cultural and religious differences were as important as geography in determining when white Americans began to practice birth control. Mormons, Missouri Synod Lutherans, and many Catholics all adopted birth control after black Americans.[6] Immigrants often kept up the birthrate in American communities. In Boston in 1880, there were 537 children under five for every

1,000 married women aged twenty to forty-nine in the native-born population; every 1,000 foreign-born wives had 880 children under five.[7] A comparable pattern existed in New York in 1920.[8] More frequent childbearing among immigrants was noticed as early as 1851 and produced considerable alarm by 1900, but as they, too, limited their families the alarm subsided.

The means by which the revolution in childbearing occurred are less certain than the change itself. Fertility can fall because women and men seek to control their lives by deliberately limiting the number of children they must care for. It can also decline as a side effect of some other change. Therefore, it is of interest to ask whether Americans in the nineteenth century consciously altered a basic rhythm of life or merely responded to external forces beyond their control.

Three possible explanations exist for the decline in fertility—a reduction in physical capacities to conceive and bear children; new marriage patterns that shortened women's exposure to the risks of pregnancy; and the control of births by married couples.

In a period when life expectancy declined noticeably a fall in fertility would be likely as marriages were broken earlier by the death of a spouse, and increased ill-health made it more difficult for parents to conceive and mothers to carry a child. If anything, however, changes in the death rate worked to increase childbearing as life expectancy improved dramatically after 1850, and so fostered longer marriages and healthier parents by 1920.

What little is known of marriage patterns in the nineteenth century suggests that changes in marriage may have caused some, though not all, of the reduction in the birthrate. In the eighteenth century, the age at which women married for the first time rose steadily, and that trend continued into the nineteenth century. Women who married between 1850 and 1900 may have been as much as two years older, on average, than brides a century earlier. This could account for a decline of perhaps one child per couple. However, between 1890 and 1920 the age at which women and men married for the first time actually dropped slightly, but the birthrate continued to fall. The proportion of bachelors and spinsters in the American population seems to have risen slightly throughout the nineteenth century, but that had no effect on marital fertility, and only a small influence on the overall birthrate.[9]

The second half of the nineteenth century saw a remarkable increase in the voluntary dissolution of marriages by divorce. At the time of the Civil War, only 1 out of 1,000 marriages ended by divorce in any given year. By 1900, the rate of divorce had tripled, and for the years 1920–1924, 7.2 divorces occurred for every 1,000 marriages.[10] This was a new and significant pattern in American family life, and continues to be so. But the emergence of divorce is more important in terms of family life than fertility. Divorced persons tend to remarry rapidly and so lose little of their reproductive potential. In addition, divorce emerged just as life expectancy began to increase so that the overall rate at which marriages were broken actually declined slightly.

The process of elimination of alternatives, combined with the evidence presented earlier regarding the childbearing experiences of 12,000 wives, leads to the conclusion that deliberate efforts by American wives and husbands to reduce the size of their families was the main cause of the revolution in childbearing. Additional evidence both reinforces this conclusion and provides some insight into how the change occurred. Earlier, we noted that a rise in the average age at first marriage might have had a slight effect on the overall birthrate. Even without this change, families would have been smaller after 1800, for, in looking at brides of the same age, one scholar has shown that women married between 1800 and 1824 had about one less child on average than women married between 1750 and 1799.[11] One sign of conscious control of fertility is when couples have children rapidly in the first years of their marriage and then slow down dramatically, ceasing at earlier ages than before to produce children. This pattern can be found among some late eighteenth-century Quakers and inhabitants of Sturbridge, Massachusetts.[12] Other Americans apparently adopted a different course. At least one group was able to delay pregnancies so that the interval between births rose from an average of thirty to forty months in the first half of the nineteenth century. Later, after 1850, they also reduced the number of years in which a woman might expect to bear children from sixteen to ten.[13]

The obvious question is how nineteenth-century American couples controlled their fertility. Clearly they knew more about sex and reproduction than the Victorian image would suggest. The answer is rather surprising. With the exception of the birth control pill, every form of family limitation currently available was known to nineteenth-century Americans. Furthermore, in the middle of that century, a vigorous debate took place regarding the most effective and morally correct means of control. The form of birth control most often used between 1770 and 1920 is not known. But it is possible to list the techniques most frequently mentioned by supporters and opponents of birth control.[14]

Letters, diaries, and court records indicate that nursing and coitus interruptus, or withdrawal, were used, at least occasionally, by eighteenth-century men and women who wished to delay or prevent conception. Information on such techniques was passed by word of mouth in the early years. In 1831, Robert Dale Owen published the first American pamphlet advocating birth control under the title *Moral Physiology*.[15] The following year Charles Knowlton's *Fruits of Philosophy* appeared in support of family limitation.[16] By 1850, other authors offered American wives and husbands advice on how to limit births. Apparently these works found a ready market, for Frederick Hollis's *Marriage Guide* went through over three hundred editions, and Edward Foote's *Medical Common Sense* sold at least 150,000 copies.[17] By mid-century, as much as one-eighth of the space of a newspaper might be devoted to advertisements for birth control aids and services.[18] Public discussion of birth control came to an end in 1873 when Anthony Comstock persuaded Congress to declare such information as obscene and illegal, but by then most Americans knew of some technique and merely wanted to know if it was the best. Certainly the Comstock Law did nothing to halt the decline in fertility.

The most extreme forms of birth control used in the nineteenth century were abstinence, which was not very popular, and abortion. If the amount of hostile writing on the subject is any indication of its practice, abortion was fairly common in the mid nineteenth century.[19] Before state legislation made the practice illegal after 1860, many newspaper ads were placed either by doctors who performed abortions or by individuals who offered medicine such as ergot or savin for home use to produce a miscarriage. Withdrawal, intercourse without ejaculation, infrequent intercourse (once a month or less), or various rhythm methods, some of which had the timing of ovulation wrong, were all suggested to those who had great self-control. Others could rely on condoms, "womb veils" (diaphragms or cervical caps), or sponges to absorb semen. Douching, either with water or with some form of spermicide, was quite common. The chemicals recommended as sperm killers included opium, prussic acid, iodine, strychnine, vinegar, and sulfuric acid. No doubt such additives had the desired spermicidal effect, but some must have done considerable damage to the women who used them.

By 1920, medical knowledge and the technology of birth control (especially regarding rubber products) combined to eliminate some of the more unpleasant and ineffective techniques from use. But in 1850, the "scientific" basis of birth control consisted of little more than the understanding that if male and female "fluids" could be kept apart, then conception would be prevented, and that if conception did occur, the fetus could be dislodged by various actions. As a result, techniques for limiting births were recommended in the nineteenth century that sound strange today. Some argued that without orgasm or intercourse in the horizontal position, a woman could not conceive. At least one author felt that infrequent sexual relations would produce shocks to the body when intercourse occurred that would kill the sperms or egg. Electrical devices to kill sperm were offered for sale. And finally, vigorous dancing or horseback riding over rough roads immediately after intercourse were suggested as contraceptives for women.

Knowledge and availability of birth control techniques and aids is no guarantee that people will use them. They have to *want* to limit their childbearing. The motivation to limit family size must have been particularly strong in the nineteenth century, for the available techniques by which to accomplish this goal were far from pleasant, safe, effective, or easy to use. Nineteenth-century men and women seldom recorded their reasons for wanting to have fewer children. Since the decision was a highly personal one (though perhaps made with the support of a few family members or friends), the motives must have varied from one person to another, or one family to another. The fact that some techniques were controlled by women, others by men, and that others required cooperation further suggests complex patterns of motives.

It is particularly important to avoid sociological explanations such as "urbanization" or "increased pressure on land" unless the specific effects of such forces on individuals can be demonstrated. It has often been claimed that the men and women who moved into America's growing cities were the first to adopt birth control because they had less need for small hands to help with the work. Such an explanation assumes that farm children were a help and that urban children were not. In fact, given the wages of many factories, urban families may have been more dependent for survival on the labor of their children than rural residents. In addition, over the course of the century, the emergence of expensive agricultural technology and commercial farming subjected rural families to all the uncertainties of the business cycle.[20] Perhaps people who were willing to move to cities were more likely to experiment with the other basic rhythms of their lives as well. However, both rural and urban fertility declined significantly between 1770 and 1920. In both environments, perceptions by individual women and men of how children would affect their future led to private actions which combined to produce one part of the revolutions in Americans' lives.

In the absence of formal surveys of the people who began to practice birth control in the nineteenth century, it is necessary to combine recent findings with the observations of nineteenth-century advocates and opponents of birth control to make some statements about the motives behind the reproductive revolution. The one fact that stands out above all else is that both men and women decided to limit childbearing because they felt it would improve their lives, as well as those of their children. They rejected the traditional notion, that God sent children and it was the parents' duty to accept these "gifts" even if they were too poor or tired to care for them. At the same time, they acted in a modern fashion by actively seeking to improve the present and future, often with the goal of increased individual freedom and dignity in mind. Family limitation was a rational action aimed at introducing a greater degree of control in one's life.

Women sought to limit childbearing (with or without their husband's knowledge) for several reasons. For many, fears of frequent pregnancies and the burden of a large family were reasons enough. This was true for women concerned with their own physical and mental health, and those who felt they could be better mothers to fewer children. Some women resented bearing children forced on them by the undesired advances of a thoughtless husband. The simple desire to pursue one's own life and interests without being tied to little ones was often noted (frequently with alarm by male physicians). Apparently at least some of the male advocates of birth control understood and supported efforts by women to gain control over their own bodies. In 1858, Edward Bliss Foote promoted the use of cervical caps as placing "conception entirely under the control of the wife, to whom it naturally belongs; for it is for her to say at what time and under what circumstances, she will become the mother, and the moral, religious, and physical instructress of offspring."[21] "Voluntary motherhood" was an important concern to American women in the nineteenth century.[22]

Many men presumably supported or at least tolerated efforts by their wives to limit the size of their families. Some must have sympathized with female goals; others found that the efforts of their wives made it easier to limit the number of offspring, an end which they desired for their own reasons. Some men became the active partners in the practice of birth control. The primary male concern was economic. Whether an individual husband wished to preserve or enhance his own standard of living or make it easier to establish his children with enough property to ensure the well-being of the next generation does not matter. Both indicate a perception of a better future achieved through present control. This concern with economic factors is understandable in a period when males were defined as providers, and women were the ones most directly involved in actually rearing the children. Perhaps a few nineteenth-century men found the day-to-day burdens of child care sufficient reason to limit births, but there is no evidence to suggest that as a common motive.

Although frequent movement was a fact of life for many Americans, new patterns of migration emerged after 1770, and especially after 1820, that set the experiences of nineteenth-century men, women, and children apart. New conditions produced significant changes in the numbers and nature of migrants and in their choice of destination. It is easier to understand the revolutions in international, rural to urban, and westward migration if they are treated separately, even though individual Americans may have participated in all three patterns, sometimes simultaneously.

Immigrants may have been less important in American history between 1770 and 1820 than at any time except the 1930s. The War of Independence brought an end to eighteenth-century migrations from Europe, and before they could resume on a large scale the French Revolution of 1789 developed into a general European conflict which further inhibited migrations across the North Atlantic. Similarly, the slave trade which had brought many African colonists to America fell off, both because of the European wars and because American efforts to prohibit this form of involuntary immigration proved generally successful after 1808.

However, after 1820 an extraordinary change occurred. During the next century, over 33 million men, women, and children moved to the United States. After a slow but steady growth from 1821 to 1845, migration surged upward between 1846 and 1850, first as a result of the failure of the potato crop in Ireland, and then in response to economic and political troubles in the German states. Thereafter, as Chart 2 shows, the number of immigrants increased over the remainder of the period, except when war or economic depression reduced the appeal of the United States. Even in the midst of the Civil War (1861–1865), the United States attracted over 800,000 people, not far below the total number of people who moved to England's colonies before 1775. Between 1905 and 1914, over 1 million people arrived in America in each of six single years. The combination of World War I and extensive legal restrictions on immigration after 1917 finally reduced the flow of people into the United States.

CHART 2 NUMBER OF IMMIGRANTS: 1821–1920

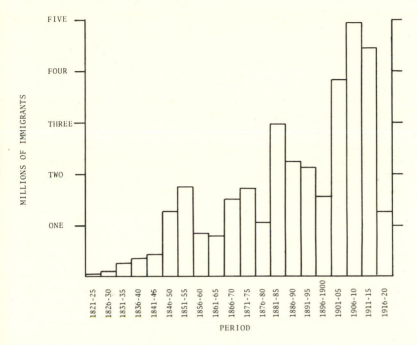

SOURCE: *Historical Statistics of the United States,* Series C 88–114.

As late as 1850, native-born Americans outnumbered immigrants and their children eight to one. But by 1920 there were only two native Americans for every first or second generation immigrant. Between 1901 and 1910, enough immigrants arrived to account for 9.5 percent of the total population in 1910. From 1840 to 1920, the lowest comparable figure for a single decade was that of 1891 to 1900 when, because of a major depression, the total number of immigrants added *only* 4.9 percent to the total population in 1900.

The spectacular nature of immigration has often so fascinated students of the subject that they have overlooked the fact that almost 7 million people (equal to about 20 percent of all immigrants) left the country during this century and a half.[23] Figures on emigration are not as accurate as those on immigration, nor

were they recorded as early, perhaps because it was not as satis-
fying to document the numbers of people for whom the American dream became a nightmare.

The colonists who preferred to remain under the government
of King George rather than participate in republican experiments in the newly independent colonies comprised the earliest
identifiable group of any size to leave the United States. Perhaps
as many as eighty thousand individuals departed during and after
the War of Independence. Considering the size of the population,
about five times as many people fled the United States during her
revolution as left France in the midst of her political upheavals.[24]
This amounted to about one year's growth by natural increase.

Throughout the nineteenth century, other groups of discon-
tented Americans left for other lands. After the Civil War, both
black and white Southerners emigrated to Mexico, Brazil, and
other parts of Latin America.[25] A small number of Mormons
moved to Mexico after federal statutes outlawed polygamy.[26] In
the latter half of the nineteenth century, the United States lost
some population to Canada as farmers pushed the agricultural
frontier north and west across the continent. Men in search of
land proved more loyal to the fertile soils of the Red River Valley
of Minnesota, North Dakota, and Manitoba than to their
nation.[27]

A new group of emigrants emerged in the late nineteenth and
early twentieth centuries. As transportation and communication
improved, industrial workers and miners frequently moved back
and forth across the Atlantic and Pacific in search of steady
employment and high wages. British and Chinese workers seem
to have followed this practice before emigration statistics were
collected.[28] Italian laborers engaged in the same sort of behavior
after statistics began to be recorded. Thus, although about
282,000 Italians arrived in America in 1907, just over 167,000
returned home the next year. Presumably a number of workers
made the journey more than once. For other groups, like the
Irish, or Russian Jews, the prospect of returning home was so bad
that only 5 to 10 percent ever left the United States.[29]

Before 1775, migrants into England's American colonies came
primarily from northwest Europe and Africa. In addition, a few

Spanish and French settlers had moved into regions which later became part of the United States. After 1820, people continued to move from northwest Europe to America, but three changes altered and enhanced the cultural pluralism that had first emerged during the colonial period. First, significant immigration by blacks ended by 1808. Second, except for the first years of the California gold rush, few Hispano-Americans became United States citizens unless they lived in territories added during the nineteenth century. The third change, involving extensive immigration of peoples who had never before moved to America, was the most important. Perhaps best known of these "new" immigrants are those who came from Poland, Italy, Greece, Russia, and other parts of southern and eastern Europe. Canada also emerged as a source of new inhabitants, sending both French and English Canadians, as well as European transients, on to the United States. Finally, for the first time in thousands of years, Asians began to move to America, as first Chinese and then Japanese arrived on the west coast.

Many native-born Americans who lived in the midst of this massive migration were alarmed by increased pluralism. Perhaps their anxieties would have been less if all the groups had arrived at even rates. But each nationality had its own peak of immigration, which often emphasized the addition of one more strain to the American population.[30] The Irish were the earliest group singled out for attention. Their peak years of immigration were in the 1840s. Most Germans came in 1852–1854, 1866–1873, and 1881–1893. This latter period was also a time of extensive immigration from Scandinavia. Most Chinese arrived between 1853 and 1883, Japanese between 1891 and 1924, and Russians and Italians between 1900 and 1914. Considering the scale and diversity of nineteenth-century immigration it is no wonder that the wisdom of continued migration became a matter of public debate.

No doubt anxieties produced by adding new strands to an already complex tapestry of people were further stimulated by the fact that newcomers continued to distribute themselves unevenly throughout the country, as they had before 1770. As early as 1850, 84 percent of the foreign-born lived north of the Ohio River and east of the Mississippi.[31] By 1900, that same region, plus the northern plains states contained 87 percent

of the foreign-born. Within this region there was still plenty
of opportunity for ethnic segregation. In 1910, 44.7 percent of
Norwegians lived in Minnesota and Wisconsin, while 49.4 percent of Italians resided in New York and Pennsylvania, and 38.3
percent of Irish immigrants lived in New York and Massachusetts. Germans preferred New York and Illinois, since 27.1 percent of them lived in those two states. The Pacific Coast states
had relatively few immigrants, partly because few Americans of
any description lived there until well into the twentieth century.
But in proportion to the total population of the Far West, foreigners were fairly common. In 1860, 39 percent of all Californians were foreign-born. Since the vast majority of Hispano-
Americans, Chinese, Japanese, and American Indians lived in
that region, it had an ethnic blend quite unlike New York, Massachusetts, or Minnesota.

Only the South was largely untouched by nineteenth-century
immigration. Parts of Texas and Louisiana attracted some immigrants, especially Germans, but east of Louisiana, native-born
whites and blacks with roots well back into the eighteenth century made up the overwhelming majority of the population.
Since southern states tried to recruit immigrants, especially after
the Civil War, this relative isolation must have resulted from a
lack of interest on their part.[32] Two factors probably sent most
foreigners elsewhere. First, there was little land available for
newcomers interested in farming. More important, the South
had few cities in which to seek employment. Scholars have
shown that even before the war immigrants were more than
willing to move to southern cities, when they existed. Charleston, South Carolina, attracted 67 percent of the foreign-born in
that state in 1860; the corresponding figure for Mobile, Alabama,
was 63 percent.[33] In Texas in 1860, about 60 percent of the free
population in Brownsville and New Braunfels was foreign-born,
while San Antonio and Galveston were 47.1 and 44 percent
foreign-born respectively. For the state as a whole, however, in
1860 only one of every ten free Texans had been born abroad.[34]

Not all the nineteenth-century patterns of migration were
new. As in earlier centuries, males tended to move more often
than females, and immigrants often were in their prime working

CHART 3 CHARACTERISTICS OF IMMIGRANTS:
1821–1920

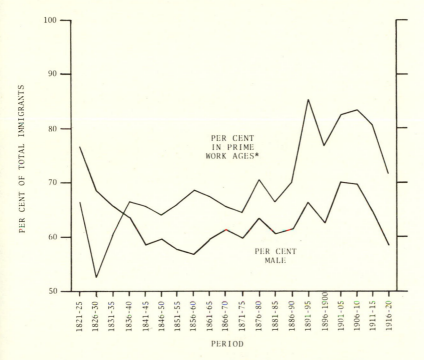

PERIOD

SOURCE: *Historical Statistics of the United States,* Series C 88-114, C 133-138.

*Ages 15–40 (1821-1898); 14–44 (1899-1917); 16–44 (1918-1920).

years. Chart 3 shows both these patterns. For the entire period from 1821 to 1920, the proportion of males among all immigrants never fell below 56.9 percent in any five-year period. In 1857, the year in which male and female immigrants were most evenly balanced, men still accounted for 53.9 percent of the total. In sixty-five years, the proportion of males in the immigrant population was 60 percent or above. This means that at least 150 men arrived for each 100 women in two of every three years.

The predominance of workers is demonstrated by the fact that the only five-year period in which less than 60 percent of all immigrants were in the prime work force years was from 1826 to 1830, when migration was still relatively slight. Once the surge of immigrants began after 1845, the proportion never fell below 64 percent. In general, women and children appeared most frequently in groups for which the commitment to move permanently to the United States was strong. Scandinavian and British Mormon converts were especially prone to move in balanced family groups. British, Chinese, and Italian male workers seldom brought their families with them, preferring to return home themselves.

Faced with a record of over 33 million individuals who came to America, it is only natural to ask why they came. To begin, the nineteenth and early twentieth centuries were periods of worldwide migration.[35] The streams of people headed for the United States were the largest and most varied at the time, but millions of other individuals moved from one country to another with no thought of America as their destination. Between 1820 and 1940, as many as 50 to 60 million Europeans crossed oceans in search of new homes. About 60 percent of them came to the United States, while 20 million or more chose destinations such as Argentina, Brazil, Australia, or the Union of South Africa. Argentina alone received 7 million immigrants between 1857 and 1940, producing a ratio of immigrant to native born three times higher than that of the United States. Between 1872 and 1940, 3,300,000 people moved to Brazil. The Chinese and Japanese who landed in California between 1853 and 1924 represented only a small part of widespread migrations around the edges of the Pacific Ocean.[36]

Additional millions of people crossed international boundaries during this period without crossing an ocean. From 1876 to 1926, while about 8.9 million Italians came to various parts of North and South America, another 7.5 million moved to other European countries.[37] Millions more in Europe disrupted their lives by leaving their farms for the lure of the city. They may not have crossed an international border, but differences between rhythms of country and city living may have been more significant than any change in language or law.

The meaning of this massive movement of people for American history is clear. Theories that attribute the large-scale immigration into the United States to the lure of free land or democratic politics do not explain the millions who chose other destinations. To fully understand immigrants' decisions, it is necessary to look at what they were leaving, as well as what they were going to.

One factor distinguishing nineteenth-century immigrants to America from their colonial counterparts is that an increased proportion of them came voluntarily. Before 1770, many individuals who moved to the New World had no choice in the matter. Many wives and children in the nineteenth century probably had little influence on decisions to migrate, but family migration was only a small part of the total picture. A study of Danish immigrants suggests that about 70 percent of them made their own decisions, either because they were unmarried or because they were heads of families.[38] The proportion of immigrants who made their own decisions to move undoubtedly varied considerably from one group to another. The choices available to the Irish who fled starvation brought on by potato blight, or the Russian Jews who sought to escape religious persecution and the pogroms of 1881 to 1906, were limited. But there is no reason to believe that, among most groups, the overall proportion of voluntary migrants from 1770 to 1920 was less than that of the Danes.[39].

What then were the factors that encouraged a young man or woman to move? Migrants often responded to very basic economic changes. Agricultural reforms and growing populations forced many to decide between a life of poverty in a rural area, and setting out for a city or a new country. Urban workers, who made up a large proportion of the migrants, often moved to areas where wages were higher. Variations in business cycles from one country to another had a profound effect on where and when people went.[40] The "free" land of the American West played a very minor role.

In order to respond to economic changes and economic incentives, individuals who made a decision to move had to believe that their actions would actually affect their future well-being. They had to have at least some of the values and attitudes that make up the modern personality. Some may have migrated with the desire to improve their lots; others undoubtedly hoped to prevent a decline in their fortunes. Some saw nearby cities as places that offered new opportunities for those willing to change; others crossed international boundaries in search of better lives; some moved first to a local city and then to a new land. The particular destination does not much matter, for all were manifestations of a willingness to change and experiment when faced with a bleak future. Voluntary migrants were people who refused to accept their fate passively when action offered the possibility of improvement. Thus, to the extent that migration in the nineteenth century was often (though not always) a manifestation of modern attitudes, the United States acquired large numbers of people for whom the future was more important than the past, and for whom significant change was an acceptable solution to serious problems. The individuals most tied to traditional ways of thought and behavior never made the voyage.

The remarkable willingness of millions of people to change their homeland may also be explained by the fact that, for many, the most fundamental change in their lives must have been the move from rural to urban areas. Compared to the adjustments to city work and city living that fundamentally altered the rhythm of life on a day-to-day and year-to-year basis, the need to learn a new language or new laws must have seemed a relatively minor problem. Since many immigrants first moved to cities in Europe and later settled in urban areas in America, it may be appropriate to view international migration as much as a part of the widespread urbanization of European populations as it was a part of the general overseas expansion of European population at the time. Certainly anyone willing to confront the urban frontier would not have been severely inhibited by a mere national boundary.

Modern values and economic incentives may have been the most important factors in the widespread migration of people in the nineteenth century. At the same time, a series of legal, institutional, and technological changes made it easier for those who might otherwise have stayed at home to actually accomplish a move.

In the nineteenth century, many nations in Europe repealed laws that had made emigration a crime. Instead, governments began to regulate the companies that provided transportation to America, making the voyage safer and more certain. In Great

Britain, labor unions actively encouraged their unemployed members to look for work abroad.

Knowledge of America improved considerably. Initially, personal letters of earlier immigrants and newspaper accounts provided most information about the United States. But by the middle of the century, well-organized efforts to recruit immigrants became more important. States all over the country established bureaus to tell potential immigrants of the virtues of West Virginia, Missouri, Michigan, or the Dakotas.[41] A few towns did the same thing. American railroads played a major role in publishing and circulating promotional literature in Europe, not only because they wanted to sell tickets, but also because they had land to sell in the West.[42] Railroad companies offered immigrants both advice and the chance to book passage all the way from Europe to a piece of land in the American West. For those who did not wish to farm, jobs could be arranged in mines or factories. Mormon missionaries in Great Britain and Scandinavia arranged passage to Utah, via New Orleans, for converts they won to the faith.[43] Under such conditions, the risks of moving were minimal.

Improvements in both rail and steamship travel in the nineteenth century were extraordinary. By 1900, voyages once long and dangerous became swift and sure, and often cheap, too. The increase in the capacity to move people across the ocean was so great that transportation companies had to actively recruit migrants to fill up their space. No doubt anxiety, disease, seasickness, and bad food continued to plague immigrants, even in the early twentieth century, but their lot was better than that of the people who came in the eighteenth century. It is unlikely that the transatlantic commuters who sought work on both sides of the Atlantic after 1850 would have appeared without the major improvements in transportation.

Adjustment to America depended on a variety of factors. Skilled British workers and well-educated Japanese immigrants refused to give up what they considered to be superior customs and traditions.[44] Many immigrants sought the security of ethnic ghettos (in both urban and rural regions) to help ease the process of learning new laws in a new land, and to preserve familiar patterns of behavior. Others desired to become "Americans" as quickly as possible, even though it was not always clear what that meant. Migrants who came in family units often had a greater commitment to establishing themselves here than did those who came alone. Perhaps those who believed the excessive claims of American propaganda aimed at recruiting immigrants experienced the greatest discontent. Instead of streets paved in gold or a stable social order, they found a confusing, complex society in which many cultures lived side by side, not always comfortably. The revolutionary changes in people's lives which frequently encouraged them to leave their native lands were also present in the New World. In fact, the immigrants themselves, taken en masse, were a central factor producing instability and change. For those who sought change the experience was exciting, if occasionally painful; for those who moved to try and protect their positions in life, America must have seemed like a strange new world indeed.[45]

The choice of 1920 to mark the end of the period of demographic revolution is perhaps most fitting with regard to international migration. Between 1917 and 1924, federal legislation expanded restrictions on the numbers and types of people who might move to the United States. Earlier, state laws, diplomatic efforts, and federal legislation, from the end of the slave trade in 1808 to the Chinese Exclusion Act of 1882, had effectively regulated immigration from Mexico, Asia, and Africa. By 1920, rising demands for a policy controlling the immigration of Europeans (especially those from southern and eastern Europe) could no longer be ignored. As a result, unrestricted European immigration came to a halt.

Migration *within* the United States was as important as immigration in changing the lives of nineteenth-century Americans and transforming their society. In 1770, most of the 2.5 million Americans lived in small rural settlements close to the Atlantic seacoast. By 1920, a majority of the 100 million people lived in cities, and the country was continental. Because the restlessness that characterized nineteenth-century Americans was a carryover from earlier centuries, it is tempting to dismiss internal migration as an unimportant part of the revolutions in Americans' lives. However, new destinations that fundamentally altered the rhythms of individuals' lives and transformed the nation as a whole, and fuller information about the process of migration, make this an important part of the story. No one set of statistics fully indicates how many people migrated within the United States between 1770 and 1920. However, four different types of data are available which together make clear both the frequency and scale of movement.

Series of censuses and city directories have often been used to see if individuals living in a community one year were present at a later date. Results show that between 40 and 60 percent of the inhabitants of a community disappeared in the span of a decade. Some undoubtedly died, but many more moved on. Especially interesting is the fact that high mobility characterized all types of communities, ranging from cities in Massachusetts, Texas, or Washington to farm communities in Wisconsin, Iowa, and Kansas.[46] The California mining towns of Grass Valley and Nevada City are the most unstable communities yet studied—only 5 percent of their inhabitants of 1850 were still present in 1856—but they were most unusual places.[47]

In the early twentieth century, settlers of some western communities were interviewed about how they came to reside there. A survey of the "prominent" pioneers of Lincoln County, in the state of Washington, showed that only about a third had been born in Washington or had moved there directly from the state of their birth. Almost one of every five pioneers had lived in four states before arriving in Washington.[48] The early residents of Woodbury County, Iowa, (where Sioux City is located) followed highly individualistic routes from their place of birth to their new home.[49]

Several scholars have taken advantage of the fact that after 1850 the federal census recorded the place of birth of all individuals, to trace the migration of families by noting the states in which the children were born. These studies may not identify all the moves a family made, but they do show an extraordinary amount of mobility among nineteenth-century families. A family living in Texas in 1860 might well have started off in Virginia, and then moved to Kentucky, Ohio, and Missouri, before arriving in the Lone Star State. Foreign-born immigrants who ended up in the West often made several stops along the way.[50]

A new, western city like Chicago could experience an increase in population from 4,470 in 1840 to 109,260 in 1860 primarily because of immigration. No one would question the fluid and unstable nature of such a community. What is surprising is that evidence from city directories has shown that older urban areas that were apparently quite stable with regard to total size were in fact subject to a remarkable turnover of individuals who lived there. Perhaps as many as 1.5 million people move in and out of Boston between 1880 and 1890, even though the total population of that city was only 448,000 in 1890, an increase of 85,000 over the previous decade.[51]

In general, the men, women, and children who combined to give nineteenth-century America a restless, rootless quality never moved very far at any one time. The gold rush to California, which attracted individuals from thousands of miles away, was unusual. The irregular but frequent short-distance moves of farm families described by Laura Ingalls Wilder or Hamlin Garland were far more common. At least 138 of the 146 Virginians who lived in Wapello County, Iowa, in 1850 had stopped in at least one state on their way from Virginia.[52] Three distinct patterns of short-distance migration were present in Iowa in 1895, including: (1) short-distance movements in eastern Iowa from farms to the emerging urban centers, (2) westward migration across the state, both to newer agricultural regions and to towns on the Missouri River, and (3) movement to the capital city involving people from all over the state, even though Des Moines was centrally located.[53] Factory workers in New England, whether they were daughters of old New England families or more recently arrived French Canadians, also moved relatively often within a regional network of communities, but never went very far.[54] Numerous explorations of how individual states were populated demonstrate that most inhabitants came from bordering states. It seems probable that a single move of over 250 miles was most unusual, even though individuals often covered far longer distances over the course of a lifetime.

Numerous studies of regional, state, county, and even town settlement patterns suggest that each place attracted particular groups of migrants who might be quite different from those drawn to nearby communities. In general, however, three differ-

ent types of migration streams emerged from the complex interaction between the forces that produced a desire to leave one
place and made one potential destination more attractive than
another. Single men and women, often relatively young, made
up one type of migration stream. Frequently certain communities attracted more members of one sex than the other. The mill
towns of eastern Massachusetts provided temporary homes for
many young women in the nineteenth century. In 1840, there
were 7,876 women between the ages of fifteen and twenty-nine
living in Lowell, Massachusetts, but only 2,841 men of the same
ages.[55] In 1860, eastern cities such as Boston, New York, Philadelphia, and Baltimore all had more female than male inhabitants; farther west, in Cincinnati, Chicago, Saint Louis, and New
Orleans, men predominated. By 1900, Cincinnati and New
Orleans had joined the four eastern cities as communities with a
female majority. Mining areas offered a strong appeal to young
men.[56] In 1850, the gold rush to California produced a local
population that was 92 percent male, with 73 percent between
the ages of twenty and forty.[57]

Family migration was common in the farming regions of the
American west. Occasionally chain migration, in which the husband and father would move a year or two ahead of his family,
gave the newest agricultural settlements an unusual demographic profile. But within five to ten years agricultural regions
generally had large numbers of couples in their thirties and
forties, with an average of over three children per family.

The third type of migrant flow involved whole groups of
people who moved to a particular place at one time. The motives
behind such colonies varied widely. Utopian schemes, community schism, religious or racial persecution, and the efforts of
individual and corporate land speculators all led to group migrations at one time or another during the nineteenth century. Such
colonies could be found all over the West, from Gallapolis, Ohio,
to Salt Lake City, Utah, or the Peters Colony in Texas.[58] In
general, families dominated the group migrations, though in
instances like the Mormon migration to Utah single individuals
were also involved.

Many of the patterns described so far best fit the experiences
of white Americans, whether native or foreign-born. Black

Americans and the surviving Indians also participated in and were affected by the great nineteenth-century transformations brought about by migration, but the experience of each of these groups was different enough from that of the white majority to require special comment.

From 1770 to 1860, blacks took part, however unwillingly, in the westward expansion of southern society. They may not have had much choice in where or when they went, but blacks as much as whites were pioneers. As in the eighteenth century, blacks made up the majority of the population in some parts of the South, and were almost entirely absent in other regions. In Texas, in 1860, local geography and the origins of the white settlers had the greatest influence on where blacks lived. Whites from the Deep South often brought along slaves; white Southerners from Virginia, Kentucky, Maryland, or Missouri tried to restrict the numbers of black neighbors.[59]

After the Civil War and emancipation, some blacks moved into what was left of the southern cities, and many more moved within the rural South. Although a few blacks left the region for places like Kansas or Mexico, most remained in the South until the second decade of the twentieth century. Then, social and economic pressures at home, and the economic lure of northern factories during World War I, combined to start a voluntary movement of black Americans off southern farms and into northern and western cities. In 1920, 85 percent of all blacks still lived south of the Ohio River, but a trend had started that dramatically altered that situation over the next half century.[60]

For the first Americans, the nineteenth century brought continued catastrophe of the sort common between 1500 and 1800. The few Indians who survived the ravages of disease found themselves under continual pressure to move off land that whites wanted. Some chose to retreat before the flood of white settlers, in the hopes that they might preserve themselves and their culture a bit longer. Others refused to move and were physically ejected. The Cherokee described their forced migration from the Carolinas to the Ozarks as the Trail of Tears, indicating that whites seldom were much concerned about Indian well-being when land was involved. By 1920, the surviving descendents of the first immigrants had been forced onto reservations generally consisting of land whites did not want. For Indians, westward migration meant contraction rather than expansion.

That westward migration could mean contraction rather than expansion for one group of Americans points out that, all too often, westward migration has been discussed using words that limit our view of the total process. Reference to the "frontier" invokes another idea that can distort our understanding of what occurred. As used by American historians, the concept of the frontier has often implied the edge of civilization, beyond which lies nothing but savagery and darkness. In contrast, geographers often refer to "zones of contact" or "borderlands" when discussing the area of contact between two cultures, and are less prone to automatically judge one culture as good and the other as bad. Finally, "free land" is a term often used in connection with westward migration that is, by and large, inaccurate, whether applied in the financial sense or used to refer to an unoccupied region. As in the colonial period, nineteenth-century whites had difficulty in perceiving the difference between land not used according to European customs, and land not used at all.

Although the millions of people who made America a mobile society in the nineteenth century were never asked why they moved, the motives that led them to alter their lives are of interest. A variety of factors contributed to the propensity to migrate, though their importance relative to any one individual or group may be hard to assess.

Coercion continued to be a common reason for moving within the United States. Blacks before 1865, Indians, children, and wives often had no say in when, where, or even if they wanted to move. Some were undoubtedly happy to go along, but for others the experience must have been unpleasant. For slaves or children, the element of coercion in their migration is clear; for others, the line between voluntary and involuntary migration is harder to determine. Unavoidable migration must often have arisen from marriage, childbearing, or the death of a parent or spouse. Restlessness seems also to have driven some Americans to move even when logic dictated staying. Hamlin Garland, in his *Son of the Middle Border*, portrays his aging father's inability to

remain in one place, even after his wife refused to move anymore
and settled in a permanent home in Wisconsin in her old age.[61]
Many may have fled from an oppressive family life or an unsa-
vory reputation, seeking anonymity and privacy in a new community. Health also was often a consideration in the decision to
move. Individuals desperately seeking a cure for the ravages of
tuberculosis were, at various times, lured to Minnesota, Florida,
Colorado, Arizona, and southern California for the reputed
health-giving qualities of their climates.[62] Some were successful
in their quest, others were not. In some instances, fears of a
region may have discouraged immigration. Before 1850, the
valleys of the Ohio and Mississippi rivers were well known as
hotbeds of malaria.[63] In the 1870s, many southern cities received
damaging attacks of yellow fever which discouraged immigration and encouraged survivors to leave.[64]

Among the migrants who were able to make their own decisions according to a rational calculation of their future well-
being, one motive stands out—money. Men and women, young
and old, single, married, or widowed sought out new lives in new
environments in order to preserve or enhance their financial
security. Cities offered high wages to those willing to adjust to
crowded conditions and new rhythms of work and play. Westward migration frequently involved a search for land to use in
raising crops or cattle, mining for gold, silver, or other metals,
cutting timber, or making a profit by passing it on to later
migrants. For some, migration ceased when they found a community in which they could prosper. Those who arrived soon
after a town began to grow often grew with it. A majority,
however, moved on after a few years in search of an ever-
improving standard of living. Most often the latecomers were
early-goers, hoping to find their own place that was just getting
started.

By the end of the nineteenth century, changes in technology
and legislation made it easier than before for people to indulge
their habit of moving. Just as a revolution in oceanic travel played
a major role in the early demographic history of America,
another revolution in transportation in the nineteenth century
opened up the interiors of continents on both sides of the Atlantic. The canals and steamboats which increased access to the

eastern third of the North American continent were built during the first three decades of the nineteenth century. With the advent of the railroad, drier areas and longer distances in the West could be crossed quickly and with greater comfort. The fact that early migrants moved in wagons and flatboats suggests many would have gone without the railroad. But there can be no doubt that travel became easier over time.

The relationship of the railroad to where people lived changed over the century. In the East, where settlement occurred before railroads, tracks were built from one population center to another. In the West, the location of rail lines frequently influenced which areas would be settled early and which would remain thinly inhabited for a long time. Western towns were especially vulnerable to the decisions of railroad companies. Kansas City, Houston, and Los Angeles all owe their eventual dominance over neighboring communities to success in attracting trains.[65] Coolidge and Shakespeare, New Mexico, are little known today, in part because when railroads deserted them, so did their inhabitants.[66] Even in the East, railroads eventually produced a shift in population. The late nineteenth-century success of Lebanon and the decline of Lyme, both in New Hampshire, can be traced to where the railroads ran.[67]

Although the most striking effects of all-weather highways on where Americans chose to live became apparent only after 1920, the pressure for improved roads began about 1860, and mounted steadily after 1890 as bicycles and automobiles became part of American life.[68] By 1920, Americans were freer to move where they wished than ever before. The tyranny of geography over transportation, and hence over where people lived, had been significantly reduced.

Legislation fostering canals, railroads, and highways was only one of two major responses by federal, state, and local governments to the propensity of the people to move. The other was in land laws. Throughout the nineteenth century, land was acquired from the Indians and rapidly dispensed to whites as governments sought to respond to public demands. Most Indian land was acquired after white expansion put pressure on a particular cultural border. As new and different environments were encountered by the whites in their move west, land laws were amended to meet the needs of the new residents. Often land policy lagged behind the realities of the environment in which whites found themselves. This required continued adjustments in terms of acres sold to any one individual, credit terms, and water and timber rights. But governments on all levels proved more than willing to accommodate their citizens in their desire to move west.

The decision on where to go was often closely related to, and as important as, the decision to go. An individual's choice of where to move was often based on an image (real or otherwise) of her or his destination. Those who left farms for the city knew that new forms of work, play, and family life would be required in the more crowded, energetic, urban environment. For many Americans, images of cities were mixed. On the one hand, they were places of activity, excitement, progress, and wealth; on the other hand, vice, poverty, death, and the toil of factory labor also characterized urban life. But cities were *not* the country, and that was appealing.

The people who moved west to rural areas also had images about where they were headed that strongly affected their decisions. Many migrants sought regions geographically similar to those from which they came. The Cherokee who were forced out of the Carolina mountains settled in similar surroundings in the Ozarks.[69] Finnish immigrants found familiar environments in northern Michigan.[70] Migrants from West Virginia and eastern Kentucky eventually located in the mountains of Oregon and Washington where they could reestablish many of the rhythms of their earlier life.[71] The Mormons are a notable exception to this pattern, for they deliberately sought out the apparently hostile environment of Utah, with the hope that others would leave them there in peace.

As a result of this tendency to seek similar environments, migrants often followed temperature, and to a lesser extent, rainfall lines. Until they reached the dramatically different regions of the West, migrants often moved east to west, but seldom north to south. Some Southerners (especially Quakers) from Virginia, Maryland, and Kentucky moved north of the Ohio River, but even so they often stayed in the southern counties of Ohio, Indiana, and Illinois. Greater mixing occurred in the Far West, perhaps because the lure of gold, and later the attraction of better health, could only be satisfied in unfamiliar surroundings. But east of the Mississippi little movement occurred along north-south lines until after 1920.

In general, migrants chose their destinations on the basis of available information. Guidebooks were published for most parts of America, testifying to the demand for such literature. In addition, travellers' accounts, novels, poems, plays, promotional literature, advertisements, and newspapers all helped create images of various regions of the United States. However, the images often contained as much myth as reality. Hence, decisions that made perfect sense to the men and women who made them seem puzzling today. One region that particularly fascinated mid nineteenth-century Americans was the territory stretching from the western borders of Missouri and Iowa to the base of the Rockies. This region was described as both a desert and a garden, two quite opposite visions. Recent studies, primarily by geographers, have shown that both images had some basis in fact, no matter how contradictory they appear. Changes in climate which occurred between 1840 and 1860, the time when this territory was beginning to attract interest, created some confusion. First, a long-term cold spell that affected the northern hemisphere from about 1550 came to an end about 1850.[72] On top of this, the region in question has had twenty-year cycles of rainfall and drought that can be traced from the 1850s to the present. Each of these influenced the perception of whether European agricultural techniques could be applied there. Since some observers approached the plains from west Texas in May, while others arrived in late summer from Wisconsin, it is easy to see how different writers presented quite varied pictures of the region. A decision to settle there or not could hinge on the accident of from where and when the author of one's guide book visited the Great Desert/Garden.[73]

Historians have often claimed that white Americans showed an initial reluctance to move out on the prairies because of a European idea that land without trees was infertile. Close examination of settlement patterns shows that farmers were more than happy to acquire prairie lands, if they could also locate near timber for housing, heat, and fences.[74] To be completely away from timber created serious problems that had little to do with the fertility of the soil. In addition, treeless land was often flat and drained poorly, making it hard to farm, no matter how fertile the mud. Decisions on where to migrate were quite rational, both in terms of the labor required to establish a farm, and the need for shelter, implements, and fuel.

The story of westward migration includes not only Indians and the whites who resettled their land, but also millions of people who moved in and out of a region after it was resettled. Many of these people were influenced by the factors already examined, but their decisions were also based on their attitudes toward the people who had already moved there. Ethnic ghettos, which provided migrants with easily identifiable customs and a familiar language, grew up on western prairies as well as in eastern cities. The contrasting images of Oregon, California, and Utah as places devoted to farms and furs, gold, and religion respectively, grew out of the initial years of white occupation and gave later migrants a chance to select a region in which they would be comfortable.[75] The struggle over Kansas in the 1850s reflects the fact that both Northerners and Southerners understood that the culture that first took hold in a region was hard to dislodge. Black, Asian, Hispanic, and Mormon Americans were among those who also learned that certain communities should be avoided for safety's sake. Once a state, county, or town was established, selective migration frequently worked to preserve or enhance its particular characteristics.

The aggregate effect of internal migration in the nineteenth century was to transform the American people into a continental, urbanized nation. Often a move west involved migration to or through a new town, but it is helpful to separate the two streams for a few brief remarks on their overall significance.

Although the general tendency for the American population to move west had been established in the eighteenth century, the most impressive distances were covered in the nineteenth and twentieth centuries. Historical atlases provide decade-by-decade maps tracing the results of the millions of individual moves that shifted the geographic center of the American population from east of Baltimore, Maryland, in 1790 to slightly southeast of Saint Louis, Missouri, in 1970. Vast quantities of statistics document this transition in detail, but Chart 4, from the 1970 United States census, illustrates the two main trends. Panel A shows that, by 1870, the Northeast Region, the most heavily populated in 1790, had been passed in total numbers by both the South and the North Central. The great increase in the West came after 1920. Panel B illustrates that the major changes in where Americans lived occurred between 1850 and 1920. Before 1850 the North Central Region had experienced some growth, but in the second half of the century the North Central and West combined to make steady inroads on the dominance of the South and Northeast.

Unlike westward migration which had long been a part of American's lives, the move to the cities was a dramatic new trend. Until 1820, cities in the United States grew along with the rest of the country, but the proportion of the total population living in urban environments increased slowly or not at all, as shown in Chart 5. After 1820, however, mobile Americans began to choose cities as their destination in ever-increasing numbers. They were reinforced by large numbers of immigrants who preferred an urban existence to life on the farm. The top part of Chart 5 traces the evolution of the United States from a nation that was 95 percent rural in 1790, to a country in which almost three of every four people live in urban areas today. The 1920 census found that, for the first time, a majority of Americans were urbanites. Many of the new city dwellers were native-born Americans; many were immigrants. The surge in the growth of cities between 1840 and 1850, visible in the bottom part of Chart 5, corresponds to the first years of sizeable immigration. Each of the ensuing decades in which urban growth was relatively low corresponds to a period of economic depression in the United States that curtailed immigration and may have discouraged native-born migrants from seeking work in towns.

Some groups of Americans and some regions of the country experienced the urban transformation earlier than others. Northeasterners became city dwellers long before Southerners demonstrated any significant inclination to move to the cities. White Americans, especially immigrants, generally moved to the cities

CHART 4 POPULATION OF REGIONS: 1790–1970

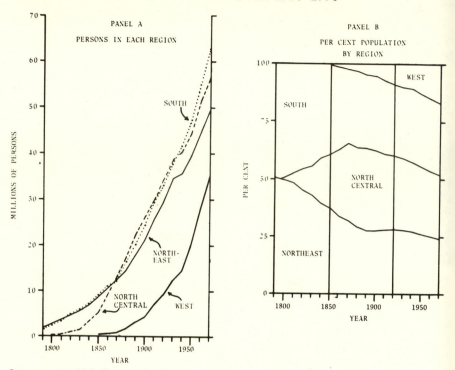

SOURCE: *1970 U.S. Census of Population*, vol. 1, pt. 1, pp. 48–51, Figures 16–18.

CHART 5 GROWTH OF CITIES:1790–1970

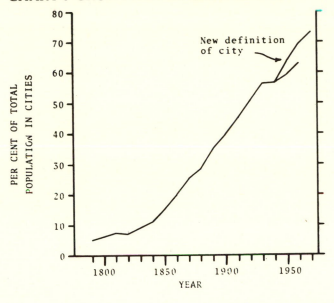

New definition
of city

PER CENT OF TOTAL POPULATION IN CITIES

YEAR

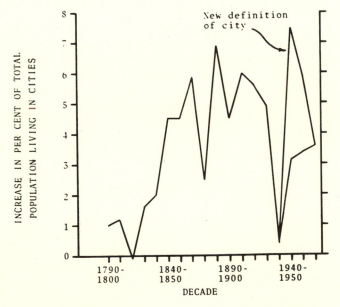

New definition
of city

INCREASE IN PER CENT OF TOTAL POPULATION LIVING IN CITIES

DECADE

SOURCE: *1970 U.S. Census of Population*, vol. 1, pt. 1, p. 42, Table 3.

before blacks, though in the North, free blacks more often than their white neighbors were city dwellers from 1790 on.[76] Eventually virtually every group and every section was caught up in the process of urbanization. It was a matter of *when* people of a particular culture would begin to move to cities, not *if* they would move. Furthermore, nineteenth-century censuses may understate the extent to which Americans were exposed to the rhythms of city life, for they recorded only the people living in cities every ten years, without indicating how many others had passed through on their way to other destinations. Surely, New England farm women who had worked in the Lowell mills in their youth knew the patterns of urban life, even though most of their days were spent on the farm.

The rich variety of life in places like Boston, Chicago, New Orleans, or Los Angeles, and concern over the problems of major metropolitan areas, encourages us to think of urbanization in terms of large cities. In fact, the vast majority of city dwellers resided in smaller communities. New York was the first American city of 1 million or more people and attained that size by 1880; by 1920, three additional cities passed that mark. However, in 1920, more Americans lived in the 219 cities with 25,000 to 100,000 inhabitants than in the four cities with 1 million or more. The 1,948 towns with 2,500 to 10,000 residents contained almost as many Americans as the four largest urban areas.[77] Life in a cattle town like Caldwell, Kansas, was far different from that in a cosmopolitan port like New Orleans. Clarence, Iowa, or Roseburg, Oregon, offered different attractions than Houston, Texas, or Schenectady, New York. Thus, although important transformations occurred in peoples' lives as they left the farm for the city, they were not always the same, since each urban community required its own pattern of adjustment depending on its geography, economic base, and demographic structure.

It is ironic that matters of health and death were the last of the basic rhythms of life to undergo revolutionary change in the nineteenth century, for, unlike other demographic transformations, health improvement was a universally approved goal. After 1870, the state of scientific knowledge finally caught up with modern desires to improve the quality of life, and produced significant achievements in combating disease and death by 1920. Curiously, however, modern attitudes may have been less important in the health revolution of the late nineteenth century than in some other changes since, unlike birth control or migration, which required an awareness by the individuals involved, better water supplies and city sewers affected people without their knowledge.

The dramatic changes in American life and health that occurred by 1920 can be demonstrated in four ways. First, life expectancy improved. The causes of health and death altered, as did the options for health care available to the ill. Finally, public and private attitudes about health and death fluctuated noticeably, especially when vehement professional debates heightened normal anxieties about the best treatment.

Nineteenth-century Americans frequently faced widely varying life chances, depending upon their race, sex, age, and place of residence. But *when* a person lived was often more important than these other factors. In the absence of epidemic infections, Americans probably survived as long as any people in the world, an advantage they had acquired by the end of the eighteenth century. But when epidemics struck, the death rate could increase sharply, especially in urban areas. Between the 1793 yellow fever outbreak in Philadelphia and the great influenza epidemic of 1918–1919, which may have killed 550,000 Americans in ten months (and at least 20 million worldwide), people were exposed to the constant but unpredictable threat of epidemics. Cholera invaded the United States in 1831–1833, 1849, and 1866 with effects that ranged from mild to disastrous from one community to another. In New Orleans, a warm weather port in which diseases easily were established, the death rate could increase from its normally high level of 35 to 40 per 1,000 (9 per 1,000 is the United States average today) to 70 per thousand or higher in epidemic years. Between 1832 and 1833, cholera and yellow fever combined to kill perhaps 10,000 of New Orleans's 50,000 residents.[78] In 1853, yellow fever helped produce over 6,000 deaths in that city, compared to a normal total of under 3,000. In August 1853, at the peak of the epidemic, 1,628 people were buried in a single week.[79] Memphis, Tennessee, took years to recover from the 1878 yellow fever outbreak. Of the town's 40,000 inhabitants, about half fled (many not to return), and 5,000 of the 20,000 who stayed behind died.[80] As in the seventeenth and eighteenth centuries, epidemics held a special terror because of their irregular occurrence and frequently spectacular visual aspects. Improvements in transportation made the spread of epidemics both faster and more predictable after 1850, but greater certainty that an epidemic was coming offered scant comfort to potential victims.[81] However, with the end of the influenza attack of 1918–1919, epidemics of the catastrophic quality of nineteenth-century plagues disappeared from Americans' lives.[82]

In addition to the eventual elimination of the worst of the short-term effects of epidemics, Americans who lived after 1870 benefitted from more general improvements in life chances. As late as 1850, life expectancy at birth for most white Americans probably was between forty and forty-five years, much the same as in the late eighteenth century. Black Americans could expect to live eight to ten years less on average. Among both groups, women lived a year or two longer than men. In mid nineteenth-century Massachusetts, whites who lived outside the major cities in years when major epidemics were absent, could anticipate nearly fifty years of life at birth, surely close to the maximum for that time.[83]

Sometime between 1870 and 1880, the chances Americans had of living long and healthy lives began to increase significantly. This change was unprecedented in human history, although it was shared by many Europeans at the time. White males, whose life expectancy at birth was just over 40 in 1850, expected to live 48.2 years on average by 1900, and 56.3 years by 1920. For women, the comparable increase was from about 43 years in 1850, to 51.1 in 1900, and 58.5 in 1920.[84]

As late as 1900, black Americans had relatively poor life chances. At the start of the twentieth century, black males could expect an average of only 32.5 years of life when they were born; for females, the figure was 35.0. By 1920, however, blacks were clearly benefitting from the changes that had affected whites earlier. In that year, black males had a life expectancy of 47.1, up fifteen years in only two decades. For women, the increase was not as spectacular. Nonetheless, they added 11.8 years to their life expectancy to produce an average of 46.8 years. In 1900, the gap between black and white life chances was probably as great as it has ever been in American history. Since then it has narrowed steadily, though rather slowly after 1920.[85]

Improved life chances for individuals are reflected in the overall death rate. The death rate in American cities fell from as much as 29 per 1,000 in 1870–1880 to 17 per 1,000 for 1910–1920.[86] In rural areas the decline may have been as much as from 23 to 15 per 1,000 in the same period.[87] For some Americans, the change occurred sooner than others. In New York City in 1920, the death rate among Germans was 13.0 per 1,000, compared to 13.7 for native-born white Americans, 14.0 for Italians, 18.1 for Irish, and 25.5 for nonwhites.[88] All these figures allow for differences in the age pyramids of the various groups.

From the evidence examined so far, it is clear that race, sex, age, and place of residence also influenced one's chances of living to a ripe old age. In general, white females living in rural New England had as good life chances as any Americans; black males in the South were relatively disadvantaged, especially if they happened to be living in a city visited regularly by epidemic diseases. But even black males had good life chances compared to the continued depopulation suffered by the first Americans.

By the start of the nineteenth century, many Indian tribes had already suffered extensive reductions in numbers. The trend was continued and enhanced by further contact with expanding white settlements. In 1837, the approximately 1,800 Mandans, Hidatsas, and Arikaras who lived on the upper reaches of the Missouri River were reduced to about 130 survivors of a smallpox epidemic.[89] Between 1830 and 1833, malaria, introduced from Oregon, killed about 75 percent of California Indians as 20,000 people died of this unfamiliar malady.[90] The Kansa tribe, whose numbers had fallen from about 4,800 to 1,600 during the eighteenth century, counted only 209 members in 1905. About 400 had died of smallpox in 1855, and 200 more perished four years later.[91] Demographic catastrophe on a similar scale occurred in the Hawaiian Islands well before they became a United States territory in 1898. In 1850, the total number of islanders was just over 84,000, between a fifth and a third the number in 1778. Epidemics had taken their toll, with more than 10,000 deaths (in a population of about 87,000) occurring in 1848–1849 alone.[92] Between 1900 and 1920, only about 240,000 Indians lived in the United States, no more than 5 percent of the best estimates for the population before Columbus made contact.

Although the precise contribution of any one factor is uncertain, an extraordinary array of items combined to produce the changes that enabled most Americans to live longer, healthier lives in 1920 than in 1870. Causes of death were eliminated; more and more people practiced actions that "caused" health.

A decline in deaths from infectious diseases was an important reason for improved life chances, especially among young people, who are frequently the victims of such disorders. In New York, Boston, Philadelphia, and New Orleans the number of deaths each year from eight major infectious killers dropped from 964 per 100,000 between 1864 and 1888, to 524 from 1889 to 1913. Cholera and yellow fever were almost eliminated during this period, as the number of deaths from these two causes decreased from 22 to 1 for each 100,000 people. More important, however, was the beginning of control over regular, if less spectacular killers. Deaths from tuberculosis and intestinal disorders dropped from 664 to 419 per 100,000.[93]

Why did infectious diseases kill fewer Americans after 1870 than before? The answer is simple. By a variety of actions, some personal and some public, Americans increasingly prevented themselves from getting sick in the first place, in the end the most effective form of disease control. Perhaps one or two diseases evolved into less dangerous infections. The gradual elimination of purging and bleeding by doctors enabled people's bodies to combat diseases more effectively by natural means. Better surgical techniques saved a few lives. But effective curative medicine was a thing of the future. Doctors attained the capacity to cure more than a handful of diseases only after 1920. The start of the health revolution came because of preventive actions consciously taken to improve life.

Public health measures, especially in cities, became an important part of late nineteenth-century life. Although limited in scope, Louisiana established the first permanent state board of health in 1855. After New York City and Massachusetts set further examples, in 1866 and 1869 respectively, permanent and powerful boards of health gradually replaced the earlier temporary, highly politicized bodies that had tried unsuccessfully to deal with matters of public health.[94] As a result of their efforts sewers were built, streets cleaned, and garbage collected more regularly by 1900 than before. Water supplies improved. In 1850, only 68 public waterworks existed in the United States. By 1880, the figure stood at 629, rising to 3,196 by 1897.[95] Inoculation, especially for smallpox, was encouraged. Public drinking cups and spitting (which spread tuberculosis) were discouraged. Statistics were collected and reports issued to mark both the distance from and progress toward a better life.

Reformers in the mid-nineteenth century began to advocate all manner of programs to improve personal hygiene and health. Apparently they received some attention, for between 1830 and 1890, at least eighty-five popular health magazines were published.[96] Many reformers had a major concern for diet. Sylvester Graham (for whom the cracker is named) was one of many who urged a better balanced diet, suggesting less animal protein and more vegetable matter.[97] Improved agriculture and inventions like refrigerator cars for trains made it possible to follow these suggestions. Bathing for skin care was recommended, even at the unheard-of frequency of every three weeks. Public parks, new sports, and bicycles all were supported as exercise and fresh air were recognized as health-giving activities.[98] Reformers even suggested, though often with little success, that clothing should fit the needs of health rather than fashion.

Other reforms involving food also contributed to improving life spans. Before 1906, when the federal government passed its first laws setting standards for pure foods, Americans were exposed to significant dangers from spoiled food, poisons left on vegetables, additives, and parasites. Gradually, and despite a great deal of resistance by food packagers and distributors, reforms occurred. Meat packing plants were inspected; the "certified milk" movement led to cleaner dairies and healthier herds of cattle.[99] After foreign importers threatened to boycott American foods, lead and arsenic insecticides, some with exotic names such as London purple or Paris green, were washed from vegetables and fruits, and pork was inspected for trichina worms.[100] American politicians generally showed little interest in improving their constituents' food supplies when reformers like Harvey Wiley, S. H. Adams, or Henry L. Coit made themselves very obnoxious, and responded only to economic pressures from abroad or widespread public outrage.[101]

Efforts to label drugs and purify the contents of patent medicines often were closely associated with pure-food reforms. The federal Pure Food and Drugs Act of 1906 also addressed itself to this problem. For years Americans had been happily dosing themselves with concoctions which ranged from harmless and worthless, to potions in which opium, morphine, heroin, or cocaine were mixed in an alcohol solution. Such medicines did not cure many people, but there must have been many who felt no pain from their ailments with such aids at hand. After 1906, labeling requirements exposed the worst frauds and most dangerous medicines for what they were, though it was difficult to actually force them off the market.[102]

Many Americans acquired better housing in the nineteenth century. Space, ventilation, plumbing, and even screens became matters of concern for reasons of health as well as convenience. The Rockefeller family contributed to an effort to build privies in many parts of the rural South in the twentieth century, surely an element as important to American health as urban sewers.[103]

Welfare movements also played their part in improving life. As industrial accidents rose as a cause of death, industrial safety became a matter of increased concern. Attacks on regional diseases such as hookworm in the South were mounted. Child welfare became a matter of public concern, first with the creation of the Society for the Prevention of Cruelty to Children in 1875 (modeled on the Society for the Prevention of Cruelty to Animals established nine years earlier!) and later, in 1912, with the federal Children's Bureau.

Some actions initiated to improve health had little effect. In the late nineteenth century, the Post Office attempted to disinfect mail in order to control the spread of epidemics. Postal clerks dipped letters in various solutions and fumigated envelopes to kill germs. In extreme cases, they used wooden mallets with nails in the end to pound holes in envelopes so the letter inside would also receive the benefit of fumigation.[104] Similarly, libraries sometimes quarantined books if a borrower became ill. Warnings were issued about green wallpaper, because the dyes in it contained arsenic compounds. These examples may seem funny today, but they indicate just how serious and widespread the search for health became in the late nineteenth and early twentieth centuries.

Before 1880, doctors continued to do as much damage as good, but eventually they also contributed to better health for Americans. Nonetheless, throughout the period Americans often chose among a variety of health care options when they became ill. Two characteristics stand out regarding those options available before 1880. First, medical care was generally poor throughout this period. Second, recognizing that no one approach to medicine could *demonstrate* its superiority over another, Americans made use of a wide range of healers when they were sick. A great deal of debate occurred between 1770 and 1880 about proper medical practice, without much being settled.

One result of this debate was the justifiable erosion of confidence in professional doctors. The first half of the nineteenth century may well be the low point in the history of the American medical profession. In the late eighteenth century, many states began to require a license to practice medicine, but by the 1840s these efforts to enforce standards had been repealed. The opening up of medical practice to anyone who could get patients was partly the result of a democratic impulse against creating a monopoly for any group, but it also reflected a realistic assessment of the abilities of licensed physicians compared to the "irregulars." Medical education was extremely poor. Most doctors learned via apprenticeship. Of the one-third who acquired degrees from medical colleges, many purchased diplomas from mail-order schools. Most of the others were exposed to a series of lectures, often lasting less than six months, but which might be repeated a second year in the case of a high-quality program.[105] Sectional hostilities were so strong by mid century that doctors in one part of the United States refused to adopt techniques developed in other parts of the country.[106] Similarly, American physicians often refused to accept medical discoveries made in countries they disliked.[107] By 1850, the worst excesses of "heroic" medicine were being abandoned, but some doctors continued to bleed via cutting or leaches, to induce vomiting and diarrhea, and to dose with medicines such as calomel or tartar emetic that contained poisons like mercury or antimony.

As professional medicine declined in importance, Americans turned to alternative forms of health care. Undoubtedly many used home remedies. Others sought out local folk healers who claimed healing "powers" that were often attributed to some unusual aspect of their birth, such as being the seventh child of a seventh child, or having been a breech birth. Those who could afford it travelled to spas for bathing in and drinking mineral water, and to different climates.

In the absence of a clearly superior choice, both groups and individuals made systematic efforts to advance their claims to holding the solution to America's health problems. Prominent among the alternative systems of medicine put forth in the nineteenth century were Thomsonians, who advocated botanic medicines for purging; Hydropaths, who urged water cures; Eclectics, who used whatever appealed to them; and Homeopaths, who treated patients with medicines that would produce symptoms similar to the illness at hand when given to a healthy person. As newspapers and magazines developed, individual "healers" made use of the new media to advance their own particular health techniques. Throughout much of the nineteenth century, proprietary or patent medicines and mechanical devices were widely advertised and sold. Some modestly claimed to solve only one or two ailments, such as "female complaints" or malaria, but others offered help for almost every imaginable form of illness known. From Perkin's Metallic Tractors in 1796, to Radam's Microbe Killer in 1886, Americans responded enthusiastically to all manner of patent medicines and devices with exotic names like Comstock's Dead Shot Pellets, or Pink Pills for Pale People, to more prosaic sounding cures like Hostetter's Bitters, or Lydia E. Pinkham's Vegetable Compound. Some of these "medicines" were little more than colored water, but others were potent concoctions including sulfuric acid, opium, arsenic, or alcohol. Many individual merchants of liquid or powdered health were accused of quackery at the time, a valid judgment, but one that was fully as true of their professional accusers.[108]

Some of the solutions nineteenth-century Americans tried in their quest for health are amusing in retrospect, but from the perspective of the sick, many of their actions were entirely logical. Whatever the actual merits of the various systems and medicines offered by alternative health specialists, their techniques were often cheaper and less violent than those used by professional physicians and surgeons. In addition, home dosage appealed to those who resented their dependence on experts in times of illness, and allayed the fears (at least temporarily) of people whom the professionals could not help. Many must actually have felt better as a result of their treatment, even if they were not physically helped. Today, almost one-third of all patients say they feel better after some medical attention, even when the treatment is known to be ineffective. Presumably human psychology was much the same in the nineteenth century. A few treatments may actually have worked; for instance, water cures could help people with certain mineral deficiencies. Medicines containing heroin in alcohol would reduce the perception of pain, even though the cause remained. Even arsenic potions, such as Fowler's Solution, had an appeal to those unaware of the principal ingredient for the first stage of chronic arsenic poisoning produces the appearance of returning health via weight gain and improved skin tone and color. Confronted with doctors who openly recommended arsenic as a tonic, or praised the smoke of Pittsburgh as beneficial for keeping the "miasmas" of rotting garbage in the streets under control, it seemed quite rational to look elsewhere for health care.[109]

Before 1880, Americans found few effective means for improving their health, but the wide range of options they explored indicates they had passed beyond a traditional passive acceptance of illness and death to a more modern idea, that health could and should be actively pursued.

Between 1880 and 1920, the range of medical techniques considered acceptable by consumer and vendor alike began to narrow as scientific and technological change made it possible for professional doctors to demonstrate actual advantages to their forms of practice. Significant advances in the capacities of doctors to cure illness came mostly after 1920, but three broad changes before then marked the emergence of a more effective system of health care for Americans.

One of the most important changes was in the way doctors looked at medicine. In the eighteenth and early nineteenth centuries, medicine was more a philosophy, or system of ideas, than a science, or way of defining a problem and seeking a solution. As a result, new knowledge was acquired slowly, partly because medical questions were posed on very general levels, and partly because new techniques were incorporated into practice only if they did not threaten a doctor's philosophy. By 1900, medicine was well on the way to becoming a science in which empirical observation of precisely defined phenomena contributed specific solutions to limited problems. Doctors could circulate and accept new findings without threatening whole systems of belief and practice.

Technical changes also began to accumulate which actually improved treatment and reinforced the scientific approach to medicine. By 1920, anesthesia, antiseptic practices, and X rays all made surgery safer and more effective. The isolation of the tuberculosis bacillus by Robert Koch in 1882, and the discovery that cholera also was caused by a single organism, were instrumental in turning doctors away from a search for general causes of illness and health, toward studies of specific causes and cures for specific illnesses. Even nonmedical technology made its contribution. By 1920, automobiles and telephones made faster, more specialized medical care available.[110] When they became sick, people could more easily get to the doctors they needed.

Institutional arrangements within the medical profession also played an important role in the gradual improvement of Americans' health. The establishment of the American Medical Association in 1846 and the creation of permanent and effective boards of health made it possible for doctors to have an influence on public health policy between the times when epidemics created a sense of urgency. In the early years of these organizations, the scientific basis of medicine was insufficient for them to have any notable effects. But as scientific knowledge began to accumulate, the new institutional arrangements made it easier for doctors to establish and enforce professional standards that were beneficial to the sick. The Flexner Report of 1910 was especially instrumental in improving medical education in the United States. This report, funded by the Carnegie Foundation, found *every* medical school in the country with the exception of Johns Hopkins lacking in some regard.[111] Throughout most of the nineteenth century the best American doctors trained in Europe, an expenditure of time and money few could afford. After 1910 Americans could seek out physicians trained at home, with increased chances of better care.

Sharp conflicts of values and attitudes were part of the nineteenth-century revolution in health care and life expectancy. Between 1770 and 1920, but especially after 1850, major efforts were made in America and Europe to reassess the social and personal meaning of disease. The magnitude of the demographic changes made it impossible to resolve all the differences satisfactorily. The vehemence of the debate sometimes hindered acceptance of new techniques, and on occasion may actually have been detrimental to health. Two aspects of this discussion are especially interesting. The first involves often striking inconsistencies in the ways in which Americans thought about health and death. The second revolves around the almost inevitable tension which exists between doctor and patient.

Like their ancestors, nineteenth-century Americans devoted attention to epidemic diseases out of proportion to their actual effect on the death rate. The irregular and often spectacular aspects of epidemic killers drew attention, and often severely disrupted normal human relationships within a community. The fears and hostilities generated in Philadelphia in 1793, New Orleans in 1853, or Memphis in 1878 created lasting problems within families, among friends, and in the communities at large. As a result, many early efforts to improve public health by means of preventive medicine focused on epidemic diseases even though many more lives could have been prolonged by control of a major, regular killer.

Religion continued to have an important influence in shaping American attitudes toward health and death in the nineteenth century. Individual men and women found support in religion when confronted with their own mortality or that of a loved one. In fact, people systematically prepared for their own death and for the need to console others when family members died. It has been suggested that this fascination with death was excessive in the context of nineteenth-century America, where life expectancy was already as favorable as anywhere in the world.[112] Perhaps ritual funerals and the continued threat of sudden death from epidemic disease gave death a reality and imminence life tables can not convey. Perhaps clergymen and middle-class women began to write consolation literature when other issues that had once concerned them disappeared. Whatever the reason, the search for health in the nineteenth century was accompanied by a search for a proper way to die.[113]

However much religion aided Americans and their families as they faced death, it may have delayed the more general search for health. Before 1850, it was common to view personal illness or the sudden appearance of an epidemic as signs of individual or communal wickedness.[114] Sickness was God's way of punishing sinners; it was not the result of germs multiplying in foul water or garbage-filled streets. Since many middle-class native-born Americans associated "sin" with the poor or immigrants, they found little reason to support public health efforts until they, too, were touched by epidemic illnesses. As a result, the response to disease often was prayer for the strayed rather than prophylaxis for the streets. Americans' 1832 responses to cholera of prayer, fasting, and other religious activities are remarkably similar to the way fourteenth-century Italians prepared for the bubonic plague. By 1866, however, a fundamental change occured as cholera came to be considered a natural process that could be controlled without interfering with God's efforts to punish sinners. Victims of disease deserved aid for their misfortune rather than censure for their immorality.[115] By 1900, many Americans willingly admitted that, although poverty and illness were closely related, neither necessarily reflected an individual's moral worth. Consequently, it was possible to take action to help the sick (especially the sick poor) without risking the anger of God or wasting one's efforts on a lost soul.

Economics also affected attitudes toward health and death, especially in the cities. Until 1850, many businessmen and politicians believed sewers, clean streets, and pure water cost more than they were worth. The presence of epidemic disease in a community often was denied for weeks because of the legitimate fear that actions taken to combat the illness would scare off business.

Between 1850 and 1880, these simple but realistic concerns were replaced by a more sophisticated analysis of the relationship of disease to the economic well-being of a town. Community leaders learned from experience that any short-term gain in prolonging trade in the face of an epidemic was more than offset by long-term shifts in trading arrangements when diseases got out of control. Outbreaks of yellow fever in southern cities like Atlanta and Memphis in the 1870s were so badly handled that coalitions of businessmen forced political and public health reforms to protect the economic welfare of their cities.[116] In addition, after 1850 individuals such as J. C. Simonds of New Orleans and organizations like the Massachusetts Board of Health began to marshal statistics to show that high rates of illness and death significantly reduced a community's potential for economic growth through the loss of workdays and the workers themselves.[117] It took a while for politicians to understand that increased productivity more than repaid taxes spent on public health matters. Once they had, spending on public health rose significantly.

In the twentieth century, Americans commonly insure themselves heavily against the results of illness and death. Given the higher rates of sickness and death in the nineteenth century, it is somewhat surprising that insurance was rather rare at that time. Some individuals and groups did seek to control the effects of illness and death by the establishment of health and life insurance plans, and by 1920 both types of insurance were available to Americans, though few took advantage of opportunities to buy policies. Part of the resistance to illness and death insurance came from identification of such measures with "socialist" immigrants, who were seen as undermining the moral fabric of the country.[118] Many, of course, could not afford the premiums. Ironically, a healthy public may be necessary before insurance premiums are low enough and family incomes steady enough to allow individuals to budget insurance payments. In the past, many Americans may not have been as rational and calculating in their efforts to control the future efects of illness and death as

are their descendants. Whatever the reasons, heavy investment
in life and health insurance occurred only after the revolution in
actual mortality was well underway.

The values and attitudes of nineteenth-century consumers of
health are important. But what of the merchants—the doctors?
They, too, had ideas about health and death, and about their
patients as well, that shaped the treatment they offered. Historians of science have demonstrated that new scientific discoveries
are often met with skepticism and resistance, especially when
they challenge established theories and concepts. Doctors in
nineteenth-century America often were reluctant to adopt new
techniques even after medicine began to move from a philosophy
to a science. Resistance to new findings often was based on
loyalty to the system one had learned in medical school or as an
apprentice. New findings were professionally and psychologi-
cally threatening when they called into question years of practice
involving matters of life and death. In addition, the nineteenth
century was so full of medical fads that most physicians must
have found it safer to wait a couple of years for new procedures
to prove themselves, rather than be made fools for too hasty
judgements. It is easier for us to identify significant advances in
medicine than it was for those who first learned of anesthesia or
the tuberculosis bacillus.

Scientific concerns were not the only source of values affecting
medical practice. Doctors exhibited a normal human tendency
when they identified most readily with patients like themselves,
and reflected concerns, especially regarding race and sex, that
were prevalent at the time. Male physicians frequently refused
to take seriously the complaints of women.[119] Native-born
middle-class doctors often ignored or gave cursory examination
to illnesses affecting primarily immigrants or the poor.[120] It was
more acceptable to treat gout or other problems of overeating
than to treat venereal disease or skin problems caused by filthy
living conditions. Religious teaching that suggested that the poor
and foreign deserved their problems reinforced doctors' tendencies to prefer the medical problems of polite, bill-paying society to
those that may have been killing more people.

The nature of the doctor-patient relationship is always one that generates tension, if not hostility. Patients turn to doctors when they are sick or dying and are forced into a very dependent relationship. Sick people literally expose their innermost problems to doctors, often with unrealistic hopes and expectations about the possibility of relief or cure. Physicians, on the other hand, cannot afford to get too close to patients who may die suddenly, and perhaps unpleasantly. It is difficult to envision an early nineteenth-century surgeon operating without anesthesia on many people for whom he held deep personal affection. Between 1840 and 1880, the multiplication of patent remedies and alternative systems of treatment, public assaults on licensing and standards, and outcries and occasional riots against "body-snatching" by medical students in anatomy classes made it clear to doctors that they were viewed with suspicion.

Although most doctors seem to have handled the tensions of their profession fairly well, some acted in ways which could have been detrimental to the health of some of their more defenseless patients, especially those from the lower classes. It has been argued that black Americans often received relatively good health care when they were slaves because white masters wanted to protect their investment. Regardless of the general merits of this argument, it is clear that some southern physicians took advantage of access to slaves to conduct rather brutal medical experiments. Most notable was Dr. J. M. Sims of Atlanta who, between 1843 and 1848, used thirty black women to perfect a surgical procedure for the genital-urinary system before he attempted the operation on white women. Sims also amputated the cancerous jaw of a male slave for benefit of his medical students even though the patient opposed the operation.[121] In the late nineteenth century, northern and southern physicians alike felt that blacks were doomed to extinction when confronted with white competition.[122] Such attitudes presumably did not improve the health care black Americans received. Similarly, northern mental hospitals treated poor and foreign-born patients more harshly than native-born middle-class sufferers.[123]

Perhaps the most difficult problems many male doctors faced arose from the issues raised by changing patterns of reproduction and sexual behavior. Here they found themselves torn by their personal goals, their professional concerns, and general attitudes which were widely shared by middle-class white males. On the one hand, some evidence suggests that doctors were among the earliest groups to limit the size of their own families.[124] On the other hand, many doctors felt it necessary to speak out, as professionals and leaders of the community, against abortion and birth control as dangerous to women, families, and society. Physicians warned of diseases such as "masturbatory insanity," and some practiced extensive and painful sexual surgery on women and men whom they feared to be out of sexual control.[125] Doctors were influential in passing legislation to outlaw abortion, both on moral grounds and to assert their professional control over childbearing, which had previously been in the hands of midwives. Although the trend did not manifest itself fully until the middle of the twentieth century, doctors helped to give a new meaning to "birth control" as they worked to make childbirth an event to be medically managed in hospitals by professionals, instead of a natural process that occurred at home in the company of family and friends.[126] This change is especially ironic since the very men who felt they were working to preserve and protect American families by opposing various forms of birth control were, by means of their efforts to control birth, undermining one of the most basic of all family activities. But then, revolutions have often confused as much as clarified, at least in the short run.

Notes

1. Frederick S. Crum, "The Decadence of the Native American Stock: A Statistical Study of Genealogical Records," *American Statistical Association Journal* 14 (1916–17): 214–22.

2. Ansley J. Coale and Melvin Zelnik, *New Estimates of Fertility and Population in the United States* (Princeton, N.J., 1963); Colin Forster and G.S.L. Tucker, *Economic Opportunity and White American Fertility Ratios, 1800–1860* (New Haven, 1972); Yasukichi Yasuba, *Birth Rates of the White Population in the United States, 1800–1860: An Economic Study* (Baltimore, 1962).

3. Ansley J. Coale and Norfleet W. Rives, Jr., "A Statistical Reconstruction of the Black Population of the United States, 1880–1970," *Population Index* 39 (1973): 3–36; Stanley J. Engerman, "Black Fertility and

Family Structure in the U.S., 1880–1940," *Journal of Family History* 2 (1977): 117–38; Reynolds Farley, "The Demographic Rates and Social Institutions of the Nineteenth-Century Negro Population: A Stable Population Analysis," *Demography* 2 (1965): 386–98.

4. Yasuba, *Birth Rates*, pp. 51–52.

5. Wendell H. Bash, "Changing Birth Rates in Developing America: New York State, 1840–1875,"*Milbank Memorial Fund Quarterly* 41 (1963): 161–82; Susan E. Bloomberg, et al., "A Census Probe into Nineteenth-Century Family History: Southern Michigan, 1850–1880," *Journal of Social History* 5 (1971): 26–45.

6. Alan Graebner, "Birth Control and the Lutherans—The Missouri Synod as a Case Study," *Journal of Social History* 2 (1969): 303–32; James E. Smith and Phillip R. Kunz, "Polygyny and Fertility in Nineteenth-Century America," *Population Studies* 30 (1976): 465–80.

7. Tamara K. Hareven and Maris A. Vinovskis, "Marital Fertility, Ethnicity, and Occupation in Urban Families: An Analysis of South Boston and the South End in 1880," *Journal of Social History* 8 (1975): 69–93.

8. Ira Rosenwaike, *Population History of New York City* (Syracuse, 1972), p. 106.

9. Crum, "Decadence"; Thomas P. Monahan, *The Pattern of Age at Marriage in the United States*, 2 vols. (Philadelphia, 1951).

10. Kingsley Davis, "The American Family in Relation to Demographic Change," in Commission on Population and the American Future, *Demographic and Social Aspects of Population Growth* (Washington, 1972), p. 256.

11. Bettie C. Freeman, "Fertility and Longevity of Married Women Dying after the End of the Reproductive Period,"*Human Biology* 7 (1935): 392–418.

12. Nancy Osterud and John Fulton, "Family Limitation and Age at Marriage: Fertility Decline in Sturbridge, Massachusetts, 1730–1850," *Population Studies* 30 (1976): 481–94; Robert V. Wells, "Family Size and Fertility Control in Eighteenth-Century America: A Study of Quaker Families," *Population Studies* 25 (1971): 73–82.

13. These statements based on reworking of data in Carl E. Jones, "A Genealogical Study of Population," *American Statistical Association Journal* 16 (1918–1919): 201–19.

14. The discussion on birth control that follows is based on Carl N. Degler, *At Odds: Women and the Family in America from the Revolution to the Present* (New York, 1980), pp. 178–248; Linda Gordon, *Woman's Body, Woman's Right: A Social History of Birth Control in America* (New York, 1976); Norman E. Himes, *Medical History of Contraception*, rev. ed. (New York, 1970), pp. 209–332; James Reed, *From Private Vice to Public Virtue: The Birth*

Control Movement and American Society since 1830 (New York, 1977); Robert V. Wells, "Fertility Control in Nineteenth-Century America: A Study of Diffusion, Technique, and Motive," paper presented to the Conference on Historical Perspectives on the Scientific Study of Fertility in the United States, Boston, 1978.

15. Robert Dale Owen, *Moral Physiology* (New York, 1831).

16. Charles Knowlton, *The Fruits of Philosophy, or the private companion of young married people* (New York, 1832).

17. Wilson Yates, "Birth Control Literature and the Medical Profession in Nineteenth Century America," *Journal of the History of Medicine and Allied Sciences* 31 (1976): 42–54.

18. Richard H. Shryock, "Public Relations of the Medical Profession in Great Britain and the United States: 1600–1870," *Annals of Medical History* 2 (1930): 316.

19. John P. Harper, "Be Fruitful and Multiply: Origins of Legal Restrictions on Planned Parenthood in Nineteenth-Century America," in *Women of America: A History*, eds. Carol Berkin and Mary Beth Norton (Boston, 1979), pp. 245–72; James C. Mohr, *Abortion in America: The Origins and Evolution of National Policy* (New York, 1977); R. Sauer, "Attitudes to Abortion in America, 1800–1973," *Population Studies* 28 (1974): 53–67.

20. In addition to the sources cited above in notes 2, 5, and 7, *see* Richard A. Easterlin, "Factors in the Decline in Farm Family Fertility in the United States: Some Preliminary Research Results," *Journal of American History* 63 (1976): 600–614; John Useem, "Changing Economy and Rural Security in Massachusetts," *Agricultural History* 16 (1942): 29–40.

21. Quoted in Vincent J. Cirillo, "Edward Foote's *Medical Common Sense:* An Early American Comment on Birth Control," *Journal of the History of Medicine and Allied Sciences* 25 (1970): 341–45.

22. Linda Gordon, "Voluntary Motherhood: The Beginnings of Feminist Birth Control Ideas in the United States," in *Clio's Consciousness Raised: New Perspectives on the History of Women,* eds. Mary Hartman and Lois Banner (New York, 1974), pp. 54–71.

23. Bernard Axelrod, "Historical Studies of Emigration from the United States," *International Migration Review* 6 (1972): 32–49.

24. Robert R. Palmer, *The Age of Democratic Revolution: A Political History of Europe and America 1760–1800,* Z vols. (Princeton, N.J., 1959), vol. 1, p. 188.

25. Alfred W. Reynolds, "The Alabama Negro Colony in Mexico, 1894–1896," *Alabama Review* 5 (1952): 243–68; 6 (1953): 31–58; B.H.C. Weaver, "Confederate Emigration to Brazil," *Journal of Southern History* 27 (1961): 33–53.

26. B. Carmon Hardy, "The Trek South: How the Mormons Went to Mexico," *Southwestern Historical Quarterly* 73 (1969–1970): 1–16.

27. Paul F. Sharp, "The American Farmer and the 'Last Best West,'" *Agricultural History* 21 (1947): 65–75.

28. Rowland T. Berthoff, *British Immigrants in Industrial America, 1790–1950* (Cambridge, Mass., 1953).

29. Thomas Kessner, *The Golden Door: Italian and Jewish Immigrant Mobility in New York City 1880–1915* (New York, 1977), pp. 26–32.

30. For this and most other matters on immigration, readers can do well to consult Maldwyn A. Jones, *American Immigration* (Chicago, 1960); and Philip Taylor, *The Distant Magnet: European Emigration to the U.S.A.* (New York, 1971).

31. In 1850, the United States Census began to record data on place of birth. Thereafter, the summary volumes of each succeeding decennial census provide ample data on the residence patterns of various ethnic groups.

32. C. G. Belissary, "Tennessee and Immigration, 1865–1880," *Tennessee Historical Quarterly* 7 (1948): 229–48; Robert F. Futrell, "Efforts of Mississippians to Encourage Immigration, 1865–1880," *Journal of Mississippi History* 20 (1958): 59–76.

33. Herbert Weaver, "Foreigners in Ante-Bellum Towns of the Lower South," *Journal of Southern History* 1 (1947): 62–73.

34. Ralph W. Wooster, "Foreigners in the Principal Towns of Ante-Bellum Texas," *Southwestern Historical Quarterly* 66 (1962): 208–20.

35. Frank Thistlethwaite, "Migration from Europe Overseas in the Nineteenth and Twentieth Centuries," International Committee of Historical Sciences, 11th Congress, Stockholm, 1960, *Rapports*, vol. 5, pp. 32–60.

36. Ibid., p. 39; Nicolas Sanchez-Albornoz, *The Population of Latin America: A History* (Berkeley, 1974), pp. 146–81.

37. Thistlethwaite, "Migration from Europe," p. 41.

38. Kristian Hvidt, *Flight to America: The Social Background of 300,000 Danish Emigrants* (New York, 1975).

39. Dutch emigrants stand out as one of the few exceptions to the rule; *see* Robert P. Swierenga, "Dutch Immigrant Demography, 1820–1880," *Journal of Family History* 5 (1980): 390–405.

40. Barry W. Poulson and James Holyfield, Jr., "A Note on European Migration to the United States: A Cross Spectral Analysis," *Explorations in Economic History* 11 (1973–1974): 299–310; Brinley Thomas, *Migration and Economic Growth: A Study of Great Britain and the Atlantic Economy*, 2d ed. (Cambridge, England, 1973).

41. Theodore C. Blegen, "The Competition of the Northwestern States for Immigrants," *Wisconsin Magazine of History* 3 (1919–1920): 3–29;

Norman L. Crocket, "A Study of Confusion: Missouri's Immigration Program, 1865–1916, "*Missouri Historical Review* 57 (1962–1963): 248–60.

42. For example, *see* James B. Hedges, "Promotion of Immigration to the Pacific Northwest by the Railroads," *Mississippi Valley Historical Review* 15 (1928): 183–203.

43. John A. Olsen, "Proselytism, Immigration and Settlement of Foreign Converts to the Mormon Culture in Zion," *Journal of the West* 6 (1967): 189–204; Philip A. M. Taylor, "Mormons and Gentiles on the Atlantic," *Utah Historical Quarterly* 24 (1956): 195–214.

44. Berthoff, *British Immigrants;* John Modell, "Tradition and Opportunity: the Japanese Immigrant in America," *Pacific Historical Review* 40 (1971): 163–82.

45. Kessner, *Golden Door;* Gilbert Fite, "Daydreams and Nightmares: the Late Nineteenth-Century Agricultural Frontiers," *Agricultural History* 40 (1966): 285–92; Virginia Yans McLaughlin, "Patterns of Work and Family Organization: Buffalo's Italians," *Journal of Interdisciplinary History* 2 (1971): 299–314.

46. Stephen Thernstrom, *The Other Bostonians: Poverty and Progress in the American Metropolis, 1880–1970* (Cambridge, Mass., 1973), 220–61.

47. Ralph Mann, "The Decade After the Gold Rush: Social Structure in Grass Valley and Nevada City, California, 1850–1860," *Pacific Historical Review* 41 (1972): 484–504.

48. Carl F. Reuss, "The Pioneers of Lincoln County, Washington: A Study in Migration," *Pacific Northwest Quarterly* 30 (1939): 51–65.

49. Frank H. Garver, "The Settlement of Woodbury County," *Iowa Journal of History and Politics* 9 (1911): 359–84.

50. Barnes F. Lathrop, "Migration into East Texas, 1835–1860," *Southwestern Historical Quarterly* 52 (1948): 1–31, 184–208, 325–48; William A. Bowen, *The Willamette Valley: Migration and Settlement on the Orergon Frontier* (Seattle, 1978).

51. Stephen Thernstrom and Peter R. Knights, "Men in Motion: Some Data and Speculations about Urban Population Mobility in Nineteenth-Century America," in *Anonymous Americans: Explorations in Nineteenth-Century Social History,* ed. Tamara Hareven (Englewood Cliffs, N.J., 1971), pp. 17–47.

52. Mildred Throne, "A Population Study of an Iowa County in 1850," *Iowa Journal of History* 57 (1959): 305–30.

53. Michael P. Conzen, "Local Migration Systems in Nineteenth-Century Iowa," *Geographical Review* 64 (1974): 339–61.

54. Tamara K. Hareven, "Family Time and Industrial Time: Family and Work in a Planned Corporation Town, 1900–1924," *Journal of Urban History* 1 (1975): 365–89.

55. U.S. Department of State, *Sixth Census or Enumeration of the Inhabitants of the United States* [1840] (Washington, 1841), p. 44.

56. U.S. Bureau of the Census, *Population of the United States in 1860* (Washington, 1864), pp. 608–15; idem, *Abstract of the Twelfth Census of the United States, 1900* (Washington, 1904), pp. 103–5.

57. Sherman L. Ricards, "A Demographic History of the West: Butte County, California, 1850," *Papers of the Michigan Academy of Sciences, Arts, and Letters* 46 (1961): 469–91.

58. Seymour V. Conner, "A Statistical Review of the Settlement of the Peters Colony, 1841–1848," *Southwestern Historical Quarterly* 57 (1953–1954): 38–64.

59. Terry G. Jordan, "The Imprint of the Upper and Lower South on Mid-Nineteenth Century Texas," *Annals of the Association of American Geographers* 57 (1967): 667–90.

60. Reynolds Farley, "The Urbanization of Negroes in the United States," *Journal of Social History* 1 (1967–1968): 241–58; Florette Henri, *Black Migration: Movement North, 1900–1920* (Garden City, N.Y., 1976).

61. Hamlin Garland, *A Son of the Middle Border* (New York, 1917).

62. John E. Baur, *The Health Seekers of Southern California, 1870–1900* (San Marino, Calif., 1959); Billy M. Jones, *Health Seekers in the Southwest, 1817–1900* (Norman, Okla., 1967).

63. Erwin Ackerknecht, "Malaria in the Upper Mississippi Valley, 1760–1900," *Bulletin of the History of Medicine,* supp. 4 (1945).

64. Thomas H. Baker, "Yellowjack: The Yellow Fever Epidemic of 1878 in Memphis, Tennessee," *Bulletin of the History of Medicine* 42 (1968): 241–64; Marshall S. Legan, "Mississippi and the Yellow Fever Epidemic of 1878–1879," *Journal of Mississippi History* 33 (1971): 199–217.

65. A. T. Brown, *Frontier Community: Kansas City to 1870* (Columbia, Mo., 1963); Robert M. Fogelson, *The Fragmented Metropolis: Los Angeles, 1850–1930* (Cambridge, Mass.,1967); Kenneth W. Wheeler, *To Wear a City's Crown: The Beginnings of Urban Growth in Texas, 1836–1865* (Cambridge, Mass., 1968).

66. Rita and Janaloo Hill, "Alias Shakespeare: the Town Nobody Knew," *New Mexico Historical Review* 42 (1967): 211–27; Irving Telling, "Coolidge and Thoreau: Forgotten Frontier Towns," *New Mexico Historical Review* 29 (1954): 210–23.

67. James W. Goldthwaite, "A Town that Has Gone Down Hill," *Geographical Review* 17 (1927): 527–52; Edward N. Torbert, "The Evolution of Land Utilization in Lebanon, New Hampshire," *Geographical Review* 25 (1935): 209–30.

68. Ballard Campbell, "The Good Roads Movement in Wisconsin, 1890–1911," *Wisconsin Magazine of History* 49 (1965–1966): 273–93.

69. Leslie Hewes, "The Oklahoma Ozarks as the Land of the Cherokees," *Geographical Review* 32 (1942): 269–81.

70. Eugene Van Cleef, "The Finn in America," *Geographical Review* 6 (1918): 185–214.

71. Woodrow R. Clevinger, "Southern Appalachian Highlanders in Western Washington," *Pacific Northwest Quarterly* 33 (1942): 3–25.

72. E. W. Wahl and T. L. Lawson, "The Climate of the Midnineteenth Century United States Compared to Current Normals," *Monthly Weather Review* 98 (1970): 259–65.

73. G. Malcom Lewis, "William Gilpin and the Concept of the Great Plains Region," *Annals of the Association of American Geographers* 56 (1966): 33–51.

74. Leslie Hewes, "Some Features of Early Woodland and Prairie Settlement in a Central Iowa County," *Annals of the Association of American Geographers* 40 (1950): 40–57; Terry G. Jordan, "Between the Forest and the Prairie," *Agricultural History* 38 (1964): 205–16.

75. Dorothy O. Johansen, "A Working Hypothesis for the Study of Migrations," *Pacific Historical Review* 36 (1967): 1–12.

76. Jane R. Wilkie, "The United States Population by Race and Rural-Urban Residence 1790–1860: Reference Tables," *Demography* 13 (1976): 139–48.

77. Warren S. Thompson and P. K. Whelpton, *Population Trends in the United States* (New York, 1933), pp. 18–32.

78. John H. Ellis, "Businessmen and Public Health in the Urban South During the Nineteenth Century: New Orleans, Memphis, and Atlanta," *Bulletin of the History of Medicine* 44 (1970): 197–212.

79. John Duffy, *Sword of Pestilence: The New Orleans Yellow Fever Epidemic of 1853* (Baton Rouge, La., 1966), pp. 59–97.

80. Baker, "Yellowjack."

81. Gerald F. Pyle, "The Diffusion of Cholera in the United States in the Nineteenth Century," *Geographical Analysis* 1 (1969): 59–75.

82. Alfred W. Crosby, Jr., *Epidemic and Peace, 1918* (Westport, Conn., 1976).

83. Jack E. Eblen, "New Estimates of the Vital Rates of the United States Black Population During the the Nineteenth Century," *Demography* 11 (1974): 301–20; S.L N. Rao, "On Long-Term Mortality Trends in the United States, 1850–1968," *Demography* 10 (1973): 405–20; Maris Vinovskis, "Mortality Rates and Trends in Massachusetts before 1860," *Journal of Economic History* 32 (1972): 184–213.

84. Rao, "Mortality Trends," p. 412.

85. Ibid.

86. Edward Meeker, "The Improving Health of the United States, 1850–1915," *Explorations in Economic History* 9 (1971–1972): 353–73.

87. Robert Higgs, "Mortality in Rural America, 1870–1920: Estimates and Conjectures," *Explorations in Economic History* 10 (1972–1973): 177–95.

88. Rosenwaike, *Population History*, p. 108.

89. Adrian R. Dunn, "A History of Old Fort Berthold," *North Dakota History* 30 (1963): 157–240.

90. Sherburne F. Cook, "The Epidemic of 1830–1831 in California and Oregon," *University of California Publications in American Archaeology and Ethnology* 43 (1946–1956): 303–26.

91. William E. Unrau, "The Depopulation of the Dhegia-Siouan Kansa Prior to Removal," *New Mexico Historical Review* 48 (1973): 313–28.

92. Robert C. Schmitt, "Population Characteristics of Hawaii, 1778–1850," *Hawaii Historical Review* 1 (1965): 199–211.

93. Meeker, "Improving Health."

94. George Rosen, "Politics and Public Health in New York City (1838–1842)," *Bulletin of the History of Medicine* 24 (1950): 441–61; Barbara Rosenkrantz, *Public Health and the State: Changing Views in Massachusetts, 1842–1936* (Cambridge, Mass., 1972); Richard H. Shryock, "The Origins and Significance of the Public Health Movement in the United States," *Annals of Medical History* 1 (1929): 645–65.

95. Howard D. Kramer, "The Germ Theory and the Early Public Health Program in the United States," *Bulletin of the History of Medicine* 22 (1948): 233–47.

96. Shryock, "Public Relations," p. 317.

97. Richard H. Shryock, "Sylvester Graham and the Popular Health Movement, 1830–1870," *Mississippi Valley Historical Review* 18 (1931): 172–83.

98. John R. Batts, "American Medical Thought on Exercise as the Road to Health, 1820–1860," *Bulletin of the History of Medicine* 45 (1971): 138–52.

99. Manfred J. Waserman, "Henry L. Coit and the Certified Milk Movement in the Development of Modern Pediatrics," *Bulletin of the History of Medicine* 46 (1972): 359–90.

100. John L. Gignilliat, "Pigs, Politics, and Protection: The European Boycott of American Pork, 1879–1891," *Agricultural History* 35 (1961): 3–12; James C. Whorton, *Before Silent Spring: Pesticides and Public Health in Pre-DDT America* (Princeton, N.J., 1974).

101. James H. Cassedy, "Muckraking and Medicine: Samuel Hopkins Adams," *American Quarterly* 16 (1964): 85–99; Waserman, "Coit and Certified Milk"; James H. Young, *The Toadstool Millionaires: A Social History of Patent Medicines in America before Federal Regulation* (Princeton, N.J., 1961), pp. 205–44.

102. Young, *Toadstool Millionaires*.

103. James H. Cassedy, "The 'Germ of Laziness' in the South, 1900–1915: Charles Wardell Stiles and the Progressive Paradox," *Bulletin of the History of Medicine* 45 (1971): 159–69.

104. K. F. Meyer, *Disinfected Mail* (Holton, Kans., 1962).

105. Martin Kaufman, *American Medical Education: The Formative Years, 1765–1910* (Westport, Conn., 1976).

106. Sanford V. Larkey and Janet B. Koudelka, "Medical Societies and Civil War Politics," *Bulletin of the History of Medicine* 36 (1962): 1–12.

107. James Eckman, "Anglo-American Hostility in American Medical Literature of the Nineteenth Century," *Bulletin of the History of Medicine* 9 (1941): 31–71.

108. Young, *Toadstool Millionaires*.

109. John Duffy, "Hogs, Dogs, and Dirt: Public Health in Early Pittsburgh," *Pennsylvania Magazine of History and Biography* 87 (1963): 295–96.

110. Michael L. Berger, "The Influence of the Automobile on Rural Health Care, 1900–1929," *Journal of the History of Medicine and Allied Sciences* 28 (1973): 319–35.

111. Donald Fleming, *William Welch and the Rise of Modern Medicine* (Boston, 1954).

112. Maris A. Vinovskis, "Angels' Heads and Weeping Willows: Death in Early America," in *Studies in American Historical Demography,* ed. Maris A. Vinovskis (New York, 1979), pp. 181–210.

113. Ann Douglas, "Heaven Our Home: Consolation Literature in the Northern United States, 1830–1880," *American Quarterly* 26 (1974): 496–515; Ronald V. Wells, "Dignity and Integrity in Dying (Insights from Early 19th Century Protestantism)," *Journal of Pastoral Care* 26 (1972): 99–107.

114. William Gribben, "Divine Providence or Miasma? The Yellow Fever Epidemic of 1822," *New York History* 53 (1972): 283–98.

115. Charles E. Rosenberg, *The Cholera Years: The United States in 1832, 1849 and 1866* (Chicago, 1962).

116. Ellis, "Businessmen and Public Health."

117. Rosenkrantz, *Public Health and the State*; Henry E. Sigerist, "The Cost of Illness to the City of New Orleans in 1850," *Bulletin of the History of Medicine* 15 (1944): 498–507.

118. Odin W. Anderson, "Health Insurance in the United States, 1910–1920," *Journal of the History of Medicine and Allied Sciences* 5 (1950): 363–96.

119. Regina Morantz, "The Lady and Her Physician," in Hartman and Banner, *Clio's Consciousness Raised*, pp. 38–53; Ann Douglas Wood, "The Fashionable Diseases: Women's Complaints and their Treatment in Nineteenth-Century America," *Journal of Interdisciplinary History* 4 (1973): 25–52.

120. Gerald N. Grob, "Class, Ethnicity, and Race in American Mental Hospitals, 1830–1875," *Journal of the History of Medicine and Allied Sciences* 28 (1973): 207–29; Charles Rosenberg, "And Heal the Sick: The Hospital and the Patient in 19th Century America," *Journal of Social History* 10 (1977): 428–47.

121. Walter Fisher, "Physicians and Slavery in the Antebellum Southern Medical Journals," *Journal of the History of Medicine and Allied Sciences* 23 (1968): 36–49.

122. John S. Haller, Jr., "The Physician Versus the Negro: Medical and Anthropological Concepts of Race in the Late Nineteenth Cectury," *Bulletin of the History of Medicine* 44 (1970): 154–67.

123. Gerald N. Grob, "Mental Illness, Indigency, and Welfare: The Mental Hospital in Nineteenth-Century America," in Hareven, *Anonymous Americans*, pp. 250–79.

124. Himes, *Medical History of Contraception*, p. 371.

125. Ben Barker-Benfield, "The Spermatic Economy: A Nineteenth-Century View of Sexuality," *Feminist Studies* 1 (1972): 45–75; Morantz, "The Lady and Her Physician."

126. Regina M. Morantz and Sue Zschoche, "Professionalism, Feminism, and Gender Roles: A Comparative Study of Nineteenth-Century Medical Therapeutics," *Journal of American History* 67 (1980): 568–88; Richard W. Wertz and Dorothy C. Wertz, *Lying-In: A History of Childbirth in America* (New York, 1977).

6

WHITHER THE FAMILY: THE GREAT DEBATE

The demographic revolutions that occurred between 1770 and 1920 profoundly affected the family life of nineteenth-century Americans. The most casual observer of American families knew that significant changes were occurring, but even the most astute students had trouble explaining what they meant, let alone prescribing what ought to happen. As a result, a wide-ranging debate on the future of American families developed in the nineteenth century, concerned with trying to describe just what was happening, and focused on whether the visible changes should be opposed, encouraged, or left alone. This debate on the family eventually raised many questions about some of the most basic aspects of life in America; the fact that the debate continues today indicates both its importance and the difficulty of finding answers. It is essential to examine some of the structural changes that helped to generate discussion before considering what people thought was happening and ought to happen to families.

The widespread reduction in childbearing among nineteenth-century American couples was sufficient to generate anxieties about the future well-being of American families, and hence, of American society. Because not all groups began to limit their childbearing at the same time, some observers became especially agitated over the prospect of fundamental changes in the "quality" of the American people. Since other aspects of family life were also affected by the demographic revolutions, the sense of urgency surrounding the debate increased.

Demographic factors play an important role in determining day-to-day living arrangements, so it is only natural to find that

Table 4 Changes in American Households over Two Centuries

	Rhode Island				U.S. Census			
	1774	1790	1860	1880	1900	1950	1970	1976
Mean Household Size (free persons only)	6.3[a]	5.7[b]	5.3[c]	5.0	4.8	3.5	3.1	2.9
% Households with 1 Person	1.4	3.7			5.1	9.3	17.0	20.6
% Households with 2–4 Persons	31.6	33.4			49.4	69.2	61.9	63.5
% Households with 5 or More Persons	67.0	62.9			45.5	21.5	21.1	15.9
% Households with Female Heads	8.9				12.2	14.9	19.7(white) 33.0(black)	22.3(white) 38.0(black)
Average Persons per Dwelling	7.2[d]	7.0	5.5[e]	5.6	5.7		2.7	

SOURCES: U.S. Bureau of the Census, *Censuses of 1790, 1850, 1860, 1900*; idem, *A Century of Population Growth* (Washington, 1909); Frances Kobrin, "The Fall in Household Size and the Rise of the Primary Individual in the United States," *Demography* 13 (1976): 127–38; Irene Taeuber and Conrad Taeuber, *The People of the United States in the 20th Century* (Washington, 1971); Robert V. Wells, *The Population of the British Colonies in America before 1776* (Princeton, N.J., 1975).

[a]Includes 0.5 slaves per household.
[b]7.0, including slaves.
[c]6.0, including slaves.

[d]For Massachusetts, 1764. Persons per family in Massachusetts in that year averaged 6.0.
[e]Down from 5.95 in 1850 (dwellings rose by 47.8 percent, 1850–1860).

household size and composition altered as the birthrate fell, life expectancy increased, and millions of men, women, and children moved from one environment to another. The information in Table 4, on household size and composition in the United States over two centuries, illustrates some of the most general changes. Perhaps the most surprising conclusion is that the average household size in the country remained remarkably stable during the nineteenth century in spite of the demographic revolutions. Between 1790 and 1900, the average number of free persons in a household declined by less than one. The decrease between 1900 and 1973 has been twice as great. Similarly, the most dramatic shifts in the proportions of single-person households, large households, households headed by women, and average number of persons per dwelling have occurred in the twentieth century. In 1900, the relatively moderate changes in average household structure that had occurred over the previous century must have seemed reassuringly stable compared to alterations in some other aspects of family life.

Although households in 1790 and 1900 were surprisingly similar, two changes of considerable consequence affected the living arrangements of many nineteenth-century Americans. The most dramatic *statistical* change in family life occurred in the 1860s, when large numbers of black families left the legal control of white households. In terms of average household size, this produced a decline of about one person between 1860 and 1870. Its significance to the ways in which black and white Americans actually lived their lives is less certain. For most whites the change was minor, because slave owners were a distinct minority. For blacks, it was a change for the better, though perhaps not as much so as one might anticipate. Blacks who lived on large plantations with many other slaves frequently had developed strong family ties independent of white control. When slavery ended, black couples often took steps to gain the legal recognition of their marriages that had so long been denied them. But, since most black Americans remained in the rural South until after 1900, white pressure on black families through economics, physical intimidation, and other means of control continued.[1] Nonetheless, once slavery ended, black families no longer faced the threat of involuntary separation because of the needs or whims of a white master. In the long run, lower life expectancy and continued high fertility among black Americans until after 1880 may have had as great an impact on black family life as slavery per se. Among nineteenth-century black families in rural Louisiana and Philadelphia, high death rates frequently disrupted family continuity and explain the relatively high proportion of black households headed by women.[2] Black Americans seem to have shared the preference of their white neighbors for husband and wife to live together with their children, but harsh demographic realities made it more difficult for them to attain this goal until the start of the twentieth century.

Although the available data are limited, it is clear that a second change of general consequence occurred as the dwellings in which Americans lived improved markedly over the nineteenth century. Space increased, allowing greater privacy and more specialized use of rooms. Construction techniques, heating, plumbing, and even the use of screens improved household hygiene. Architects tried to provide appropriate settings for new family patterns through innovations in interior and exterior designs.[3] No one style of architecture dominated American life as families lived in buildings as varied as New York tenements, prairie sod huts, sharecroppers' shacks, or Frank Lloyd Wright designed homes. Nonetheless, houses clearly changed as much as the families who lived in them, and in general the changes were for the better.

The statistics that suggest relatively stable household patterns among nineteenth-century Americans mask a rich variety in the actual experiences of individual families visible in both urban and rural settings. In 1880, middle-class white Chicago families averaged 3.0 persons, only slightly below the 3.8 persons living in black New Orleans families in the same year. However, black residents of New Orleans had to share their living quarters often enough that there were 6.0 persons in each "Negro family dwelling," a situation unknown to the isolated middle-class white families in Chicago.[4] The crowded living quarters in New Orleans's black neighborhoods would have been more familiar to Boston's white families of 1845, when the influx of Irish raised the average number of persons per dwelling to over 10.[5] Within a given city striking contrasts might exist. In 1875, the average number of persons per family in New York City ranged from 4.3 in Ward 10, to 7.3 in Ward 2; in Albany wards the range was not as great, but it still went from 4.5 to 5.8.[6]

The reasons why urban households differed are numerous, but two stand out as having special importance. The first involves the ways in which various groups experienced the demographic revolutions. Migration patterns produced quite different living arrangements among Italians and Russian Jews in New York because the vast majority of the former were young males travelling alone, while many of the latter came to the United States in family groups.[7] In Philadelphia in 1880, black households more often than white were headed by women, primarily because black mortality was high enough to produce a significantly larger proportion of widows.[8] Immigrants in the cities frequently had more children than did native-born whites.[9] The need for migrants to find housing and residents to supplement low wages meant that boarders became common in many lower-class urban households in the second half of the nineteenth century.[10]

The economic base of the community also played an important role in shaping living arrangements. Lowell, Massachusetts, cotton mills attracted many single women who lived in company-run boarding houses.[11] In Cohoes, New York, an unusually high proportion of households were headed by women because widows found work in textile mills there that enabled them to keep their families together.[12] In contrast, in Homestead, Pennsylvania, the site of a major steel mill, female household heads were rare because company housing was available only to the men who worked in the mills.[13] George Pullman attempted to force his vision of family life on his railroad-car builders by providing different types of housing for operatives with various skills and incomes in a carefully planned community. His efforts failed when many of his employees sought cheaper rents or homes to buy in surrounding communities.[14]

Variations in household patterns were equally impressive outside the emerging urban-industrial centers where different regions attracted particular types of migrants. California illustrates this well. Households in Los Angeles County in 1850 were characterized by rather complex patterns related to the relatively recent American conquest of the territory. The older, Hispanic families frequently lived in either nuclear households, or, when wealth permitted, in rather complex units of parents, children, relatives, and laborers. Recently arrived Anglo residents of Los Angeles lived either in boarding houses or nuclear families with boarders.[15] Both these forms reflect recent arrival, relative youth, and lack of money among the Anglos. This contrast between Hispanic and Anglo households is of some interest, for it suggests that in agricultural areas wealth and permanence of residence fostered larger households, whereas poverty and recent arrival seem to be related to larger, complex households in the city. In contrast to Los Angeles, the inhabitants of Butte County, California, in 1850 were composed of 3,463 males and 104 females. Although 87.5 percent of the females appear to have lived in relatively stable households, it is clear that in that mining region the sex ratio made family life remarkably rare.[16] Presumably the fact that males were in the overwhelming majority among Chinese immigrants produced a similar situation in neighborhoods in the California cities where they settled. Finally, late nineteenth-century health seekers who sought to restore their physical strength by moving to California frequently brought their families with them, and settled into relatively permanent and stable habits.

   In midwestern agricultural settlements stretching from Indiana and Iowa down to Texas, family life quickly came to dominate after an early period of unusual household patterns. In the initial years of white resettlement, a region might well experience some demographic abnormalities. For example, Nueces County, Texas, in 1850 was characterized by high sex ratios (177 males for each 100 females) and low fertility.[17] As in Los Angeles in the same year, the more normal patterns of the older Hispanic residents moderated the effects of young single male Anglo immigrants on the living arrangements of the population. The settlement of the Peters Colony in Texas from 1845 to 1850 involves much the same story. During that five-year period, 896 householders moved into the region, each with an average of 3.3 children. In addition to these family migrants, there came 698 single persons, 97 single persons who married after migrating, 45 widowers, 41 widows, and 10 remarried widows.[18] The 896 householders with children probably soon came to dominate, for their family pattern of two adults living with slightly over three children on average is remarkably similar to other farming communities, in Indiana in 1820, in Iowa in 1850, and in Michigan in 1850.[19] Some single persons may have moved on, but if the pioneers of Lincoln County, Washington, are typical, most married quickly and began to have children at a relatively rapid rate.[20]

Even groups that, on the basis of cultural differences, might be expected to have unusual households, seem to have conformed to this pattern when they lived in established agricultural communities. The Cherokee of the southern Appalachians in 1835 and the Mormons of Kanab, Utah, in 1874 had households that averaged 6.3 and 5.1 persons respectively.[21] The average for the Mormon community is especially surprising in view of the presence of more than one wife and numerous children in at least a few households.

Interestingly, rural-urban differences in households seem to have emerged rather quickly in the west.[22] In 1820, the tiny "urban" center of Vincennes, Indiana, had a median household size of 3.3 persons, compared to 6.0 persons for the rest of the county in which the town was located, partly because of lower fertility in the town, and partly because more individuals lived alone. In Michigan in 1850, rural households averaged 3.1 children, compared to 2.4 in the villages and towns, much the same as in Iowa the same year, where farm households in Wapello County averaged 3.5 children in contrast to the 2.4 children found in an average nonfarm household.

The early existence of rural-urban differences among households in the west should not be taken as evidence that later reductions in household size (and in fertility) were the result of people moving from rural to urban areas. In Michigan, as elsewhere in the west, the number of children per household declined with time in the rural areas as well as in the cities. In fact, in Detroit the average number of children per household remained remarkably stable between 1850 and 1880, until it was higher there in 1880 than in surrounding rural areas.

Thus, the most common household pattern among the people living in rural, agricultural regions in the west was the nuclear family with large numbers of children. But when the reason for moving west was unusual, be it a search for gold, health, or city excitement, individuals often accepted unusual living patterns, especially in the early years of resettlement.

Life cycles of American families were also affected by the demographic revolutions. As fertility and mortality came under greater control, the rhythms by which families developed over time altered. Some of the greatest changes became apparent only in the twentieth century, but the process clearly began before 1920.

The most obvious change in family life cycles was that child-bearing and childrearing became less dominant in the overall purpose for a family's existence. Between 1770 and 1920, the combination of fewer children and longer lives meant that men and women who married toward the end of the period could expect more time together alone; the earlier pattern of widow-hood with children still present became less common. By 1950, adult companionship became a central, if not *the* central, purpose for marrying.[23]

Less apparent, but no less important to individual family members, was the fact that as the number of children in a fam-ily dropped and health increased, the number of transitions family members went through declined. Among one group of American families, the times between births increased by almost a year in the first half of the nineteenth century. After 1850, women stopped having children altogether at increasingly younger ages.[24] As life expectancy improved after 1870, families experienced the addition or loss of members at increasingly longer intervals. Children and parents could be more confident of stable family relationships by 1920 than ever before, a trend only slightly offset at that time by rising rates of divorce.

Of course, individual experiences with birth and death varied enough that the actual life cycles of separate nineteenth-century American families differed considerably. The youngest children of Massachusetts women born about 1830 had about an equal chance of losing a parent before they married as they did of seeing both parents at their weddings. The children of women born in 1890 had a more stable family situation. For every ten children in this latter group who had lost at least one parent by the time they married, seventeen could expect to have both mother and father alive when they wed.[25] In mid-nineteenth-century Buffalo, New York, ethnic preferences also contributed to when and how often transitions in the life cycle occurred.[26] In the twentieth century, enough Americans had experienced the changes brought on by the new demographic patterns that the variety in family cycles common in the nineteenth century began to disappear.

The debate on the future of American families which emerged as the demographic revolutions began to affect individual Americans directly and through their families was both wide-ranging and complex. Old assumptions about family relationships proved no more stable than the demographic realities upon which they were based. But until new demographic patterns became clear, it was anyone's guess as to what might happen to families. Since many people entered the debate, often with more passion than understanding, it is difficult, if not misleading, to present their positions in neat analytical categories. The participants were uncertain about what the family had been, was, and ought to be, and any discussion of the debate must reflect that fact. The most fundamental issues are perhaps clearer in retrospect than they were at the time since the debaters themselves were trying to resolve very basic tensions, while confronted with realities of life in American families that were complex and often bore tenuous relationships to the ideals under consideration. If what follows seems very familiar, that is because the debate is still in progress today. Little new by way of issues or answers has been added since 1900. Only the balance of opinions has changed.

In practice, none of the contributors to the debate on the family approached it in general terms; instead they focused on very specific issues such as childrearing, divorce, or birth control. However, in reading the literature on and from this debate, it becomes clear that several very fundamental questions about human nature and society were central in determining both the specific problems that interested an individual author and how he or she might suggest solving them. In order to make the specific issues and arguments more intelligible, it is necessary first to examine these broader concerns that disturbed those who were uneasy about America's families and America's future.

Almost all participants in the debate had some idea about the cause of the problem with which he or she was concerned. One group saw social and institutional arrangements such as laws, churches or schools, or even cities as either causing or inhibiting change. For these people there was hope for the future. Laws could be amended or repealed; churches and schools could be altered by evolution or revolution; cities could be improved or people could be educated to their dangers. There was no need to accept the current situation as inevitable. For others, American families faced problems rooted in human nature. The oft-noted tendencies for men and women to seek their own economic or sexual gratification at the expense of their family or community were of special concern. Those who felt that human nature was a constant had little hope that significant improvements could be made in the future—a most depressing, if not alarming, prospect. On the other hand, those who took a more positive view of the possibility of changing human behavior found themselves confronted with a particularly perplexing problem. If people could change for the better, they might also become worse, so recommendations for social reform had to be formulated with special care.

A second issue central to the debate involved the proper relationship between individuals and society. The most conservative thinkers felt that individuals ought to continue to subordinate their own interests to the needs of family, community, and state, as they had in the past. The alternative was anarchy and chaos. At the other extreme were those who felt anarchy led to freedom, not chaos. For them, the time had come to break the bonds of social convention and legal arrangements so women and men could develop as free individuals along whatever lines they wished. The majority occupied a middle position, believing that individual needs must be recognized, but only to a limited extent. According to these participants in the debate, individuals should be set free from the worst social and legal limits to their advancement, but not for the sake of unfettered individualism. Rather, individuals should learn self-control and discipline in order to achieve a better future for themselves, *and* for their families, communities, and the state. New freedoms and opportunities carried with them new responsibilities and dangers. Every new chance for progress and success carried with it an equal chance for mistakes and failure. To make the best of this dangerous situation individuals had to be clever and disciplined.

A third attitude, closely related to the previous two issues, involved authors' ideas about the exercise of control over human behavior. No doubt some Americans accepted the "traditional" view that life could not be controlled, but could only be endured. However, such people did not participate in the debate on the family for the obvious reason that discussion would do no good. Those who felt some sort of control was possible can be divided into two groups—regulators and eradicators. Eradicators were those who believed that, with sufficient effort, undesirable actions could be eliminated; preferred behavior could be established. Less optimistic observers accepted the notion that some control was possible, but not to the extent of remaking humanity. According to them, bad behavior might be channeled into less destructive courses by proper regulation; it could never be eliminated altogether. For regulators, the most sensible approach to any problem was to work with it rather than against it.

Obviously, all three of these concerns are closely related to the attitudes and values that are part of the "modern" personality. Matters of human dignity and individual worth, a desire to exercise control in one's life, and a feeling that progress was possible by rational action all are visible here. Only a few of those who participated in the debate on the family can be described as holding "traditional" attitudes that stressed passivity, subordination, and a disregard for individual merit. Most of the debate was carried on by women and men who accepted some, but perhaps not all, of the "modern" ideals. Frequently they argued more about the means than the ends. There was no point, for example, to changing laws if human nature was to blame for prostitution, divorce, or increased use of birth control. Likewise, efforts to improve individuals were pointless if the urban environment was the source of the difficulty. The fact that some saw the future in terms of either perfection or catastrophe, high stakes by anyone's standards, added heat to an already warm debate. A wrong choice could destroy individuals, families, and even civilization. Others recognized that improvement (or at least change) was possible, but felt that heaven or hell on earth were unlikely outcomes of any course of action.

Underlying these concerns were racial and sexual prejudices prevalent in nineteenth-century America. It should come as no surprise that Americans paid special attention to matters of race and sex in the midst of demographic revolutions that added over thirty million new inhabitants to an already segmented society, and halved the rate of childbearing by means of birth control that were neither pleasant nor reliable. The existence of these prejudices is important to remember for they gave coherence and consistency to some of the ideas expressed that otherwise appear illogical. For example, in the second half of the nineteenth century most native-born white Americans considered themselves to be superior to both immigrants and black Americans. However, racial and ethnic hostilities were so strong that no one saw the obvious inconsistency in fearing that native whites would commit "race suicide" by reducing childbearing in the face of waves of "inferior" immigrants, while expecting the "inevitable" disappearance of black Americans as they failed to compete successfully with "superior" whites. Similarly, white Americans developed considerable anxieties about the possible debilitating effects of excess sexual activity on their physical well-being in general and on their sexual organs in particular. Yet, it was apparently equally appropriate to marvel at the presumed sexual prowess of "weaker" black Americans, and to comment on the growth of blacks' genitals through use.

Although individual outlooks on the future of families varied widely, depending upon both general and specific concerns, it is possible to identify three broad groups who by work or deed took part in the debate; (1) utopian philosophers, who wished to abolish the family as it was known, (2) reformers, who hoped to improve existing family relationships, and (3) defenders of past patterns as they perceived them.

Utopian philosophers who wished either to abolish the family or else reform it radically were more important to the debate on the family than their numbers might suggest, for they were the only ones to question seriously the utility of monogamous marriage as a primary social institution.[27] They suggested that, rather than being their victims, families might be the source of many social and personal problems. The role families played in inhibiting individual development, especially among adults, was of particular concern. Children had little place in utopian plans. Although utopian thinkers might agree that families created problems in any effort to attain a perfect society, they differed dramatically over solutions. Noyes's Oneida community attempted to improve the human condition by establishing complex marriages with multiple sexual partners, and a form of birth control featuring extreme male self-discipline (extended intercourse without ejaculation). The Shakers and Rappites advocated celibacy and the segregation of the sexes. The Rappites believed that social perfection would be accompanied by the actual disappearance of male and female sex organs. Two groups that were less extreme but that still can be classified as utopian were the Mormons and the Swedenborgians. The Mormons advocated polygamy as a means for improving society. This gave them an undeserved reputation for unlicensed sexuality, for in matters of adultery, masturbation, and premarital sex they were very strict. The Swedenborgians emphasized the spiritual nature of sex and the civilizing aspect of marriage, assuming that with perfect unions war and disease would end and that world order under a reign of love would follow.

Most family reformers expected more modest results from the changes they wished to make. They accepted the idea that new roles for family members were desirable, but expected families to continue to play an important, if altered, part in society. Curiously, most of the debate focused on women and children; man's place in the family was seldom considered, even though any change for wives had to affect husbands, and new attitudes toward children certainly involved adults.

In opposition to utopian thinkers and moderate reformers stood a group who wished to preserve family relationships as they had existed (presumably) in the past. Expressions of concern for the future of American society came both from native-born Americans and from foreigners who had not yet been fully exposed to the changes wrought by the demographic revolutions. An inability to distinguish between self-centered individualism and the stress on individual advancement through order and self-discipline led many to react strongly against new free-doms acquired by some women and children. Instead of strong individuals who would work for human progress, these critics saw only rude, unmannerly, and passionate people who had no respect for their betters.[28] At best such individuals were distaste-ful; at worst, they threatened the very existence of society if family order broke down. Although they gradually lost ground to moderate reformers, the conservative participants in the debate on the family argued strenuously that individuals were not important and that family order had to be maintained for the good of society.

One set of specific questions raised by the debate on the family involved the proper relationship between parents and children. About the time of the American Revolution, the assumption that children had strong obligations to their parents and family was challenged by the idea that the major family obligations actually were those owed by parents to children. Property, which had once been used as a weapon in intergenerational conflict to bind children to parents, became a means by which parents could fulfill their obligation to insure their children's well-being. Sim-ilarly, marriage occurred more for love and less as the result of economic bargains between families. The future happiness of individual sons and daughters took precedence over the per-petuation of the family reputation.

Approaches to childrearing also evolved as Americans debated how best to prepare their offspring for a world that was clearly changing. Gradually parents accepted the idea that children were not wicked, small adults to be broken and controlled; instead childhood was a stage in which character could be shaped, and innocence and happiness prevail.[29] In addition, the age at which girls and boys were expected to become women and men gradu-ally increased, with the result that a new stage between child-hood and adult life was often recognized. That, of course, was adolescence. Parents who accepted these ideas felt a tremendous burden of responsibility for their children's futures—failures as well as successes. Differences of opinion about how best to pre-pare a son or daughter for the struggle of the adult years were common, though most reformers agreed that order and self-discipline were necessary habits for young and old alike. These ideas became so widespread that childrearing manuals published by the federal government in the first decades of the twentieth century stressed the need for order, discipline, and conformity if children were to be successful in a competitive world. They advocated hardening children physically, both by toilet training at three weeks (!), and by never allowing young ones in rooms warmer than 50°F.[30]

The precise relationship between new ideas about children and the demographic revolutions is uncertain. But several ties seem likely. In some instances both parental control and demographic behavior were voluntarily altered. Several scholars have argued that the decline in childbearing was at least partially the result of parents' wanting to give the best possible economic start to their offspring.[31] Obviously, it was easier to provide for fewer sons and daughters. Similarly, as parents accepted responsibility for the character development deemed essential for their children's future well-being, it became preferable to have smaller families so more time could be devoted to each child. Other parents may have found demographic changes forcing them to adopt new relationships to their children. As cities grew and industrialization offered opportunities to work for wages, the promise of the family farm became less effective as a means to command obedience. Among immigrant families, children often learned the new language and customs before parents, thus reversing the normal situation in which age provided greater knowledge and ability to cope.

Most family reformers believed it was important to reexamine relationships between the sexes and felt that women's roles in the family and in society at large could be improved, but that was as far as agreement went. In the late eighteenth century, women began to exercise more control over their lives than before. Sometimes this involved the choice of a husband; sometimes it meant greater chances to work or control property.[32] Formal education for women became more acceptable, at least in the North.[33] After 1800, the debate focused on whether and where change should continue, and how much further it should go. A few radicals argued that marriage ought to be abolished as legalized prostitution in which women became slaves to men. The majority, however, took a more moderate view. The efforts of women in the nineteenth century to expand their rights to work, vote, and control property are well known. However, most nineteenth-century reformers accepted marriage as the necessary and even desirable state for women, and concentrated their efforts on improving women's lives within marriage.

Efforts to improve the place of adult women in their families, known as domestic feminism, were probably more important to most nineteenth-century American women than were matters like suffrage or the ability to bring suit in court. Certainly the movement touched on many of the day-to-day relationships that affected the rhythm of a woman's life. It also contained some dangerous traps that, in the long run, served to limit women's advancement.[34]

Much nineteenth-century support for women's rights grew from the idea that women were the guardians of civilization, both as wives and mothers. If they were to fulfill this role properly, then they had to be educated and free enough to challenge corrupt men who might pose a threat to society. Many women and a few sympathetic men seized upon this idea to urge reforms in the family. By the second half of the century women claimed the right, as guardians of society, to participate in any reform organization whose goal was to improve society. Initially these ideas were useful in efforts to free women from earlier restrictions, but in the long run they, too, proved limiting because they based women's claims to power over social matters on new sex roles rather than on the fact that female reformers were individuals with special abilities and training.

Three roles women normally filled were subjected to special scrutiny in the nineteenth century. The combination of new occupations which took men out of the home and the view of women as guardians of civilization shifted the burdens of child-rearing increasingly toward wives. As mothers, women were expected more and more to ensure the proper upbringing of the next generation by taking an active role in the discipline and education of their children. Obviously, they would bear a great responsibility for any failures. In this context, formal education for women made a great deal of sense to those who did not wish to rely on innate talents for childrearing. Advocates of female education faced a major dilemma, however, since some doctors taught that schoolwork took blood and energy to the brain and away from developing reproductive organs. Thus, better educated mothers presumably ran the danger of producing physically weaker children.

Sexual relations between husbands and wives occupied a central place in the debate on the family. Almost everyone accepted the idea that sex was part of marriage. There was less agreement as to how often sex should be part of marriage and on whose terms. Many nineteenth-century Americans believed that people had only a limited supply of vital energy and that what was used in sexual activity could not be used elsewhere. In particular, some reformers feared that if too much of a woman's vital forces was spent on sex rather than childrearing it would diminish her capacity to act as the guardian of civilization within her own family. Equally serious was the concern that sex might undermine female purity which was the foundation of society. At best, too much sexual activity might weaken a woman's efforts to guide her children; at worst, she might be corrupted and transformed into a self-indulgent, passionate, pleasure seeker—the antithesis of the "modern" person. Such a woman could never teach her children order and self-discipline. Given these ideas, it is easy to see why efforts to limit family size generated so much concern in the nineteenth century. Many thought it appropriate for a couple to have fewer children in order to care for them better, but if birth control led to sexual passion and personal pleasure it presented a danger to society that had to be eliminated. The motives for birth control became as important as the practice itself.[35]

Finally, many reformers advanced the idea that women should become household executives, sharing with their husbands the responsibilities for creating a successful family.[36] This meant that when men went out to work, women had to develop the personal and intellectual abilities to run an orderly, economic, and efficient household. They had to manage people and money as skillfully in their own sphere as any man did in his. No doubt this idea appealed primarily to urban women whose husbands could afford to keep them in their own "doll house." It gave them a weapon to argue for their education and activity, as well as a sense of purpose and accomplishment. Most nineteenth-century

American women would have found this notion strange, either because their husbands were still at home, or because they were already working hard enough to ensure the survival of their family and did not need to take on any additional burdens.

The attitudes of the most conservative participants in the debate were remarkably similar regarding both women and children, and were in striking contrast to those interested in family reform. They believed children should be firmly controlled and strictly disciplined by their parents. For conservatives, society still revolved around the interests, needs, and achievements of the current generation rather than the next. Similarly, women should remain firmly under the control of their husbands. A partnership of husband and wife was unthinkable—authority could not be shared. Conservatives presented the greatest danger to domestic feminists when they seized upon the idea that women were important as defenders of civilization to stress that this could only be accomplished by strict attention to domestic duties in which a woman acted as the helpmate of her husband, freeing him for more mundane matters. If women wished to take on greater responsibilities for childrearing, that was acceptable, for it freed men for other concerns and tied women closer to home unless they wished to be blamed for the failures of their children. The defenders of traditional family relationships found the demographic revolutions alarming enough without questioning whether family patterns ought also to change. They failed to realize that basic demographic structures were so closely related to family relationships that a shift in the former automatically rearranged the latter.

The prominence of age and sex roles as issues in the debate on the family should not obscure the fact that many other issues attracted the attention of the participants. A close examination of three additional matters sheds brighter light on the concerns that occupied Americans as their lives were transformed. The first is divorce. The second involves human sexuality. The third includes the extent to which family affairs were a matter for public action as well as public interest.

During the second half of the nineteenth century divorce, long a rare phenomenon, became an increasingly common part of American family life. In 1860–1864, only 1.2 of every 1,000 existing marriages ended in divorce in any given year. This was probably well above the level of the eighteenth century, but it posed no severe threat to family life in general. Over the next sixty years the rate rose dramatically, until by 1920–1924, 7.2 of every 1,000 marriages ended in divorce. The impact of divorce on American family life was even greater than these figures suggest, because improvements in life expectancy during this period significantly reduced the chances of marriages ending early by the death of a spouse. In 1860–1864, only 3.5 percent of the marriages disrupted in a year were ended by divorce; by 1920–1924 divorce accounted for 24.6 percent of all the marriages that came to an end.[37]

By the time this trend began, the debate on the future of the family was well underway, and it is only natural that divorce was quickly included. The positions people took on the matter were predictable. Utopian thinkers saw rising divorce rates as evidence of the need for a fundamental overhaul in family relationships. Moderates viewed divorce as an acceptable choice in marriages in which a husband and wife simply could not get along. From their perspective, neither adults nor children benefited from perpetuating a personal relationship that was destructive to all concerned, though just what constituted a destructive relationship generated considerable difference of opinion. As might be expected, the conservative position stressed divorce as one more threat to families and society, especially if it encouraged individuals to indulge their own whims and weaknesses.

Anyone who attempts to penetrate the vast body of nineteenth-century American writing involving human sexuality must surely feel that somehow Freud should have been an American. Doctors, lawyers, feminists, clergy, and reformers of all sorts wrote extensively on sexual matters. It is not surprising that sex became a source of great concern for individuals. Efforts to control reproduction by unsure and unpleasant means, medical theories that saw sexual activity as physically dangerous, and the traditional Western hostility toward sex on a moral basis combined to produce great tensions as individuals confronted their personal needs and desires. For those who had great hopes and fears for human progress and civilization, uncontrollable sexuality presented grave dangers.[38]

Writing on male sexuality was remarkably rare, especially within the context of marriage. Male masturbation was a source of some concern, both as a threat to personal health and because the "private vice" might endanger the formation of future families. But most nineteenth-century thinkers assumed that men had animal-like sexual urges which might be controlled by great self-discipline or by alternative outlets in work or play, but could never be eradicated. Wives were expected to accommodate their husbands' needs.

Women, on the other hand, were divided into three categories. Presumably the existence of these sexual stereotypes caused considerable trauma to individuals seeking to accommodate their personal feelings and behavior to what they felt was expected of them. The ideal woman in the nineteenth century was a pure and wholesome individual who accepted sex in marriage as a duty but found it neither pleasant nor desirable. This image may have had its origins (or at least its widest acceptance) among couples who were practicing uncertain, unpleasant birth control techniques. Damage to the vagina, withdrawal, and the possibility of unwanted pregnancies must often have made sexual intercourse something to be avoided for physical and psychological reasons. Likewise, the sexual surgery which some doctors urged their female and male patients to undergo to control sexuality may have been very effective, but for reasons of pain rather than correct medical practice. In addition, the belief that a woman could avoid pregnancy if she avoided orgasm also contributed to efforts to limit women's sexual response, if not activity. In a more indirect fashion, an emphasis on the purity of wives may have made it easier to rationalize mens' visits to prostitutes, a very effective means of controlling family size.

A small collection of surveys of nineteenth-century women indicates that many found sex both pleasant and desirable.[39] Perhaps the majority of American women remained unaware of or unconcerned with the stereotype of the pure woman. If not, the potential for guilt arising from enjoying sex when one ought not to was significant. The idea that only wicked women enjoyed sex provided the most direct source of guilt. More complicated, but equally damaging, was the idea that in indulging in sex one spent the vital fluids of self and spouse, even to the extent of mortgaging the happiness of future generations. Doctors advised that frequent sex was very dangerous, with "frequent" defined as anywhere from more than once a week to more than once every three years. Widows whose husbands died of mysterious failings were suspicious characters to some who feared the consequences of uncontrolled sexuality. Sylvester Graham advocated his famous cracker not only for nutrition, but also because he believed that proper diet controlled the sexual passions. Many women must have found it difficult to bear the tensions between the obvious physical pleasures of sex, and ideas that stressed its dangers, especially since their husbands were not expected to share the burden of self-control as fully. It is a measure of female courage and adaptability that so many managed so well.

A second, less flattering image of women was that of abandoned pleasure seekers. Such women indulged in sex for their own immediate pleasure, with no thought of their families or their own future. By refusing to conserve vital fluids, these women proved to many thinkers the dangers of individualism. Current pleasure could only lead to future social catastrophe. The idea that uncontrolled sex led to disaster was reinforced by the fact that many authors saw only women of racial and ethnic groups considered inferior falling into this category. Black women in the South, Hispanic women in the Southwest, and immigrant women in the Northeast were subject to this unflattering stereotype.[40] The same interaction of sexual and racial anxieties also raised fears in various parts of the country that black, Chinese, or Japanese males posed threats to the purity of white women.[41] Attacks on presumed Mormon sexual excesses arising from polygamy and the "degradation" of women included descriptions of Mormon offspring that were almost identical to stereotypes of Negroes.[42] It is not necessary to be a sophisticated psychologist to recognize both the sexual and racial fears expressed by this second portrait of women.

The third stereotype was a combination of the first two. It portrayed women ruined by excessive sexual activity, but through no fault of their own.[43] According to this image, pure women could be corrupted and turned into dangerous members of society by vicious men. As with the previous image, the women depicted as belonging to this category frequently were members of racial or cultural minorities. The story of Maria Monk was one of the first of a series of popular novels that described the sexual corruption that was supposed to exist in Catholic convents. Abolitionists and others expressed concern over the real and imagined sexual exploitation of black women in the South. Single female immigrants, isolated from their families and poorly paid, were potential victims for unscrupulous men who lived in the cities.

Fears of loose women, uncontrolled sexuality, and the end to sanctity of the family led to an increasing concern with prostitution in the second half of the nineteenth century. This issue also reflected anxieties about the evils of urban life, the wisdom of unrestricted immigration, and the threat to health of venereal diseases. But sex was the major concern. One of the earliest studies of prostitution was done by Dr. William Sanger in New York City in 1858.[44] It is not clear if prostitution was actually on the rise or if the debate on the family simply brought it to attention. What is clear is that the reformers who concerned themselves with "white slavery" were almost relieved to find that low wages, ignorance, isolation, and, occasionally, male betrayal were the major reasons for young women becoming prostitutes. These conditions could be changed. More alarming was the fact that a sizeable minority of the women interviewed (almost 32 percent in Sanger's study) reported "inclination" or an "easy life" as their reason for turning to prostitution, raising the possibility that however hard reformers worked, they might never eliminate this vice altogether. As a result, much of the debate on prostitution revolved around whether it could be eradicated or only regulated, serious matters when the future of families and civilization was at stake.[45]

Public interest in the future of the American family led increasingly to public action by the end of the nineteenth century. Governments gradually accepted greater responsibility for matters once considered the exclusive preserve of the family. By 1920, the state had assumed many responsibilities in the area of police and education that had been handled by families in the eighteenth century. A White House conference on the family in 1909 was followed by the creation of a federal children's bureau in 1912 and a woman's bureau in 1920. In 1921, the Sheppard-

Towner Act offered federal aid to states that established programs for maternal and infant welfare. Governmental involvement in the debate on the family extended to writing and publishing childrearing manuals.

One of the most interesting examples of the response of public policy to the debate on the family was in the evolution of ideas on how to care for orphans and other dependent children.[46] Prior to 1820, dependent children were commonly bound out to heads of households, where they would be cared for at minimum expense to the community. The main concern was to hold down costs at the local level; if the children received any benefit, so much the better. In the 1820s, the increased emphasis on childhood as a distinct stage in life combined with the idea that children's characters could be shaped for the future benefit of themselves and society to introduce reforms in the treatment of dependent children. In particular, children were placed in asylums built to provide moral and economic protection from the corrupting influences of bad homes. The earliest asylums were organized as quasi-military units in which children could learn organization, discipline, and self-control, traits they should have learned at home. The assumption at the time was that families that broke down did so because of their own inherent weakness, so the logical response was to remove a child from a harmful environment rather than try the impossible task of raising the quality of home life. In the 1870s, states began actively to interpose in family life when they gained the power to remove children from "bad" homes which threatened society, instead of having to wait for children to be placed in asylums voluntarily. Specialized bureaucracies developed whose sole concern was child welfare, such as the Society for the Prevention of Cruelty to Children.

Between about 1890 and 1915, the treatment of dependent children changed. Part of this was spurred by soaring costs of child care in asylums. New York alone reported 29,909 dependent children under state care in 1893. This figure was especially disturbing since the number of dependent children rose by 96 percent in ten years even though the state's population had increased by only 38 percent.[47] At the same time, reformers began to recognize that children grew better in a family environment than in military-like barracks. As a result, both foster care and adoption were advocated whenever appropriate parents could be found. Support for families was provided in order to keep homes together so children might become better, more productive citizens. Cottage asylums were built that provided more private and intimate living arrangements for children who had to remain in an institution.

Direct aid for families was at least partly an outgrowth of the Spanish-American War, for even the most callous observers did not want to blame the hardship of war widows on flawed character. This change in attitude which challenged the assumed connection between poverty and moral weakness was similar to and contemporary with the one in which Americans decided that disease was not always a sign of sin.

Interestingly, all the public reforms were debated and put into practice primarily by welfare professionals. The future of the family had become a matter of public and professional interest. It was too important to leave to the amateurs who had begun the discussion.

The debate on the family paralleled and overlapped several other discussions fostered by the demographic revolutions of the nineteenth century. The title of David Pivar's book on efforts to control prostitution, *Purity Crusade,* suggests the broader context of the debate. Between 1840 and 1920, there was a widespread "purity crusade" aimed at cleansing American society of various problems (real and imagined) brought on by demographic transformations. The fact that the debate on the family and human sexuality occurred in conjunction with these other movements serves to emphasize how disturbing the revolutions in Americans' lives really were. From 1840 to 1920, people attempted to improve food, drugs, and health care; to control immigrants as well as the general impact of immigration; to alleviate, if not eliminate, the worst results of moving to urban environments; to end slavery, first black and then white; and to protect and/or improve family life. Some parts of the broader purity crusade involved relatively clearcut problems and solutions. Concerns for personal health led directly to efforts to list the contents of medicines on labels. Other issues were more complex. Advocates of eugenics and forced sterilization moved beyond efforts to control one's own life toward plans to perfect society. In addition, eugenics in one way or another touched on matters of reproduction, sex, health, death, race, and immigration.

Even reforms that at first glance appear to have little connection to the debate on the family were linked together via the purity crusade. Questions of suffrage reform addressed the social impact of both immigration and changing women's roles. Prohibition was a matter of great concern to both defenders of family stability and those who feared the influence of foreign cultures. Not long after movies became popular, efforts to censor them began as part of the campaign to control sexual urges.

The purity crusade has a coherence to it, not only because of the similarity of the arguments from one reform movement to another, but also because individuals like Catherine Beecher, Sylvester Graham, Jane Addams, Dio Lewis, or James Mann were personally interested and involved in several parts of the movement. A reformer like Loring Moody, who was involved in the Massachusetts Anti-Slavery Society, the American Society for the Prevention of Cruelty to Animals, the American Society for the Prevention of Cruelty to Children, and the Institute of Heredity, was far more representative than Margaret Sanger, who concentrated her efforts on the birth control movement. Thus, the debate on the family was only part of a more general debate on the future of American society engendered by the demographic transformations of the nineteenth century.

Defining the boundaries and internal contours of the debate on the family is a complicated task. Family roles were questioned in the midst of demographic changes unique in human history in scale, direction, and intensity. Before 1920, at least, the number of questions far exceeded the number of answers that could satisfy large numbers of women and men. In part, answers were hard to come by because Americans had to adjust to a whole array of new rhythms in their lives. In part, the day-to-day struggle for survival in what was still a very hostile environment occupied the attention of most adults to the extent that they had little time to participate in the resolution of the debate. Their descendents whose lives were lived mostly after 1920 have had more opportunity to decide on the best response to new demographic realities. Finally, old notions of a stable society based on hierarchical principles and adult male dominance have died slowly. These ideas have been a staple part of European culture for millenia; any culture that survived centuries of epidemics and high death rates had to develop effective values and customs that stressed the production of "next" generations. There is no reason to expect that even profound demographic changes could overturn such values in the span of 150 years or less. Nineteenth-century Americans began a debate that has not yet ended on one of society's most fundamental institutions.

Notes

1. Eugene D. Genovese, *Roll, Jordan, Roll: The World the Slaves Made* (New York, 1974), pp. 443–584; Herbert G. Gutman, *The Black Family in Slavery and Freedom, 1750–1925* (New York, 1976).

2. Frank Furstenberg, Jr., et al., "The Origins of the Female-Headed Black Family: The Impact of the Urban Experience," *Journal of Interdisciplinary History* 6 (1975): 211–34; C. Peter Ripley, "The Black Family in Transition: Louisiana, 1860–1865," *Journal of Southern History* 41 (1975): 369–80.

3. Clifford E. Clark, Jr., "Domestic Architecture as an Index to Social History: The Romantic Revival and the Cult of Domesticity in America, 1840–1870," *Journal of Interdisciplinary History* 7 (1976): 33–56; Carl Condit, *American Building Art: The Nineteenth Century* (Chicago, 1960).

4. John W. Blasingame, *Black New Orleans, 1860–1880* (Chicago, 1973), pp. 79–105, 236–40; Richard Sennett, *Families Against the City* (New York, 1970), pp. 71–83.

5. Oscar Handlin, *Boston's Immigrants*, rev. ed. (New York, 1969), pp. 88–123, 329.

6. New York, Secretary of State, *Census of the State of New York for 1875* (Albany, 1877), pp. 254–62.

7. Thomas Kessner, *The Golden Door: Italian and Jewish Immigrant Mobility in New York City 1880–1915* (New York, 1977), pp. 127–60.

8. Furstenberg, et al., "Origins of the Female-Headed Black Family."

9. Tamara K. Hareven and Maris A. Vinovskis, "Marital Fertility, Ethnicity, and Occupation in Urban Families: An Analysis of South Boston and the South End in 1880," *Journal of Social History* 8 (1975): 69–93.

10. John Modell and Tamara K. Hareven, "Urbanization and the Malleable Household: An Examination of Boarding and Lodging in American Families," *Journal of Marriage and the Family* 35 (1973): 467–92.

11. Richard P. Horwitz, "Architecture and Culture: The Meaning of the Lowell Boarding House," *American Quarterly* 25 (1973): 64–82.

12. Daniel J. Walkowitz, "Working Class Women in the Gilded Age: Factory, Community and Family Life Among Cohoes, New York Cotton Workers," *Journal of Social History* 5 (1972): 464–90.

13. Margaret Byington, *Homestead: The Households of a Mill Town* (1910; reprint ed., Pittsburgh, 1974).

14. Stanley Buder, *Pullman: An Experiment in Industrial Order and Community Planning 1880–1930* (New York, 1967), pp. 60–91, 205–227.

15. Barbara Laslett, "Household Structure on an American Frontier: Los Angeles, California, in 1850," *American Journal of Sociology* 81 (1975): 109–28.

16. Sherman L. Ricards, Jr., "A Demographic History of the West: Butte County, California, 1850," *Papers of the Michigan Academy of Science, Arts, and Letters* 46 (1961): 469–91.

17. Sherman L. Ricards, Jr. and George M. Blackburn, "A Demographic History of the West: Nueces County, Texas, 1850," *Prologue* 4 (1972): 3–20.

18. Seymour V. Connor, "A Statistical Review of the Settlement of the Peters Colony, 1841–1848," *Southwestern Historical Quarterly* 57 (1953–1954) 38–64.

19. Susan Bloomberg, et al., "A Census Probe into Nineteenth Century Family History: Southern Michigan, 1850–1870," *Journal of Social History* 5 (1971): 24–45; John Modell, "Family and Fertility on the Indiana Frontier, 1820," *American Quarterly* 23 (1971): 615–34; Mildred Throne, "A Population Study of an Iowa County in 1850," *Iowa Journal of History* 57 (1959): 305–30.

20. Carl F. Reuss, "The Pioneers of Lincoln County, Washington: A Study in Migration," *Pacific Northwest Quarterly* 30 (1939): 51–65.

21. William G. McLoughlin and Walter H. Conser, Jr., "The Cherokees in Transition: A Statistical Analysis of the Federal Cherokee Census of 1835," *Journal of American History* 64 (1977): 701; Dean L. May, "People on the Mormon Frontier: Kanab's Families of 1874," *Journal of Family History* 1 (1976): 169–92.

22. *See* note 19.

23. Robert V. Wells, "Demographic Change and the Life Cycle of American Families," *Journal of Interdisciplinary History* 2 (1971): 273–82.

24. Carl E. Jones, "A Genealogical Study of Population," *American Statistical Association Journal* 16 (1918–1919): 201–19.

25. Peter R. Uhlenberg, "A Study of Cohort Life Cycles: Cohorts of Native Born Massachusetts Women, 1830–1920," *Population Studies* 23 (1969): 407–20.

26. Laurence A. Glasco, "The Life Cycles and Household Structures of American Ethnic Groups: Irish, Germans, and Native-born Whites in Buffalo, New York, 1855," *Journal of Urban History* 1 (1975): 339–64.

27. Readers can begin exploring these ideas in Sidney Ditzion, *Marriage, Morals and Sex in America: A History of Ideas* (New York, 1953); Raymond L. Muncy, *Sex and Marriage in Utopian Communities: 19th Century America* (Bloomington, Ind., 1973); Gilbert Seldes, *The Stammering Century* (New York, 1965); Ronald G. Walters, ed., *Primers for Prudery: Sexual Advice to Victorian America* (Englewood Cliffs, N.J., 1974).

28. William G. McLoughlin, "Evangelical Child-Rearing in the Age of Jackson: Francis Wayland's View on When and How to Subdue the Willfulness of Children," *Journal of Social History* 9 (1975): 21–34; Richard L. Rapson, "The American Child As Seen by British Travelers, 1845–1935," *American Quarterly* 17 (1965): 520–34.

29. Bernard Wishy, *The Child and the Republic: the Dawn of Modern American Child Nurture* (Philadelphia, 1968).

30. Two volumes compiled by Arno Press, part of the *Family in America* series, advisory eds. David J. Rothman and Sheila M. Rothman, are helpful here: *Child Care in Rural America* (New York, 1972); and *The Childrearing Literature of Twentieth Century America* (New York, 1972).

31. Richard A. Easterlin, "Factors in the Decline of Farm Family Fertility in the United States: Some Preliminary Research Results," *Journal of American History* 63 (1976): 600–614; idem., "The Economics and Sociology of Fertility: A Synthesis," in *Historical Studies of Changing Fertility*, ed. Charles Tilly (Princeton, N.J., 1978), pp. 57–133. *See also* J. A. Banks, *Prosperity and Parenthood* (London, 1954).

32. Carl N. Degler, *At Odds: Women and the Family in America from the Revolution to the Present* (New York, 1980); Mary Beth Norton, *Liberty's Daughters: The Revolutionary Experience of American Women, 1750–1800* (Boston, 1980).

33. Linda Kerber, "Daughters of Columbia: Educating Women for the Republic, 1787–1805," in *The Hofstadter Aegis*, eds. Stanley Elkins and Eric McKitrick (New York, 1974), pp. 36–59.

34. In addition to Degler, *At Odds, see* Nancy Cott, *The Bonds of Womanhood: "Woman's Sphere" in New England, 1780–1835* (New Haven, 1977); Mary Hartman and Lois Banner, eds., *Clio's Consciousness Raised: New Perspectives on the History of Women* (New York, 1974); Gerda Lerner, "The Lady and the Mill Girl: Changes in the Status of Women in the Age of Jackson," *American Studies* 10 (1969): 5–15; Carroll Smith-Rosenberg,

"Beauty, the Beast, and the Militant Woman: a Case Study in Sex Roles in Jacksonian America," *American Quarterly* 23 (1971): 562–84; Barbara Welter, "The Cult of True Womanhood: 1820–1860," *American Quarterly* 18 (1966): 151–74.

35. Graham Barker-Benfield, "The Spermatic Economy: A Nineteenth Century View of Sexuality," *Feminist Studies* 1 (1972): 45–72; John S. Haller and Robin Haller, *The Physician and Sexuality in Victorian America* (Springfield, Ill., 1974).

36. Kathryn Kish Sklar, *Catherine Beecher: A Study in American Domesticity* (New Haven, 1973).

37. Kingsley Davis, "The American Family in Relation to Demographic Change," in Commission on Population and the American Future, *Demographic and Social Aspects of Population Growth* (Washington, 1972), pp. 254–62; William L. O'Neill, *Divorce in the Progressive Era* (New Haven, 1967).

38. In additon to the works cited in notes 27 and 35, *see* Vern Bullough and Bonnie Bullough, *Sin, Sickness, and Sanity: A History of Sexual Attitudes* (New York, 1977).

39. Carl Degler, "What Ought To Be and What Was: Women's Sexuality in the Nineteenth Century," *American Historical Review* 79 (1974): 1467–90.

40. Egal Feldman, "Prostitution, the Alien Woman, and the Progressive Imagination, 1910–1915," *American Quarterly* 19 (1967): 192–206; James M. Lacy, "New Mexican Women in Early American Writings," *New Mexico Historical Review* 34 (1959): 41–51; Ronald G. Walters, "The Erotic South: Civilization and Sexuality in American Abolitionism," *American Quarterly* 25 (1973): 177–201.

41. John S. Haller, Jr., "The Physician Versus the Negro: Medical and Anthropological Concepts of Race in the Late Nineteenth Century," *Bulletin of the History of Medicine* 44 (1970): 154–67; Hart H. North, "Chinese and Japanese Immigration to the Pacific Coast," *California Historical Society Quarterly* 28 (1947): 343–50.

42. Charles A. Cannon, "The Awesome Power of Sex: The Polemical Campaign Against Mormon Polygamy," *Pacific Historical Review* 43 (1974): 61–82.

43. Margaret Wyman, "The Rise of the Fallen Woman," *American Quarterly* 3 (1951): 167–77.

44. William W. Sanger, *The History of Prostitution: Its Extent, Causes, and Effects Throughout the World*, rev. ed. (New York, 1897). *See also,* Jane Addams, *A New Conscience and an Ancient Evil* (New York, 1913).

45. John C. Burnham, "Medical Inspection of Prostitutes in America in the Nineteenth Century: The St. Louis Experiment and Its Sequel,"

Bulletin of the History of Medicine 45 (1971): 203–18; David J. Pivar, *Purity Crusade: Sexual Morality and Social Control, 1868–1900* (Westport, Conn., 1973).

46. Arthur E. Fink, "Changing Philosophies and Practices in North Carolina Orphanages," *North Carolina Historical Review* 48 (1971): 333–78; Olivette Simmons, "The Care of America's Dependent Children" (Senior Thesis, Union College, 1976).

47. Simmons, "Dependent Children," p. 27.

7

NEW AMERICANS AND A NEW AMERICA

The revolutionary changes in Americans' lives must have had effects on economic, political, and social developments between 1770 and 1920. The question is, what were they? To fully answer this question would require far more than a chapter in this book. However, it is of interest to use the perspectives of demographic history to consider briefly three topics that have long attracted the attention of historians. First, did demographic trends help produce any of the economic changes that so clearly distinguish the world of 1920 from that of 1770? Second, did changes in the basic rhythms of life have any effect on the evolution of American politics in the nineteenth century? Third, have Americans exhibited particular character traits that can be explained, at least in part, by population patterns?

The American economy was profoundly transformed during the nineteenth century. In 1800, Thomas Jefferson was elected president of a nation devoted to agriculture and a modest amount of trade. By 1921, when Warren Harding succeeded Woodrow Wilson to the same office, the majority of Americans lived in cities, where many of them worked at tasks unknown a century before. Industrial, commercial, and service occupations provided livings for millions of people. Furthermore, most people in 1920 lived better than their ancestors had in 1800.

Clearly many Americans changed their style of life and prospered as a result of economic growth and development. But had the American economy benefitted from demographic changes? In reality, demographic and economic patterns interact extensively so that both are causes and effects of change. Because economic historians have devoted considerable efforts to demonstrating how the economy influenced population in matters ranging from health and birth control to migration, the focus here will be on the other side of the interaction—how population influenced the economy.

At least one old and one new economic theory suggest that rapid population growth should have prevented the American economy from developing the way it did in the nineteenth century. Between 1800 and 1920, the number of men, women, and children in the country rose from 5.3 million to 105.7 million, an almost twentyfold increase. From 1800 to 1860, there were about a third more Americans at the end of every decade than there had been at the start. Between 1860 and 1890, population increased by just over 25 percent every ten years. As the birthrate declined, so too did the overall rate of growth, but there was still an increase of over 20 percent between 1890 and 1900, and 1900 and 1910. Lower fertility, and immigration restricted by war and legislation, finally reduced population growth to only 14.9 percent between 1910 and 1920.

As early as 1798, Thomas Robert Malthus expressed concern that economic growth could never keep up with such rapid increase in people.[1] He feared that any rise in economic output would quickly be offset by an equal or larger increase in population because people could not effectively control the size of their families. Later, Malthus admitted birth control was possible. What is important here, however, is the distinction he made in his first *Essay on Population* between what we now call gross national product, and per capita income. Malthus warned that increases in the total economic output of a nation meant very little if they only resulted in more people living on the edge of starvation. What was needed were improvements in the well-being of each individual.

Recently, scholars have shown that economic growth that results in higher living standards per capita is extremely difficult when population increases rapidly.[2] Obviously, if the number of people increases by 3 percent every year, the economy must grow an equal amount just to maintain the standard of living. To raise per capita income requires levels of savings and investment

that will allow economic output to grow faster than the population. A particularly serious problem emerges when rapid population increase comes from a high birthrate. Frequent childbearing
leads to a younger population in which 40 to 50 percent of the
people are too young to contribute to the economy; all they can
do is consume income that might otherwise be saved and
invested to foster further economic growth. Futhermore, when
moderately high death rates accompany high fertility, many
younger consumers die before they produce much. Thus, where
population growth is rapid, high rates of savings and investment
are both especially necessary for economic growth and especially
difficult to attain.

How then did Americans manage to combine both large
increases in numbers and a significant improvement in their
standard of living? To begin, the United States had several economic advantages that other developing nations seeking to
escape this demographic trap have not had. One is that the North
American continent offered an extraordinary amount of easily
exploited natural resources. When resources are abundant, the
amount of investment necessary to bring them into production is
lower than when land and mineral wealth are scarce. Thus,
increasing numbers of Americans in the nineteenth century did
not present the same pressure on resources and investment that
growth does in some countries today. In addition, the American
economy also benefitted at various times from sizeable influxes
of foreign capital, when European wars made America seem a
safer place for investment, or when the demand for cotton in
England gave the American economy an unexpected new com-
modity for export. Technological improvements in production
and distribution of commodities were unusually frequent. But
along with these economic advantages, basic demographic patterns existed that combined to give America an unusually productive labor force in the nineteenth century.

Migration patterns made the most important demographic
contribution to American economic development. International
migration in the nineteenth century provided the United States
with a highly productive population in two ways. Because the
young, adult males who predominated among nineteenth-
century immigrants had been reared and educated in other coun-

tries but spent their productive years in the United States, the American economy received the benefit of their training and talents with virtually no investment. According to one estimate, the human "capital" that arrived between 1790 and 1860 equalled all the pounds, marks, or francs of foreign investors.[3] The age and sex pyramids of native and foreign-born whites in 1900, presented in Chart 6, clearly show that if rapid growth had resulted from natural increase alone (the native white experience) then the productive part of the population would have been much smaller. The United States was able to combine rapid population increase with economic growth because growth was at least partially the result of an influx of potential laborers. The shift to an older, more productive population, brought about by immigration and a declining birth rate, is evident from the fact that from 1770 to 1900 the proportion of the population between 16 and 60 rose from 47.4 percent to 57.2 percent (see Chart 1, Chapter 4). Over the same period, the number of persons dependent on each worker fell from 1.10 to 0.75. In a land where labor was traditionally in short supply, immigration provided many new workers without the wait or cost of raising them from infancy.

Changing the age composition of the American population was only one way in which immigration stimulated economic growth. Many immigrants brought with them skills and talents learned at home but of use in the United States. British immigrants, who between 1820 and 1870 brought many of the organizational and technological skills that had made Great Britain the first major industrial nation, were especially important.[4] In 1789, Samuel Slater memorized the construction of a loom (a British national secret at the time), moved to America, and became an important figure in the establishment of America's textile industry. Later British immigrants were not as famous, but between 1820 and 1870, 58 percent of the Welsh, 50 percent of the English, and 36 percent of the Scotish arrived with industrial skills. In contrast, only 15 percent of non-British immigrants claimed such training. After 1870, about 76 percent of all immigrants from the United Kingdom came from urban areas.[5] As a result, British managers, technicians, and workers dominated the early development of textiles, mining, and metalworking, all important industries in a

CHART 6 WHITE POPULATION BY AGE AND SEX: 1900

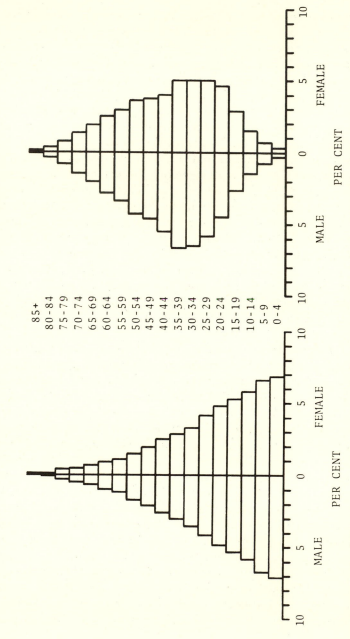

SOURCE: Bureau of Census, *Twelfth Census of the United States*, "Population, Part II" (Washington, 1902), p. liii.

nation establishing an industrial economy. Later immigrants also provided important labor to build factories and run machines after the initial changes were underway. The contribution of Irish, Chinese, and Italian workers to the creation of America's transportation network is well known. From New York to New Mexico and California, immigrants fulfilled an important economic role by assuming control of much of the commercial activity of the nation. As in the eighteenth century, immigrant farmers often brought with them new crops and techniques that enhanced agricultural productivity.

Internal migration also fostered rapid economic growth. The tremendous mobility of nineteenth-century Americans had two significant economic results.[6] First, the supply of workers in any one region of the country generally bore some reasonable relationship to the work available there. This was accomplished both by the willingness of Americans to migrate in search of a better life and by governmental action that encouraged migration. Second, the willingness of Americans to take up residence in cities, at least temporarily, made possible economic specialization that otherwise might never have developed. Transportation changes that encouraged nineteenth-century migration in general also aided the growth of larger cities with more complex economic activities, both by allowing particular towns to increase their areas of economic influence, and by making it possible for workers to live at greater distances from their place of employment.[7]

Other demographic factors also had important effects on the American economy. In particular, changes in fertility and mortality improved the labor force. The economy benefitted in two ways from declining death rates and general improvements in health after 1870. The loss of skilled workers from epidemic and endemic diseases declined, so that time and effort spent in training people was less often wasted. Furthermore, healthier workers missed fewer days on the job, benefitting both employers and workers' families, who were less exposed to a sudden drop in wages. At least three contributions to economic growth can be attributed to lower fertility. The lower birthrate led to an age pyramid more conducive to economic growth. Second, as their childbearing responsibilities declined, more and more women were able and willing to participate in the labor force. Finally, children growing up in smaller families in the twentieth century tend to be both healthier and smarter. Given the rather dramatic changes in nineteenth-century childbearing, it seems probable that American families produced American workers who by 1920 were both stronger and more talented than their counterparts a century before.

Stressing the impact of demographic change on economic development does a deliberate injustice to reality. In practice, demographic and economic factors interact closely. For example, changes in health that produced stronger, healthier workers were at least partially the result of a rising standard of living which migrants both responded to and helped create. No doubt the industrial and demographic revolutions of the nineteenth century reinforced each other extensively in a complex chain of cause and effect. Both may be seen as concurrent manifestations of modern attitudes, for values that encouraged smaller families, a search for greater health, and a willingness to seek out environments with more opportunities also were conducive to saving income for investment for the future, and the search for and adoption of innovative ways to produce and consume. In short, it is difficult to imagine either the demographic or the economic transformation of American society without the other.

Politics, at its most basic level, is concerned with the allocation and use of power. As such, the debate on the family was clearly a political debate about personal or domestic power. However, American politics on the public level was also profoundly affected by the nineteenth-century demographic revolutions. International relations, the structures of government, and political issues all were shaped by the aggregate effects of millions of individual decisions regarding birth, death, marriage, and migration. Thus, American politics, both personal and public, can only be understood fully if one has a grasp of the demographic patterns of the time. However, in looking at interactions between public politics and population, it is important to remember that public political decisions rarely have as much consequence to individuals as do marriages, deaths, births, or changes in residence.

Recall that in the colonial period both imperial and local officials were confronted by problems generated by cultural pluralism and internal migration. As new groups were added to the already complex blend of cultures, and as migration within the country continued and perhaps even increased, nineteenth-century American politicians found many of the issues facing them similar to those that perplexed officials before 1776.

One of the most striking political achievements of the century was the creation of a continental nation out of a nucleus of British colonies clustered along the Atlantic seacoast. As politicians responded to the desires of their constituents to move west, the American government frequently acquired territory, not to stimulate expansion, but because expansion was already underway. Diplomacy that transferred land often ratified demographic reality.

This process was at work in the earliest and most spectacular territorial transfer under the new nation—the Louisiana Purchase. In the Treaty of 1763, ending the Seven Years War, Spain obtained Louisiana from the French. This region was thinly settled by Europeans, a situation the Spanish hoped to change, but not by recruiting people from the English colonies.[8] During the American Revolution, the Spanish made efforts to ensure that the westward boundary of the United States would be set at the Appalachian Mountains. When the actual boundary became the Mississippi River, Spanish officials began to worry about the future of Louisiana. In the 1780s, Spanish officials expressed fear that their colonies would be lost to Americans, "hostile to all subjection, advancing and multiplying in the silence of peace and almost unknown, with a prodigious rapidity."[9] They tried to prevent this by prohibiting American immigration, by diplomatic efforts to slow down settlement of the Mississippi Valley by shutting off access to the Gulf of Mexico with the Jay-Gardoqui Treaty (1786), and by negotiating with Americans like James Wilkinson whom they thought might be persuaded to lead a rebellion in the west. All efforts to stop the American influx failed, with the result that Spain finally returned Louisiana to France in 1800; the latter sold the region to the United States in 1802. Demographic reality was finally matched by diplomatic exchanges.

This pattern was repeated again and again in the nineteenth century. Often Indian tribes were the victims of the westward thrust of European settlers. But Florida, Oregon, Texas, and

California were all added to the union as a result of the process in which colonization preceded annexation. In 1846 the Mexican government resisted America's annexation of Texas and population pressure in California with war, but in Florida, in 1819, and Oregon, in 1846, potential conflicts with Spain and Great Britain were solved by diplomacy. It was easy for European nations to recognize America's demographic imperialism in their colonies, for their homelands were protected from similar encroachment by the Atlantic. The Mexicans and Indians who resisted physically faced starker choices if their homelands were overrun. In 1898 the pattern was repeated once again when Hawaii was added to the American empire after a revolt by white settlers in 1893 ended native rule. Only Alaska, of all the eventual fifty states, was added without actual or imminent demographic occupation. Perhaps that is why many saw the purchase of that territory in 1867 as "Seward's Folly."

Besides Hawaii, 1898 saw two significant additions to the American empire—the Philippine Islands and Puerto Rico. Both of these were added via more traditional, military forms of empire building. In the absence of colonization from America, the Philippines was granted its independence within half a century. Puerto Rico remains a territory of the United States with a curious demographic relationship to the mainland. Unlike most territories that received population from the established states, Puerto Rico has been a source of immigrants. The establishment of demographic ties of an unfamiliar form has led to political uncertainty about the future bonds between Puerto Rico and the fifty states.

Over the course of the nineteenth century, a rhetoric developed which was used to justify the acquisition of new lands from Indians and Europeans alike. This rehetoric, which included the idea that Americans had a "manifest destiny," was heavily laden with demographic imagery, as the first use of the term shows. Writing in the *Democratic Review* in the summer of 1845, John L. O'Sullivan commented that it was "the fulfillment of our manifest destiny to overspread the continent allotted by Providence for the free development of our yearly multiplying millions."[10] In that same year, O'Sullivan also proclaimed that "Texas has been absorbed into the Union in the inevitable fulfillment of the general law which is rolling our population westward."[11]

The idea of manifest destiny linked the long tradition of geographic expansion of the white population to an equally old
American habit of seeing America as a place with a special mission in the world. Demographic expansion came to be seen as an
obligation to civilization and to God. In the face of such ideas,
Spanish, Indian, or Mexican claims to territory seemed minor, if
not sinful.

Although the term "manifest destiny" was used first in 1845,
the ideas involved began to emerge a generation earlier. Before
the Revolution, men like Benjamin Franklin and Ezra Stiles
already were interpreting American growth as a sign of American superiority.[12] In 1795, a traveller in the American west by the
name of C. F. Volney discovered that settlers along the Ohio
River were referring to the Atlantic seaboard as the "Back Country."[13] These people clearly saw their future lying on the continent to the west rather than eastward across the Atlantic. In
1822, in the midst of an early debate over Oregon, Francis Baylies
of Massachusetts observed, "our natural boundry is the Pacific
ocean. The swelling tide of our population must and will roll on
until that mighty ocean interposes its waters, and limits our
territorial empire. To diffuse the arts of life, the light of science,
and the blessings of the gospel over a wilderness, is no violation
of the laws of God; it is no invasion of the rights of man to occupy
a territory over which the savage roams, but which he never
cultivates. . . . " George Tucker of Virginia also felt the inevita-
bility of westward expansion when he commented in the same
debate that, "we cannot arrest the progress of our population to
the West. In vain may the Government attempt to set limits on
its course."[14]

At the very least, the future of civilization required American
expansion, but for some it was a religious duty as well. Caleb
Cushing, writing around 1830, saw "a deluge of civilized men
rising unabatedly and driven onward by the hand of God."[15]
Three decades later this theme was picked up by William Gilpin, a
governor of Colorado and western booster. In a passage rivaling
some utopian thinking on marriage and sex for its expectations
for social change, Gilpin claimed that

the *untransacted* destiny of the American people is to subdue the
continent—to rush over this vast field to the Pacific Ocean—to animate

the many hundred millions of its people, and to cheer them upward—to set the principle of self-government at work—to agitate these herculean masses—to establish a new order in human affairs—to set free the enslaved—to regenerate superannuated nations—to change darkness into light—to stir up the sleep of a hundred centuries—to teach old nations a new civilization—to confirm the destiny of the human race—to carry the career of mankind to its culminating point—to cause stagnant people to be re-born—to perfect science—to emblazon history with the conquest of peace—to shed a new and resplendent glory upon mankind—to unite the world in one social family—to dissolve the spell of tyranny and exalt charity—to absolve the curse that weighs down humanity, and to shed blessings round the world.[16]

As the ideas of Darwin began to be known and accepted in the late nineteenth century, the justification for expansion took a new turn. Those who did not care whether God had ordained a continental United States could take comfort in demographic expansion as the natural result of a "superior" race replacing "inferior" peoples. Scientific racism portrayed Indians and Mexicans as people who lost their land because they were not fit to compete. As such, they had no right to control territory which a "superior" race could use to spread civilization. When offered the chance to see themselves as a superior people fulfilling God's will or nature's destiny rather than greedy expansionists who had a ruthless disregard for the rights of others, it is only natural that many Americans preferred the former self-image. It was both more flattering and more conducive to continuing the process. Ironically, when these same "superior" people were confronted by millions of people rushing westward across the Atlantic they began to fear "race suicide" and the collapse of civilization if they in turn were replaced. Public comments on migration patterns in the nineteenth century clearly demonstrated more concern than consistency.

Acquisition of territory was only one manifestation of the influence population patterns had on American diplomacy. As various immigrant groups achieved significant size within the American population, their presence frequently influenced the nation's diplomatic dealings with their homeland. This was most apparent after 1870. Perhaps the best-known example of this were efforts by British-Americans and German-Americans to force the United States government to favor one side over the other in the early years of World War I. Attempts by Pacific Coast states to limit the number of Chinese and Japanese immigrants also created diplomatic difficulties. The Burlingame Treaty of 1868 guaranteed Chinese immigrants equal access to the United States. White westerners unhappy with this treaty eventually forced a modification of the agreement, and in 1882 persuaded Congress to pass a bill prohibiting further Chinese immigration for ten years. This "temporary" exclusion later became more basic policy, much to the unhappiness of the Chinese.[17] As Japanese immigrants replaced the Chinese, California whites responded to them as a new threat. From 1906, when white Californians asked the federal government to limit Japanese immigration, to 1913, when the state passed a law restricting Japanese ability to hold land, the federal government found itself involved in touchy negotiations with a nation that felt itself insulted by California's actions. These negotiations were complicated by the fact that after 1905 Japan and the United States were both interested in expanding into the same parts of the Pacific.[18]

Considering the tremendous changes occurring in the rhythms of peoples' lives during the nineteenth century, it is only natural that some manifestations of the demographic revolutions appeared on the domestic as well as the international political scene. Population patterns not only generated many of the issues the political system was expected to solve, they also affected basic structures of government such as constitutional arrangements and the way parties formed and functioned.

The Constitution of 1787 is a complex document reflecting the historical and political experiences, intellectual heritage, and social and economic interests of the men who wrote and ratified it. However, careful reading of the Constitution itself and the debates surrounding its creation and adoption also shows the influence of the demographic realities of the world in which the founding fathers lived. Hence, the influence of population is evident in the most fundamental political structure of the period.

To begin, the Constitution established a government that was federal instead of national in character. That is, Americans ordered their lives by several levels of government. Local and state governments were not and are not administrative units of a central authority. Instead, they maintain independent control over issues Americans prefer to handle locally, recognizing that there are considerable regional differences and preferences regarding the line between public and private affairs. Until recently, local and state affairs have been more important to most Americans than national matters. Based on cultural pluralism, the federal system also enhanced it by enabling individuals to search out communities in which they could be most comfortable instead of forcing accommodation to national standards.

The demographic patterns related to slavery generated a series of constitutional arrangements.[19] Although the words "slave" and "slavery" are missing from the Constitution, it is clear that the presence of almost three-quarters of a million black Americans living as slaves, mostly in the South, was a factor important in shaping the new government. Within the first weeks, convention members divided sharply over whether representation should be based on population (and perhaps wealth as well) or whether states should also be represented. Initially, advocates of state representation raised the possibility of serious differences between large states and small, a position that persuaded the proponents of representation by numbers alone that there was no reason to compromise, for they did not see what residents of Massachusetts, Pennsylvania, and Virginia could wish to do together that would damage their neighbors in New Hampshire, New Jersey, or Maryland. Early in July, however, the debate took a fundamental turn when the members realized that large versus small was not the source of friction; instead, they understood the country was divided into free states versus slave states (and, to a lesser extent, new states versus old). Once they admitted that the population was not homogeneous, and accepted the necessity of protecting sectional (cultural) interests via representation, they quickly arrived at the Connecticut Compromise, whereby one house of the legislature would have representatives of people while the other would have representatives of states (that is, sections or cultures).

The *men* who wrote the Constitution also provided for a census to be used in apportioning representatives to males in different parts of the country. Curiously, they felt that children, women, and slaves should be counted along with adult white males, even though these dependents had no other role in government. Efforts to change these relationships occupied a central place in nineteenth-century politics. No one ever questioned the logic behind counting women and children for the purposes of allocating power to men, perhaps because they were fairly evenly distributed throughout the country. However, many Northerners objected strenuously to counting all black Americans in the South for purposes of representation when only white males would hold power. The result of these objections was the Three-fifths Compromise, whereby five slaves would be considered equivalent to only three free persons when it came time to apportion representation and taxes.

In addition, the Constitution recognized the existence of slavery and sectional differences by arranging for the return of fugitive slaves to their owners. Once again, reference to slaves and masters was carefully avoided as Article IV, Section 3 reads that any "person held to service or labor in one State ... shall be delivered up on claim of the party to whom such service or labor may be due." Finally, southern delegates to the Constitutional Convention managed to prevent the federal government from prohibiting "the migration or importation of such persons as any of the States now existing shall think proper to admit" (that is, slaves) until 1808.

The tendency of Americans to migrate within and beyond the boundaries of the original thirteen states also received constitutional recognition. Common citizenship and equal protection for any free American under the laws of each state guaranteed continued freedom of movement.[20] Similarly, the Constitution provided for the admission of new states to the Union as equals of the old, in spite of the fears of delegates like Elbridge Gerry (for whom the demographically inspired process of gerrymandering was later named) that new states would be inhabited by immigrants and so would introduce a foreign element into the government. Only a New Englander could seriously have raised such an objection, for elsewhere foreign influences were already strong.

The provision for the admission of new states is not surprising in view of the fact that ratification of the Articles of Confederation had been delayed several years until the national government gained control over most western lands. Several of the most notable achievements of the Confederation government included the Ordinance of 1784, arranging for the admission of new states; the Land Ordinance of 1785 which established procedures for transferring public lands into private hands; and the Northwest Ordinance of 1787 which organized the first territorial governments. Unlike the British officials who had tried to prohibit expansion, American politicans saw it as inevitable (and, in most cases, desirable) and merely sought to make it as orderly a process as possible.

During the debate over ratification of the Constitution many men expressed fears that the proposed government would be either unworkable or tyrannical because the American people were too diverse. Republics, they argued, had to be small enough so the people could observe and control their representatives, and should be homogeneous in population as well if serious conflicts were to be avoided. To many, the prospects for survival, let alone success, of a nation of almost 4 million people of varied backgrounds spread along a thousand miles of seacoast, seemed slight.

In one of America's greatest political essays, known as the Tenth Federalist, James Madison addressed these fears and made strengths out of dangers. Madison recognized that most politically active Americans in the late eighteenth century feared governments that were too strong rather than too weak. He argued that one way to keep a government weak was to combine so many conflicting factions that they would have trouble agreeing or acting on anything but the most basic principles and pressing problems. Madison was correct, for American government has been a politics of catastrophe; that is, problems have been addressed only when ignoring them further would invite disaster for a large portion of the population. Madison's great political discovery was that a pluralistic republic is a remarkably conservative form of government. His essay, along with other arguments, alleviated enough fears about the size and complexity of the nation to ensure ratification of the Constitution. In the nineteenth century, technological improvements in transportation and other forms of communication combined with the rhetoric of manifest destiny to transform Americans' fears of too large a population into a glorification of size and growth.

Although it is doubtful that the men who drafted the Constitution in the summer of 1787 had any idea of the extraordinary changes that would soon transform the lives of their heirs, they did understand that societies change. In recognition of this, they established procedures by which the Constitution could be amended to conform with new needs and realities. The first twelve amendments established protections for the citizens against excesses of government, and altered awkward constitutional procedures. Six of the next seven amendments, passed between 1865 and 1919, were in one way or another connected to the demographic concerns of the day. Four of them, Amendments XIII through XV, and XIX, were designed to establish black and female Americans as the political equals of white males. Amendment XVI, passed in 1909, allowed the government to ignore population as the basis for apportioning taxes so it could concentrate on incomes instead. This amendment recognized that international migration and internal movement (especially to the cities) had produced distinct income disparities from one part of the country to another. As a result, taxes levied on population alone would be far more burdensome for the residents of some sections than others. Amendment XVIII, prohibiting the sale of alcoholic beverages, was part of the purity crusade. It aimed at improving health and family life, and was also part of the effort to limit the "undesirable" influence of foreigners. The Seventeenth Amendment, passed in 1912, which removed the election of Senators from the state legislatures and gave it to the people directly, is the hardest to tie to demographic change. Election by the people was more a democratic than a demographic issue, for the principle of representation of states (sections) was maintained. In view of the fact that the greatest demographic changes occurred between 1770 and 1920, it is interesting that virtually all successful amendments since 1919 have dealt with procedural matters. The one exception, the Twenty-first Amendment, repealed Prohibition and so ended efforts to enforce cultural uniformity via the Constitution.

The same demographic realities that shaped the general structures of government also affected the day-to-day functioning of the political system. In recent years, historians have demonstrated that individuals often aligned themselves with one party or another on the basis of their ethnic backgrounds.[21] Whigs, Republicans, and Democrats all relied on philosophical-theological issues to attract individuals with certain cultural values. In the late nineteenth century, for example, the Republican party appealed primarily to Protestant groups that emphasized individual responsibility, self-help, purity reform, and the assimilation of immigrants into a national culture. Black Americans who voted also allied themselves to Lincoln's party at this time. The Democratic party often attracted Catholics, Jews, and those Protestants who believed in strong community life, mutual aid, state assistance for unfortunate people, and the recognition of different cultures. This last concern led many Democrats to oppose the purity crusade on the grounds that purity by homogenization was undesirable. Issues like Prohibition, foreign language in schools, or church-state relations often gave a specific focus to the fundamental divisions.

Occasionally, parties attracted the support of ethnic groups simply because hated rivals associated with the opposition. Irish and English immigrants gravitated to opposite parties in New York in the 1840s.[22] A similar arrangement existed in the 1893 Wisconsin Assembly.[23]

The influence of immigrants on particular elections could be critical. German support for Lincoln, in the Midwest in 1860, has often been noted.[24] Sometimes small groups of immigrants were important because they tipped the balance of votes one way or another. But often the political influence of immigrants as a whole was based on the same migration patterns that made them such a valuable addition to the labor force. For example, in Burlington, Iowa, in 1860, just over one-third of the people were foreign-born, but because of age- and sex-selective migration, slightly more than half of the adult males (the voters) had been born abroad.[25]

The frequent mobility of many Americans raises one of the most intriguing questions about nineteenth-century political history. How was it possible for political parties and local communities to achieve any sort of stability when only a few Americans remained anywhere long enough to understand local issues or command local support? A study of Paris, Illinois, in the first half of the nineteenth century answers one part of this question by stressing the important role that the relatively few long-term residents played in the governance of a community.[26]

But what about political parties? How did they attract voters when few people lived in a community long enough to know or care what local interests were? How did parties survive when their parts kept changing rapidly? Parties began to appeal to a voter's ethnic identity, a characteristic that was transported wherever he went, rather than relying on economic interests arising from occupation or property, both subject to sudden change. An appeal to a voter based on his religious or ethnic background had a greater chance to win support than one based on local issues which might have great importance to the town or county, but had little meaning for a transient. In short, American politics came to be dominated by political leaders of some permanence in a community who obtained support by appealing to voters on issues such as alcoholic beverages, foreign language in schools, ethnic and racial hostilities, and religious matters, none of which necessarily had much to do with a community's most pressing needs.

Quite probably this process was widespread, but it was most obvious in the political machines that often dominated the big cities. Ethnic politics concerned many reformers who felt that government should be based on informed individuals judging local issues; migrants found the system far more to their liking. In exchange for help in cutting through local governmental bureaucracy and red tape, for finding jobs, and providing temporary relief, voters were willing to support whomever their fellow ethnics indicated were friends. If political bosses were corrupt and took advantage of their knowledge of local affairs to enhance their wealth, it made little difference to transients. The men who kept track of the needs of the people and provided help for families and individuals were as important to the successful functioning of nineteenth-century American politics as judges, senators, and presidents.

Demographic revolutions produced many of the specific conflicts the political system had to resolve. Most were managed successfully; a few proved so basic and so threatening that one or

more of the groups involved resorted to violence. Listing some of
the issues raised in local, state, and federal governments illustrates how widespread and complex the political manifestations
of the demographic changes were. Ironically, many states and
localities passed laws encouraging immigration, for the presence
of different ethnic groups frequently generated political conflict.
In California, efforts to inhibit immigration ranged from high
taxes on foreign miners in the gold rush years to laws prohibiting
certain aliens from owning valuable agricultural land. Wisconsin,
Nebraska, and Oregon all had vigorous political struggles over
whether foreign languages should be prohibited in the schools as
a means to force outsiders to "Americanize." Compulsory school
attendance for the same reason produced similar controversies.
Labor legislation and Prohibition both involved anti-immigrant
stands at times. Over the course of the nineteenth century,
federal laws restricting who and how many people might immi-
grate were extended, but not without heated debate. Westward
migration required governmental action on matters ranging
from diplomatic and military efforts to control or eliminate the
first Americans; land surveys and sales, support for roads, canals,
and railroads; water rights, irrigation, and drainage; and the
acquisition of new territory to the admission of new states. The
latter frequently generated controversy when one party or
another expected political support from a new state. The struggles over admitting slave and free states from 1820 to 1860 are
well known; but the same pattern can be observed with regard to
Ohio in 1803 or the Dakota Territory in 1889. Racism in America
produced tremendous amounts of legislation aimed at maintaining white dominance over blacks whether by the slave codes of
the early years, or the Jim Crow laws that followed the Supreme
Court decision of 1896, in *Plessy* v. *Ferguson*, granting constitutional protection for segregation. The purity crusade involved
legislation to improve public health by establishing boards of
health and controls over food and drugs, and regulating medical
education and practice. Concern for the family and over sexual
license led to laws on divorce, birth control, abortion, prostitution, child labor, orphans, and obscenity. In addition to questions
of community moral and physical health, the movement of people into cities raised political problems regarding who should

build needed transportation, the most appropriate tariffs and taxes, banking procedures to best meet the county's needs, and how to provide industrial safety.

It is amazing that the political system responded to as many of these basic issues as well as it did. The changes in the demographic underpinnings of society were unprecedented, and the political structures were designed to respond slowly. It is not surprising that politics occasionally failed to resolve conflict and violence broke out.

Frequently, violence was directed toward ethnic minorities in a community, especially when more powerful groups felt the government was protecting the minorities against the will of the majority. From the burning of the Irish-supported Ursuline Convent in Charlestown, Massachusetts, in 1834, to antiblack riots in Cincinnati in 1829 and 1841, Comanche County, Texas, in 1886, and Elaine, Arkansas, in 1919; from assault on the Mormons in Nauvoo, Illinois, in 1844, to the widespread anti-Chinese riots in the Pacific Coast states in 1885–1886; from attacks on Italians in New Orleans in 1891, to the use of force against Greeks in South Omaha in 1909, American history has been dotted with sporadic clashes between ethnic groups.[27] The one common denominator has been an unwillingness on the part of the majority (frequently white Protestants) to accommodate themselves to neighbors who for one reason or another seemed too different. The most frequent victims of white violence in the nineteenth century were Indians and blacks, who suffered both extralegal assaults and attacks from *within* the political system by means of the army or police.

The Civil War marks the greatest failure of the political system to resolve conflict in the nineteenth century. The constitutional issue of secession may have been the immediate cause for the outbreak of fighting, but the underlying issues were at heart demographic. From the late seventeenth and early eighteenth centuries, when the South made a major commitment to slavery based on race as a major form of labor, the various sections of what became the United States developed markedly different cultures.

To see the Civil War as the result of immigration patterns that brought large numbers of blacks to only part of the country is accurate, but insufficient. After all it was not the blacks who brought about the war, but their white owners. The conflict lay in the fact that North and South gradually developed different cultures and rhythms of life, with slavery the prime distinguishing factor, until neither side could envision living with the other without major change. The conflict between the two cultures was effectively repressed until 1820, when Missouri petitioned to be admitted to the Union as a slave state. This awakened fears, in both North and South, that unless a free state was also admitted one section would gain political dominance over the other. At the time of the Constitutional Convention, many Southerners had expected their interests would be protected in the House of Representatives, for the southern colonies had grown more rapidly than the northern in the eighteenth century. But the South had suffered a relative decline in population after 1800. As a result, the Senate, where states (cultures) were represented, became the focus of Southern hopes. Many of the most volatile national issues between 1820 and 1860 revolved around maintaining a sectional balance in the Senate. The urgency of the matter became clear in Kansas in the mid 1850s when both sections tried to rush immigrants into that territory in order to establish a political claim to the new state via demographic dominance.

The Civil War broke out in the spring of 1861, when southern men felt they could protect their way of life only by separation from the North. By this time, the stakes were more than just a farming society based on race slavery versus one of free agriculture. The rise of cities and the influx of immigrants in the North had increased the sectional differences that had emerged in the eighteenth century. The North was growing rapidly in numbers, and people were living and working in places Southerners saw as threatening. Many of the demographic changes that occurred in the nineteenth century were the product of attitudes that stressed individual merit, self-discipline, dignity, and a desire to change the future. Such attitudes must have been very threatening to a society seeking to maintain a past in which social roles were assigned by accidents of birth, and control was based on the almost complete denial of dignity and worth to a large part of the population. Many Northerners pointed to real or imagined sexual excesses in the South as evidence of what unfettered attention to individual pleasure could do to corrupt a society, a concern many Southerners found insulting as well as potentially dangerous to their way of life.[28]

Ultimately, the war itself decided very little. One immediate outcome was the end of slavery; the broader cultural differences between the sections, and the racial prejudices that permeated American society have not been so easily eliminated. In the end, the war simply settled the fact that the North had more military manpower than the South, and so, in this instance at least, regional differences would be solved not by separation, but by accommodation. In the long run, the South has become more like the rest of the country, though the change is still in process and racism has been shown to extend well beyond the boundaries of the Confederacy.

In the end, however, what is surprising about American politics in the nineteenth century is not the failure of the system that led to the Civil War, but its successes in managing issues generated by basic demographic changes. This appears all the more startling in view of the fact that the multifaceted nature of the American population interacted with the Constitution to produce political responses slowly, and only under great pressure. But perhaps this was also the strength of the system, for while the nineteenth century was a time of great demographic changes, few understood where they would end and what they meant. Rapid political action might well have produced more problems rather than fewer, especially if the decisions of the politicians had been at odds with what the American people were doing. As Anthony Comstock found out after 1873, birth control could be declared obscene and its advocates might be harassed in the courts, but wives and husbands would continue to consider their own needs as most important when it came time to decide on the size of their family.

The idea that the inhabitants of a particular country often exhibit a "national character" is one that has intrigued travellers, historians, sociologists, and other serious or casual commentators on social issues. Since Crèvecoeur first asked, in 1782, "What is an American?" many have attempted to answer that question.[29] There have been as many answers as authors. On first thought, any discussion of "American character" appears out of place in this book. The wide variety of American experiences with birth, death, marriage, and migration based on differences of age, sex, race, and culture, as well as where and when one happened to live, suggest that although there may be American characters, *the* American character does not exist. Close examination, however, reveals several character traits, often mentioned in the nineteenth century, which became visible because of the demographic processes that were altering the rhythms of Americans' lives.

By combining recent discoveries in anthropology and nonverbal communication, it is possible to explain how demographic trends may have functioned to emphasize certain forms of behavior over others.[30] In relatively homogeneous, stable societies, a great deal of communication occurs without words. Body language, communal and private celebrations, rituals of religion, work, and play, physical symbols, and even the basic rhythms of daily life create and reinforce an individual's sense of identity within the broader community. So long as contact with people of other cultures is at a minimum, nonverbal communication helps maintain a stable, smooth-functioning society. But when two or more cultures establish close contact, serious friction can arise from messages of friendship or hostility sent but not received. Similarly, actions that appear quite innocent to one group may be interpreted as insulting or threatening to another. Efforts by neighbors to express sympathy for a death in a family can lead to community antagonism rather than understanding when rituals for dealing with the transitions brought about by death are significantly different.

These discoveries have tremendous importance for understanding American history. Extensive international migration and rapid movement within the country meant that many Americans found themselves living near people whose patterns of life they did not fully understand. At best, the communication necessary to establish and maintain a stable community had to occur via an increased use of words, which was not always easy because of language differences. At worst, unintended messages transmitted from one person to another, or one group to another, could generate fears and anxieties of all sorts.

The racial and sexual tensions that were so central in American life were at least partially the result of this problem. Racial and ethnic antagonisms were easily aroused when group actions were misinterpreted. Similarly, at a time when concerns over sex were already common because of fears for health, social purity, and too-large families, the possibility of crossing the bounds of acceptable behavior were tremendous, for sexual relations may involve more nonverbal communication than any other human activity. The amused shock of British officers in the eighteenth century, when they discovered that proper American families allowed their daughters to "bundle" with young men, was repeated many times in the nineteenth with greater alarm as immigrants practiced sexual and courting rituals that appalled native-born Americans.[31]

In response to the need to establish some sort of stability in their communities, Americans adopted two ways of identifying an individual's worth which transcended most cultural barriers. First, they turned to highly visual, easily interpreted physical features as a means of assessing and communicating a person's worth and social standing. Possessions, age, sex, and skincolor all provided such measures. Second, they relied heavily on words, rather than shared experiences and understandings, to carry messages. These were the social equivalents of the mathematical notion of the lowest common denominator, offering means of communication when all else failed.

A result of relying on visual and verbal modes of communication was that certain messages were more easily transmitted than others, and so certain character traits appeared to be common to many Americans. Six will be discussed here, though readers may wish to add to or delete from the list.

The first is an emphasis on physical features. Although modern values stressed judging individuals on their talents and personality, the need for simplified forms of communication slowed the spread of modern standards by encouraging judgments based on visible characteristics such as sex, age, skincolor, or wealth. Long before Marshall McLuhan discovered television, the medium had become the message. Groups in American society were identified by shared visual characteristics, rather than similar ways of responding to death, common understanding of a symbol, or equal talents. By 1920, the emphasis on physical features as a measure of worth combined with a concern for personal health and hygiene to produce a market for the perfect toothpaste, hair dye, skin conditioner, and other aids by which one could become a success.

The need for economic success was important, especially for males. This is easy to understand when visible wealth becomes an important measure of one's standing in a community, and other possible forms of achievement are not widely accepted because of cultural differences. However, it was not sufficient only to acquire wealth; it had to be spent in such a way as to convey the message of one's worth to all concerned. In this context, a wife who could manage efficiently and get the most display for the money was a valuable marriage partner. Americans became conspicuous consumers because they had few other ways to establish their place in society. Keeping up with the Joneses had to be done in ways that the Joneses, as well as the Browns, Olsens, DeMarcos, and Rabinowitzes, would understand. This was particularly frustrating in the nineteenth century, when rising standards of living meant that possessions which once conveyed the message of considerable worth kept losing their value, so new products had to be found to set one apart from the crowd.

One trait foreigners often mentioned was the willingness of Americans to engage in conversation. Some found this pleasant; others felt it was offensive, especially when they were told all manner of personal matters. In homogeneous societies many personal matters are communicated, but in a subtle, almost subconscious fashion. Since Americans could not rely on shared culture to establish who they were nonverbally, they had to tell others. Similarly, in order to find out anything about other people, many Americans developed the habit of asking strangers rather personal questions. Many travellers also found this custom annoying, though perhaps as much because they felt their worth should be obvious as because of any impropriety.

Many Americans joined organizations with purposes ranging from serious reform to personal pleasure. The need for voluntary associations in nineteenth-century America in which a person could express his or her identity and find the company of like-minded individuals, indicates the extent to which society was "segmented."[32] Automatic knowledge of one's place in society, and with whom one might wish to associate, was missing, as were institutions that accepted a person on the basis of birth alone. In addition to providing a sense of identity and belonging, voluntary associations like fire companies, temperance societies, immigrant banks, and children's aid societies enabled Americans to solve problems by formal arrangements that in more homogeneous communities might have been handled informally.

The need for extensive verbal communication emphasized logical, structured thought. Rational action was respected; emotional responses were considered signs of weakness—the animal side of human nature was feared, even to the point of denying it. Of course, the rejection of man as animal was part of a long tradition in Western thought. The desire to establish control over their lives also led many Americans to reject anything that appeared to threaten this goal. But rational thought that could be expressed verbally also was valuable in a society where other forms of communication might either fail to get the message across, or worse yet, send the wrong signal. As a result, education became an important goal for many Americans, both because it provided needed verbal skills, and because it helped control emotional responses that might easily be misinterpreted.

The final trait to be mentioned is the oft-noted American penchant for violence. In close-knit communities of people and other animals, force and hierarchy are present, but violence frequently is not, because ritual conflicts and symbolic submission either take the place of actual assault, or prevent it from extending to physical harm. In American society, the multiplicity of cultures made it difficult for conflict to be ritualized. When verbal communication, either within or outside the political system, failed to resolve an issue, then violence or separation were the only alternatives. So long as space was available, high mobility worked both to create situations in which misunderstanding could occur, and to prevent violence from resulting by offering opportunities for retreat. But when separation was difficult, violence became more likely. No doubt, violence also broke out when the communications network worked efficiently, but conveyed messages that were perceived as more threatening than they were intended to be.

By 1920, Americans' lives, and hence their families and society, had undergone a century and a half of revolutionary change. Rhythms of life had been altered by demographic realities previously unknown in human existence. It is a tribute to the adaptability of human nature that these changes were both brought about and accommodated to as easily as they were.

Notes

1. Thomas Robert Malthus, *An Essay on the Principle of Population, as It Affects the Future Improvement of Society* (London, 1798).

2. Ansley J. Coale, "Population and Economic Development," in *The Population Dilemma,* ed. Philip M. Hauser (Englewood Cliffs, N.J., 1963), pp. 46–69.

3. Paul Uselding, "Conjectural Estimates of Gross Human Capital Inflows to the American Economy: 1790–1860," *Explorations in Economic History* 9 (1971–1972): 49–61.

4. Rowland T. Berthoff, *British Immigrants in Industrial America, 1790–1850* (Cambridge, Mass., 1953).

5. C. J. Erickson, "Who Were the English and Scots Immigrants to the United States in the Late Nineteenth Century?" in *Population and Social Change,* eds. D. V. Glass and Roger Revelle (New York, 1972), pp. 347–81.

6. Simon Kuznets, et al., *Population Redistribution and Economic Growth, United States, 1870–1950,* 3 vols. (Philadelphia, 1957–1964); Stanley Lebergott, "Migration Within the U.S., 1800–1960: Some New Estimates," *Journal of Economic History* 30 (1970): 839–47.

7. Allan R. Pred, *The Spatial Dynamics of U.S. Urban-Industrial Growth, 1800–1914: Interpretative and Theoretical Essays* (Cambridge, Mass., 1966); Sam Bass Warner, Jr., *Streetcar Suburbs: The Process of Growth in Boston, 1870–1900* (Cambridge, Mass., 1962).

8. Gilbert C. Din, "Spain's Immigration Policy in Louisiana and the American Penetration, 1792–1803," *Southwestern Historical Quarterly* 76 (1972–1973): 255–76.

9. Quoted in John C. Parish, "The Emergence of the Idea of Manifest Destiny," in his work, *The Persistence of the Westward Movement and Other Essays* (Berkeley, 1943), p. 64.

10. Ibid., p. 48.

11. Quoted in Albert K. Weinberg, *Manifest Destiny: A Study of Nationalist Expansionism in American History* (Chicago, 1963), p. 120.

12. Parish, "Idea of Manifest Destiny," pp. 56–57.

13. John G. Clark, *New Orleans 1718–1812: An Economic History* (Baton Rouge, La., 1970), p. 208.

14. Both Baylies and Tucker are quoted in Dan E. Clark, "Manifest Destiny and the Pacific," *Pacific Historical Review* 1 (1932): 4–5.

15. Ibid., p. 5.

16. William Gilpin, *Mission of the North American People, Geographical, Social, and Political* (Philadelphia, 1873), p. 124.

17. Elmer C. Sandmeyer, "California Anti-Chinese Legislation and Federal Courts: A Study in Federal Relations," *Pacific Historical Review* 5 (1935): 189–211.

18. Roger Daniels, *The Politics of Prejudice* (Berkeley, 1962).

19. Most of my remarks here are based on my reading of standard sources on the Constitutional Convention. Interested readers should also consult Donald L. Robinson, *Slavery in the Structure of American Politics, 1765–1820* (New York, 1971).

20. Frank H. Garver, "The Attitude of the Constitutional Convention of 1787 Toward the West," *Pacific Historical Review* 5 (1936): 349–58.

21. For example, *see* Lee Benson, *The Concept of Jacksonian Democracy: New York as a Test Case* (Princeton, N.J., 1961); Ronald Formisano, *The Birth of Mass Political Parties, Michigan, 1827–1861* (Princeton, N.J., 1971); Richard Jensen, *The Winning of the Midwest: Social and Political Conflict, 1888–1896* (Chicago, 1971); Paul Kleppner, *Cross of Culture: A Social Analysis of Midwestern Politics, 1850–1900* (New York, 1970).

22. Benson, *Jacksonian Democracy*, p. 185.

23. Ballard C. Campbell, "Ethnicity and the 1893 Wisconsin Assembly," *Journal of American History* 62 (1975): 74–94.

24. Hildegard B. Johnson, "The Election of 1860 and the Germans in Minnesota," *Minnesota History* 28 (1947): 20–36.

25. George H. Daniels, "Immigrant Vote in the 1860 Election: The Case of Iowa," *Mid-America* 44 (1962): 146–62.

26. Richard S. Alcorn, "Leadership and Stability in Mid-Nineteenth Century America: A Case Study of an Illinois Town," *Journal of American History* 61 (1974): 685–703.

27. John G. Bitzes, "The Anti-Greek Riot of 1909: South Omaha," *Nebraska History* 51 (1970): 199–224; Oscar Handlin, *Boston's Immigrants: A*

Study in Acculturation, rev. ed. (New York, 1969), pp. 187–89; Alexander Karlin, "New Orleans Lynchings of 1891 and the American Press," *Louisiana Historical Quarterly* 24 (1941): 187–204; J. A. Karlin, "The Anti-Chinese Outbreaks in Seattle, 1885–1886," *Pacific Northwest Quarterly* 39 (1948): 103–30; Billy Bob Lightfoot, "The Negro Exodus from Comanche County, Texas," *Southwestern Historical Review* 56 (1952–1953): 407–16; O. A. Rogers, Jr., "The Elaine Race Riots of 1919," *Arkansas Historical Quarterly* 19 (1960): 142–50; Richard C. Wade, *The Urban Frontier* (Chicago, 1959), pp. 224–29.

28. Ronald G. Walters, "The Erotic South: Civilization and Sexuality in American Abolitionism," *American Quarterly* 25 (1973): 177–201.

29. Michel-Guillaume Jean de Crèvecoeur, *Letters from an American Farmer* (London, 1782).

30. Eliot D. Chapple, *Culture and Biological Man: Explorations in Behavioral Anthropology* (New York, 1970); Clifford Geertz, *The Interpretation of Cultures: Selected Essays* (New York, 1973); Edward T. Hall, *The Hidden Dimension* (Garden City, N.Y., 1966).

31. Henry R. Styles, *Bundling: Its Origin, Progress and Decline in America* (Albany, 1871).

32. Robert H. Wiebe, *The Segmented Society: An Introduction to the Meaning of America* (New York, 1975).

PART III

AMERICA SINCE 1920: INDIVIDUAL CONTROL AND SOCIAL UNCERTAINTY

8

THE REVOLUTIONS CONTINUE

By 1920, the old order of demographic realities had been overturned, but the new had yet to be firmly established. Significant increases in life expectancy were still to come. In the 1930s, patterns of childbearing and migration both showed sharp breaks from the trends of the previous century. As might be expected, family life continued to evolve in response to new demographic realities, accompanied, of course, by the same vociferous debate on the future of the family that had first emerged in the nineteenth century. As demographic chance gave way to choice as the prime influence on the lives of most Americans, new social problems emerged, at least in part because it was no longer as easy to predict what the American population as a whole would look like in the future. Whatever the advantage has been to individual men and women and their families, personal whims have not produced aggregate demographic patterns as regular as those that resulted from traditional social and biological pressures. Thus, as the revolutions continue in Americans' lives, it is possible to bring the story to the present, but not to complete it.

Americans of all ages, sexes, and cultural backgrounds have always been restless, but since 1920 new patterns of migration have emerged that have reduced the extraordinary regional and ethnic pluralism that earlier characterized American society. The tendency for radio, television, newspapers, and magazines to convey standard news; a national economy offering common material goods; and the emergence of the national government as the most prominent political entity in most persons' lives, have aided movement toward a national culture. But migration and other demographic patterns have also been fundamentally involved.

One of the most important changes to occur since 1920 has been the decline in immigration (see Chart 7).[1] After World War I, immigration experienced a brief resurgence in the early 1920s before restrictive legislation and other factors began to have their effect. From 1931 to 1945, fewer people moved to the United States than at any time since 1836. In fact, during the period 1931 to 1935, about 324,000 people left the country, while only 220,000 arrived. This may be the only period of American history, with the possible exceptions of the early 1640s, when some Puritans returned to England to join in the English Civil War, or the 1780s, when the loyalists fled, when America has had more emigrants than immigrants. After World War II, immigration began to pick up gradually, until it now stands at just under 4 million persons per decade.[2]

Although 4 million new arrivals is a lot by any standard, their impact is less today than that of the nineteenth-century immigrants, because the total population now is over twice as large as in 1920, and over four times greater than in 1880. In 1910, foreign-born Americans accounted for 16.3 percent of all residents; today, the comparable figure is about 3 percent. In 1910, at least 39.5 percent of all Americans had at least one parent who had been born abroad; today the figure is less than 20 percent.

At present, the future importance of immigration into the United States is uncertain. As birthrates have fallen, legal immigrants have become an increasingly larger part of overall population growth, currently accounting for one of every five Americans added in a decade. Unrecorded immigrants from Mexico may make the actual figure much higher. Although it is difficult to envision a "nation of immigrants" ever closing its doors altogether, it seems equally unlikely that limits on immigration will ever be lifted significantly.

As the number of immigrants fell after 1925, several important changes began to occur in those likely to move to America (see Chart 7). Starting in 1930, and continuing to the present, more women than men moved to the United States for the first time since records began to be kept in 1821, and quite likely for the first time since 1607. At the same time, immigrants who

CHART 7 NUMBER AND CHARACTERISTICS OF IMMIGRANTS: 1921-1975

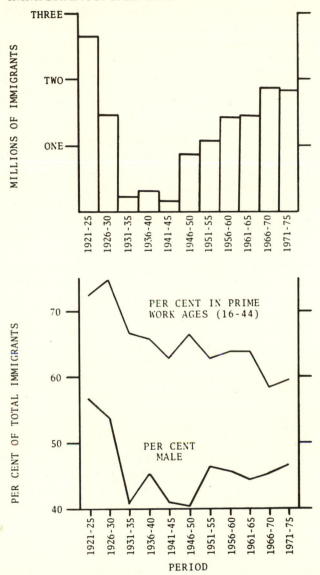

SOURCES: *Historical Statistics of the United States,* Series C 133–138; *Statistical Abstract of the United States, 1977,* p. 81; Taeuber and Taeuber, *People of the United States,* pp. 96–97.

because of age were best able to contribute to the work force became a smaller part of the total. Revisions in immigration laws in 1965 seem to have pushed the proportion of potential workers still lower. In the period covered by records, only the time from 1826 to 1830 had fewer immigrants of prime labor force ages than have arrived since 1965. Initially, this decline occurred because of a shift to older immigrants, but, since 1950, children have become more common as migrants to America.

Skills of immigrants have also changed dramatically over the last half century. As women, children, and older people have become more prominent, the proportion reporting no occupation at the time of arrival has risen from 25.7 percent between 1901 and 1910, to 55.9 percent from 1961 to 1970. Considering the importance of immigrants to American economic growth in the nineteenth century, this change would appear to hurt the American economy. Fortunately, other changes have helped to offset any damage. A combination of legal requirements by the United States, and the persecution of intellectuals in various other countries since 1920, has produced a steady influx of highly trained individuals since 1930. In the period 1901 to 1910, only 1 percent of all immigrants were professionals and technical workers; this proportion rose to 2.7 percent in the twenties, before jumping to 7.2 percent between 1931 and 1940. From 1961 to 1970, 10.2 percent of immigrants who listed occupations fell into this category. In contrast, the proportion of unskilled laborers dropped from 26.1 percent to 3.9 percent over the same period.[3]

The contributions of highly trained immigrants to American life have been impressive, but the drain of talent from other nations has been equally striking. In 1965, over 800 Korean Ph. D.s resided in the United States, compared to 80 in their homeland. In 1962, 40 percent of Israel's medical school graduates moved to America, as did about 20 percent of Chile's new engineers. As in the nineteenth century, the United States has continued to benefit from talented people raised and trained in other countries.[4]

For many immigrants, motives for moving to American remained much the same as in earlier periods. Economic well-being, a desire to escape persecution, and family ties continued to be important to individuals. But with the advent of more exten-

sive, restrictive legislation in 1917, the personal choices of potential immigrants have had to interact with American social policy.
Thus, to fully understand why the people who moved to the
United States after 1920 differed so clearly from those who came
before, it is necessary to examine the laws that encouraged some
and prohibited others.

Restrictions on immigration began in the nineteenth century
with prohibitions against Africans and Asians.[5] By the 1890s,
more and more native-born Americans wished to limit European
immigrants as well. In 1907, Congress established what became
known as the Dillingham Commission, to study the question of
possible new limits on immigration. In 1911, the commission
published forty-one volumes of reports on the subject which
enhanced the already growing concern about differences between
older and more recent immigrants. In 1917, a literacy test for
immigrants was established, but that kept out only a few of the
people restrictionists found undesirable. In 1921, quotas were
established whereby the number of immigrants from any nation
in a year could not exceed 3 percent of people born in that
country who were living in the United States in 1910. This, too,
proved unsatisfactory to those who feared immigrants from
southern and eastern Europe, and so, in 1924, new quotas were
established. No limits were placed on immigrants from other
countries in the Western Hemisphere, at least in part to allow
easy entry for low-paid Mexican farmworkers. But only 154,000
people a year could come from elsewhere in the world. Furthermore, quotas for each nation were to be based, not on recent
immigrants, but on all the inhabitants of the United States who
traced their ancestry to that land. Shifting the basis of the quotas
from recent immigrants to the national origins of the total population meant more could move from Great Britain, Germany, and
Scandinavia, and fewer from Italy, Greece, or Poland. With the
exception of Filipinos, who at that time were wanted as laborers
in Hawaii and were subjects of the American empire, Asian
immigrants were prohibited.

Quotas based on national origins went into full effect in 1929.
As a result, we know surprisingly little about how they might
have functioned, since the Great Depression, World War II, and
the cold war intervened, severely disrupting international migra-

tion worldwide. After World War II, refugees were admitted under special exemptions, a policy that has continued with regard to Hungarians, Cubans, and Vietnamese. Perhaps the period between 1956 and 1965 is indicative of what might have happened.

In 1965, a new law significantly altered American immigration policy. Numerical limits for each year were established for the Americas (120,000) and the rest of the world (170,000). For the first time, Canadians, Mexicans, and West Indians could not move freely into the United States. Selection among potential immigrants continued, but preference was based on family ties to American residents, and job skills. Choice by national origin was eliminated, except that no one nation could send more than 20,000 people in any one year.

The effects of this new legislation have been surprising. Major shifts in the age and sex composition and occupations of immigrants occurred about 1930, long before this new law went into effect. What have changed are the geographic and racial origins of immigrants. Immigrants from southern Europe jumped from 9.5 to 18.9 percent of the total between 1961-1965, and 1970; Asians saw their share increase from 7.2 to 24.9 percent during the same period. West Indians doubled their share of the total from 8.2 to 16.4 percent. Nonwhite immigrants from all parts of the globe increased from 8.6 to 19.7 percent of newcomers as a result of the new law, suggesting that racism in America's past does not necessarily deter immigration by nonwhites in the present.[6].

The establishment of quotas for countries in the Americas has had the most direct effect on Canada and Mexico. Imposition of restrictions on Mexicans is a particularly touchy question at present. Before 1965, migration from Canada seemed to be declining naturally; that from Mexico was on the increase, and some argue it continues today on an illegal basis. Because Puerto Rico is a territory of the United States, migrants from there have been exampt from quotas, but after over 450,000 people moved from that island in the 1950s, migration to the mainland slowed to an estimated 165,000 people during the 1960s.

Clearly, freedom to move to the United States has been significantly reduced in the twentieth century. Potential immigrants now must both judge and be judged, with the standards for being judged open to change. At the moment, there does not seem to be any great pressure to alter the law as fundamentally established in 1965 (enforcement of the statutes against Mexicans is another matter), but if the past is an indication of the future, one would hesitate to use the immigrants of 1975 to predict who will be moving to the United States in 1995.[7]

After 1920, Americans continued to move within the country at a rapid pace, but many of them chose destinations that were unfamiliar in earlier decades. In so doing they began to break down the regional differences that earlier migrants had helped create and perpetuate. In 1970, only 53 percent of people lived in the same house as in 1965. Many of those who moved travelled short distances—23.3 percent were still in the same county— nevertheless, almost half the people had changed their residence in five years. Black and white Americans were equally mobile, as only 51.4 percent of the former and 53.3 percent of the latter remained in one place for five years. However, unlike the nine- teenth century, when rural and urban Americans all moved often, about three of every four farm residents remained in the same place from 1965 to 1970.[8]

One of the patterns that contributed most heavily to regional differences disappeared as Americans abandoned their previous tendency to move almost exclusively from east to west. Since 1920, and particularly since 1950, Americans have moved from south to north, west to east, and north to south. In addition, black and foreign-born Americans left regions where they had concentrated before 1920. Finally, movement into cities has spread from the Northeast, where it first emerged, until now the majority of people in every region of the country are urban dwellers.

The decision by millions of black Americans to give up life on southern farms for life in cities in all parts of the country pro- duced one of the few important demographic changes to emerge in the twentieth century.[9] In 1910, almost nine of every ten black Americans lived in the South; about three of every four resided in a rural area. Then, a combination of Jim Crow laws, agricultur- al problems, labor shortages and high wages in the North during

World War I, and the desire for adventure persuaded many to try to improve their lives elsewhere. Once again, the cumulative effects of many short-distance moves was impressive. By 1930, about 20 percent of the black population lived in the North; almost 90 percent of these people lived in cities. Blacks who remained in the South joined the trend to urban residence, as the proportion of southern blacks living in cities doubled between 1890 and 1930, from 15.3 to 31.7 percent. By 1970, only 53 percent of all black Americans still lived in the South; about 20 percent lived in the Northeast, and a similar proportion resided in the North Central region. During and after World War II, many blacks began to head west, so that by 1970, 7.5 percent lived in that part of the country. Movement out of the South continued to mean movement into the cities. By 1970, fully 97.1 percent of blacks who lived in northern and western states were city dwellers. Many blacks who remained in the South also experienced the major shift in the rhythms of life that urban living requires. In 1970, the proportion of southern blacks who lived in cities stood at 67.3 percent.

Until 1900, foreign-born Americans tended to be as concentrated in the Northeast and North Central parts of the country as blacks were in the South. Eighty-seven percent of the foreign-born lived in the North at the turn of the century. During the twentieth century, the foreign-born also moved into regions they once avoided, though the shift was not as dramatic as among blacks. By 1970, the proportion of all foreign-born Americans who lived in the South and West had risen from 12 percent in 1900 to 32.6 percent. The West has appealed to foreigners more than the South, for in 1970 6.6 percent of Westerners had been born abroad, but only 2.1 percent of Southerners could make the same claim. The blending of foreign and native-born populations is far from complete, however. In Massachusetts, in 1970, one-third of the residents had been born in another country or had a parent who was an immigrant; the comparable group in Mississippi included only 1.4 percent of the people. Furthermore, not all the foreign-born migrated willingly. During World War II, Japanese-Americans were forcibly removed from the Pacific Coast states and sent eastward.[10] Mexican-Americans have also been subjected to harassment, even to the point of repatriation in the 1930s.[11]

With the exception of the 1930s, when the Great Depression slowed virtually all migration into and within the United States, cities have grown throughout the twentieth century, further blurring regional distinctions (see Chart 5, p. 123). As early as 1850, 28.8 percent of the people who lived in New England resided in cities, a striking contrast to the 4.2 percent in the region composed of Kentucky, Tennessee, Mississippi, and Alabama.[12] A century later, these two regions still were among the most and least urbanized populations in the country, with figures of 75.2 and 39.1 percent respectively. By 1970, a majority of the people (54.6 percent) living in the east south central region, as it is known to the census bureau, lived in urban areas. New England had changed little since 1950, but in both the Middle Atlantic states and the Pacific Coast region, over eight of every ten people lived in cities. Here, as with other of the demographic revolutions, the question was *when* they would affect a particular group or region, not *if* they would occur.

In spite of the importance of urban environments to the lives of twentieth-century Americans, few actually live in large cities. This has become increasingly true over the last half century. In 1920, when just over half of all Americans lived in cities, four places with a million or more people accounted for 9.6 percent of the total population. Fifty years later, an additional 20 percent of people were urban dwellers, but only 9.2 percent of them lived in the six cities of over 1 million inhabitants. Over the same period, the number of communities with 10,000 to 25,000 residents rose from 466 to 1,385. The proportion of the total population living in towns of that size increased from 6.6 to 10.5 percent. By 1970, almost the same number of people lived in the 4,134 towns with 2,500 to 10,000 inhabitants. In 1920, communities with between 25,000 and 100,000 people attracted about as many people as the urban giants; by 1970, the 760 smaller centers had almost twice as many residents as the places with a million or more.[13]

Part of the growth of smaller cities occurred as Americans in rural areas like Mississippi or South Dakota decided to move into cities close to home. But much of it reflects another major aspect of twentieth-century migration—suburbanization. By 1970, 55 million Americans lived in suburbs, compared to 64 million in central cities, and only 54 million in rural areas. The remaining 31 million lived in small towns.

The meaning of life in the suburbs to the people who live there is a subject of some interest. Three comments are in order here. First, the main appeal of suburbs has often been as a place to live while raising a family. These are residential communities, many of whose residents are in similar stages of the family life cycle.[14] Second, suburbs often have separated various groups of Americans from each other.[15] Racial segregation may be the most obvious, for in 1970 blacks accounted for 22.5 percent of people living in the central cities, but only 5.7 percent of suburbanites. At the same time, housing costs in various developments have produced equally strong class segregation. Suburbs have also contributed to segregation on the basis of age and sex, as well as race and class. The separation of residence and place of employment has created a situation in which suburbs become the major focus in the lives of women and children, but are only part of the daily and weekly rhythms of life for adult males. Third, the decisions of millions of Americans to spend part of their lives in suburbs offers an excellent example of how individual control has introduced social instability. Many of the problems currently facing America's major metropolitan areas have been created and compounded by the loss of many of the most prosperous and best-educated people to the suburbs.[16] The task of providing the necessary water and energy to millions of individuals and families who have chosen detached single-family housing as part of their plan for a better future, is generating problems that have been less evident, but may, in the long run, be the most serious of all.

The future of internal migration is hard to predict. In the nineteenth century, individuals made decisions on where to move on the basis of the image they had of a region or community. Recently, sectional differences in income, ethnic variations, or access to city life which, prior to 1920, encouraged or inhibited potential migrants, have disappeared. As a result, interregional migration may decline, except for that caused by constant attractions such as climate.

One characteristic of twentieth-century Americans, which clearly distinguishes them from the vast majority of people who have ever lived, is the attainment of levels of health and life expectancy that were almost beyond imagination even a century ago. The age-old dream of a long and healthy life is a reality for most Americans, who live today isolated from the ravages of the worst enemies of humanity—smallpox, tuberculosis, cholera, typhoid fever, and the like.

Examination of the actual levels of health and death experienced by twentieth-century Americans reveals several important trends. Between 1920 and 1950, Americans continued to improve their life chances as rapidly as they had from 1880 to 1920.[17] Among white females, the most favored group in the population, life expectancy at birth rose from 55.6 to 72.2 years over this thirty-year period. Their male counterparts experienced a corresponding increase from 54.7 to 66.5 years. Life expectancy among black Americans also rose rapidly, going from 45.2 to 62.9 for women, and from 45.5 to 59.1 for men. Since 1950, however, improvements in life chances have slowed noticeably. The figures for 1975 show that in the twenty-five years since mid century, white females have added only five years to their life chances, to 77.2, a striking contrast to the gain of 16.6 years over the previous three decades. Among white males, the gain was even smaller, with only 2.9 years (for a total of 69.4) added to life expectancy since 1950. Black males fell in between whites of both sexes, improving their life chances by 4.5 years, to 63.6. Only black women maintained relatively rapid rates of improvement. In 1975, they could expect to live 72.3 years at birth, an increase of almost ten years since 1950. One interesting result of these changes is that, among black and white Americans, sex has replaced race as the principal source of variation in an individual's life chances.

The first Americans, who for centuries suffered from extremely poor life chances, began to participate in this part of the revolutions in the twentieth century. After reaching a low of only 237,000 people in 1900, Indians increased in number slowly until after 1920, and then more rapidly, with large gains made since 1940. In 1970, the census recorded 792,000 Indians; most of the increase must have come from improved life expectancy, since childbearing has been high among Indians for most of this century.

To fully appreciate what these changes meant to the individuals involved, it is helpful to look at the chances any one person had of living from birth to some other age. Although the actual figures vary slightly, between 1870 and 1970, white women experienced improved life chances very close to the changes indicated in the columns for life expectancy at birth of 45 and 75, in Table 1, page 31. In 1870, 3 of every 10 female babies could expect to die before reaching the marriageable age of twenty. By 1970, fully 98 out of 100 will live to that point in the life cycle. In 1870, only a little over half the women could expect to survive to the end of their childbearing years (about age forty-five). Since men died at comparable rates, the chances for a long marriage were slight. A century later, almost every girl born survives to the end of her reproductive period, as only 5 of every 100 females born are expected to die before forty-five. Almost 9 of every 10 women alive today will live to what was in the past an old age (that is, sixty); a century ago just over 4 of 10 could look forward to that accomplishment. Perhaps the most striking change of all is that a white girl baby today has a greater chance to live to sixty than her counterpart born in 1870 did of surviving to her first birthday, truly a revolutionary change by any standard. The uncertainty of life brought on by the ever-present possibility of death in 1870 has been virtually eliminated for most Americans today. Life is now more controllable and predictable.

The establishment of extensive control over death has had important effects not only on individuals, but also on society. As health and life chances have improved, the productivity of Americans has risen, both because illness takes less of a toll, and because fewer skilled workers die before effectively utilizing their training. On the other hand, this may only be a temporary benefit, since we are now immune to all but the most severe processes of natural selection. Genetic weaknesses that once were eliminated because afflicted individuals did not survive to reproduce themselves, can now be perpetuated and expanded within the population. In the future, American society may face a situation analogous to an army in conflict that discovers that wounded soldiers are often more of a drain on resources than dead ones.

The possibility of establishing new relationships between men and women, and new attitudes toward families may be the most important result of greater life chances. So long as life expectancy was low, a society had to develop customs that would insure a reasonably high rate of reproduction. Any other pattern would quickly lead to extinction. Thus, every society that survived to the twentieth century has, of necessity, emphasized family life and childbearing as essential parts of the lives of most adults. The revolution in mortality has significantly reduced this pressure, and, in fact, has reversed it in favor of patterns of low levels of childbearing. What new arrangements will emerge remain to be seen, but the effects on the ongoing debate on the family will be evident below.

Causes of health and death have shifted dramatically in the twentieth century. Elimination of epidemics with the devastating physical and social impact of cholera, smallpox, or even influenza on the scale of 1918–1919, is among the most obvious. But changes in the ten most frequent killers of Americans have been equally impressive, and probably more important to life chances as well. Deaths from infections have declined, and have been replaced by degenerative diseases and what might most appropriately be called social deaths. In the years 1900 to 1904, Americans succumbed to tuberculosis, pneumonia and influenza, and diarrhea and enteritis more often than to any other cause of death.[18] These infections accounted for about one-third of all deaths. Of these major killers, only pneumonia and influenza remain in the ten most unwanted list in 1975, accounting for only 2.9 percent of all deaths. Of the other major killers at the start of the century, nephritis and diphtheria have disappeared from the current list of the top ten; cerebral hemorrhage and bronchitis remain, but are included with related illnesses. The major cause of death among Americans today is heart disease, which accounts for 37.8 percent of all mortality, a significant increase from 8 percent in 1900. Together with other cardiovascular problems (including strokes, which are third on the list), over half (51.3

percent) of all American deaths in 1975 were from these illnesses. Cancers have the dubious honor of second place on the list of 1975 killers, as 19.3 percent of all American deaths were caused by them, a remarkable increase from 3.7 percent in 1900.

Clearly, degenerative diseases are the major cause of death in America today. But the single most dangerous enemy may be the people themselves. Accidents, cirrhosis of the liver, suicide, and homicide rank fourth, seventh, eighth and eleventh as causes of death, accounting for 8.7 percent of the total. Considering the number of deaths that appear as heart problems or cancers, but which are self-inflicted through diet, smoking, pollution, or over-work, it would appear that we have replaced any germ or virus as our own worst enemy.

Reflection on changes in the causes of death suggests that the future will see only small gains in life expectancy. By 1950, most of the easily preventable and curable infectious diseases had been controlled. Lower infant mortality from reduced infections accounted for many of the early gains in life expectancy. Between 1920 and 1950, the number of children who died in the first year of their life fell from 86 to 29 for every 1,000 live births. The figure for 1920 was already about half that of the mid-nineteenth century. Since 1950, improvements in infant mortality have been much slower, with 16 out of every 1,000 babies still failing to reach their first birthday. The rate may eventually fall to around 10 per 1,000, especially when black children and mothers receive the same medical care as their white peers, but further improve-ments will be difficult. Significant future gains in health must come from persuading adult Americans not to damage them-selves. Whether the human enemy will be as easily controlled as other foes is a moot question.

As in the nineteenth century, the causes of better health are many, though it is hard to pinpoint the specific contribution of each. Preventive medicine and public health measures have con-tinued to expand since 1920. In the nineteenth century, only smallpox could be prevented by vaccination. Today diphtheria, whooping cough, typhoid fever, cholera, and polio are among the age-old killers children no longer fear. In fact, control over some of these diseases has become so extensive that parents who were born after this demographic revolution was almost complete now neglect to immunize their children. High infant and child mortality may be a matter of history for Americans, but they are also still very much a possibility without proper precautions.

Making standard public health measures available to more and more people has been as important as adding new techniques. In the decades after 1920, visiting nurses and public health officials brought lessons of diet, hygiene, and child care, as well as vaccination and sewage treatment to new groups of Americans.[19] The struggle to provide Americans with pure food and drugs continued. The years between 1927 and 1932 saw success in the campaign to have lead and arsenic washed from fruits. In 1938, a new federal law strengthened provisions of the Pure Food and Drugs Act of 1906.[20] Campaigns to improve Americans' health have even extended beyond our borders, via such efforts as the movement to increase the health of Mexican livestock between 1946 and 1951, and the more recent, and apparently successful, attempt to eliminate smallpox worldwide.[21]

Unfortunately, efforts to provide a healthy environment seem always to lag behind our capacity to discover new ways to pollute air, water, and food. Some aspects of industrial pollution are clearly detrimental to health, and so can be attacked directly. But other pollutants, such as insecticides, offer more difficult choices, because decreasing damage to our bodies may increase damage to food supplies. Here, too, individual choice and control with beneficial or neutral effects on a private level may combine to produce potential or actual social disasters.

Although preventive medicine is still the best cause of health, there is a greater chance in the twentieth century of actually being cured if one gets a disease, because of both more skilled medical practice in treating symptoms and providing life-support systems while the body's own healing powers work, and better curative technology. Drugs that effectively combat specific illnesses are now common; more general chemical cures such as sulfa drugs and penicillin have been important in medical practice since the 1940s. Surgery is safer now than before 1920, and, in addition, offers new chances for health via delicate operations on hearts and brains. Machinery has made a contribution, both in hospital treatment and by means of devices such as heart valves and pacemakers that allow their owners to return to a partially normal life. However, it is important not to overemphasize the value of curative, as opposed to preventive, medicine, because many of the most spectacular achievements of medicine in the twentieth century occurred after the major improvements in life expectancy took place. Pediatricians who vaccinate children are far more important to general good health than the most skilled transplanters of hearts and other organs. Curative medicine is a twentieth-century addition to the health revolution; it is not the main cause.

Medical technology is of value only if the sick have access to it. Several factors have made it easier than ever before for Americans to get the care they needed. Doctors have been able to specialize and become more skilled in the treatment of certain types of illness because, first automobiles and telephones, and now helicopters and computers, provide quick links between consumers and providers of health care.

Since World War II, major changes in the financial structure of medicine have also made health care more accessible. In 1950, Americans spent a total of $12 billion a year on health care. This amounted to $76 per person each year, or 4.5 percent of the gross national product. By 1960, total dollars spent on health had increased to $25.9 billion, or $137 per person, equalling 5.2 percent of the gross national product. The next fifteen years saw more spectacular changes. In 1975, Americans committed $122.2 billion to their health through public and private sources. The proportion of the gross national product devoted to health almost doubled from 1950, as it rose to 8.4 percent. In 1974, the amount of money spent per person stood at $485, over six times as much as in 1950. Some of the money went to support medical research, as federal investments to advance medical knowledge rose from $73 million in 1950, to over $2 billion in 1975, but much of it was spent to provide medical services to the people who needed them. In 1950, only one of every two Americans had insurance to cover hospital costs; just over one-third had surgical insurance. Since 1970, better than eight out of ten Americans have been covered by these forms of medical insurance, allowing them greater access to care.[22]

Since the major improvements in life expectancy came before and not after this great increase in spending on health, it is fair to ask just what it is that Americans have been buying. Obviously, inflation had some effect on costs, but that explains only part of the change. Much of the increase in spending on health care can be attributed to voluntary (and often unnecessary) medical treatment of patients who previously would have suffered minor problems; to the increased access among older and poor Americans to health maintenance via Medicare and Medicaid; and to new forms of "heroic" medicine involving rare and expensive treatments that prolong the lives of a few individuals, but have little impact on life expectancy in general.

One of the most notable differences from the nineteenth century, when Americans had many equally bad options for health care, has been the ability of scientific medicine to demonstrate its advantages over other forms of treatment. Since 1920, the medical profession has increasingly dominated the market for health services, both by offering clearly superior results, and by the reestablishment of professional controls over who is allowed to treat the ill.

Nevertheless, many Americans still prefer alternative forms of health care, both because of their desire to achieve better health at a low cost, and lingering hostilities toward doctors. The growth of television and magazines as national media have allowed sellers of health to reach a wide market. Advertisements for pain killers, cough medicines, skin conditioners, foot aids, and tranquilizers are common in almost any magazine and on almost every television station. Many newspapers, magazines, and radio stations regularly dispense medical advice. The message is clear, that people can treat themselves cheaply and at home; doctors can be avoided.

Often advertisements for health aids carry messages reinforcing old links between various parts of the purity crusade and the debate on the family. Products such as soap and toothpaste are sold both for personal hygiene and as social necessities. Health care is promoted as enhancing physical beauty and personal worth, as well as physical comfort and safety. Advertisements cast men, women, and children in clearly defined roles. For example, toothpaste offers increased sex appeal between men and women; only children are expected to use it to prevent decay, and they must be bribed with good taste. Many advertisements for health products portray men as scientifically knowledgeable, while women are caring mothers.

Fads in health care have emerged from other changes in society.[23] Quacks quickly exploited discoveries in radio, electronics, and radiation by appealing to people's faith in technology. This faith is sometimes extraordinary, for individuals occasionally have died waiting to testify to the efficacy of a particular cure. Recent interest in Asian cultures and religion in general has had its medical parallels in the interest in acupuncture and mind control as ways to health. Rejection of the artificial quality of American material culture has contributed to natural-food fads for health, and the use of natural poisons like laetrile instead of laboratory chemicals for treatment of cancer. It is entirely possible that, in certain situations, some of these treatments provide relief. But it is equally true that Americans in the twentieth century are often no more careful in their choice of health care options than were their nineteenth-century counterparts who sought cheap, sure cure-alls which kept the doctor away.

American attitudes toward health and death continue to be complex and occasionally paradoxical, although concern with establishing control over death, to allow a happier, more predictable life, predominates.

Twentieth-century Americans have manifested their interest in control through their efforts to insure themselves against the possibility of sickness and death. On the surface, insurance seems very rational and future-oriented, the epitome of modern behavior. It is designed to reduce risks, and maintain both choice and dignity in time of trouble. Yet, Americans' adoption of insurance is in some ways curious. In the early decades of the twentieth century, when insurance was particularly needed because life was still relatively uncertain, it often was rejected, not on its own merits, but because it was advocated by foreign "radicals." It was widely adopted only after the revolution in health made it far less necessary. Furthermore, insurance is often sold on an emotional rather than rational basis. Advertisements for life insurance frequently show families whose lives have been ruined (though never too much) by the death of a careless husband and father who failed in his duty to provide. We carefully avoid mentioning the main purpose for insurance (the fact that we get sick and die) by buying *health* (medical) and *life* insurance.

As death has been removed as an ever-present part of life, nineteenth-century efforts to provide men and women with guidance on how to die with dignity were replaced by an outright rejection of death, and a denial of the fact that human beings are still animals with limited life spans. Among the most curious, yet logical, manifestations of this rejection of death, are the heroic efforts made in hospitals to prolong the "life" of severely ill patients by permanent use of mechanical life-support systems. The search for control over death has been an unattainable goal of humanity for so long that we are unprepared to face modern technical possibilities that threaten us with the occasional need to welcome rather than resist the end of life. Even when the reality of death can not be denied, Americans in the twentieth century increasingly have tried to isolate the process from the rest of life. Hospitals and nursing homes became places to die, away from home and life. In institutions, death can be antiseptic and organized, rather than messy and upsetting. The dying are isolated from more "normal" people. After death, bodies are transported to funeral "homes" that specialize in the quick and tidy disposal of any reminder of our own mortality. Few expect to question very seriously any of the costs associated with these services. Only recently, experts on dying have appeared, whose main purpose is to reacquaint Americans with how to accept death with dignity.[24]

The greater skills and capacities of twentieth-century doctors to actually help their patients has led to some reduction in tension between consumers and providers of health care; nonetheless, hostilities still remain. Efforts by some doctors, and scientists in related fields, to manipulate the "quality" of the population have been relatively rare, but they often have aroused considerable suspicion. From the eugenicists of the 1920s and 1930s, to modern researchers attempting to develop new forms of life, or overzealous advocates of sterilization, there have been doctors who have crossed the boundary between what most Americans consider to be a legitimate search for control, into areas that threaten, rather than comfort, many individuals. Less threatening, but perhaps more common, is the callousness many doctors have displayed toward subordinate groups. The American Medical Association has opposed public health insurance which would allow more poor and elderly access to its members' services. Birth control pills received extensive testing in Puerto Rico before being put on the market in the United States. A group of black males in the South were allowed to develop all three stages of syphilis in order to provide medical knowledge.[25] The manufacturers of Valium, a popular tranquilizer, have perpetuated sex stereotypes through advertisements that portrayed men as having legitimate tensions, while women suffered from ill-defined nervousness and anxiety.[26] Spurred by the women's movement in recent years, and by criticism regarding the excessive interference by doctors in the natural processes of childbirth, midwives are making a comeback from their decline in the early twentieth century, as some women have sought out female help in childbirth in reaction to what they felt to be hostile and patronizing behavior on the part of male doctors. Suspicion of doctors' motives has in recent years led several state legislatures to allow use of laetrile in cancer therapy, even though the efficacy of that drug remains unproven. Most of the time, modern values stressing individual choice and greater control have been in accord with modern medical practice, but individual choice and professional standards are not always compatible. Presumably, they will remain in partial conflict in the future. Social and psychological advances have yet to match the remarkable biological achievements in health care since 1880.

Marriage and childbearing have always been closely associated, but in twentieth-century America relationships between the two have become both less clear and somewhat paradoxical. In general, marriage is the one basic aspect of Americans' lives that has been least affected by revolutionary changes. The most unpredictable of all demographic patterns in the twentieth century have been those associated with the basic rhythm of life that is subject to the greatest personal control—childbearing. The decisions of women and men about when to marry, whom to choose, and how long to live with a spouse, have altered. But all this has occurred within the framework (as solid now as in the eighteenth century) that the married state is to be preferred. In contrast, Americans have shifted their preferences and practices about family size several times since 1920, often suddenly and with little warning.

Throughout most of American history, one of the most predictable decisions that men and women would make was that they would marry if they lived long enough and in a community where there were enough members of the opposite sex to provide a partner. From 1900 to the present, less than 10 percent of all men and women lived to sixty-five without marrying, much the same as in eighteenth-century America. Recently, the number of couples who live together without being married has risen sharply, from about 520,000 in 1970 to about 960,000 in 1977. It is not clear whether this marks the onset of a rejection of marriage on the part of younger Americans, or is simply a reflection of more tolerant sexual customs. However, the facts that about 40 percent of couples who live together marry, and that many couples who live together without marrying include divorced men and women, suggest that marriage is still the accepted practice. Ninety-eight percent of all households with couples still include husbands and wives, indicating that a revolution against marriage is still a long way off, though it may be beginning.[27]

The decision about when to marry for the first time has remained remarkably stable, except for the two decades during and after World War II. From 1920 to 1940, the average age at marriage for both men and women was remarkably close to the average found in the eighteenth century. Then, for about twenty years, men and women decided to marry earlier than their parents. It is hard to tell whether this was the result of prosperity after World War II, the emphasis at the time on family life and "togetherness," or some other factor. Whatever the reason, the median age at which men married for the first time stood at 22.8 in both 1950 and 1960, three years younger than in 1900, and probably younger than at any time in our history. The change among women was not as great, for in 1900 they already married at the relatively young age of 21.9, on average, but in 1950 and 1960 the comparable figure fell to 20.3 years.

Another way to show the change is to look at the proportions remaining single between the ages of twenty and twenty-four. Until 1940, at least 72.6 percent of all men between twenty and twenty-four had yet to marry; in 1960, the comparable figure was 52.6 percent. At least 47.5 percent of all women remained unwed between twenty and twenty-four until 1940. Thereafter a decline set in until, in 1960, only 27.4 percent were single at those ages. Since 1960, decisions about marrying for the first time have been postponed, with the result that young men and women today are rapidly returning to the patterns common between 1900 and 1940. It is possible that the move to earlier marriage after 1940 is being followed by an equally unusual pattern of late marriage, but it will probably take a decade before the outcome of the current trend becomes clear.

One of the most striking aspects of American marriages since 1920 has been the continuation of the trend that emerged after 1860 for couples to end their unions by choice. In the century between 1870 and 1970, the proportion of all marriages broken in a year that were ended by divorce has increased from 5.2 to 44.0 percent.[28] The divorce rate is currently higher in the United States than in any other country in the world. Curiously, increases in life expectancy that tended to prolong unions have been offset by voluntary decisions to separate, so that the proportion of marriages coming to an end in any one year has been remarkably stable. This stability in the rate at which marriages end may soon disappear since additional declines in the death rate will be slow, but there is little evidence that the trend to more frequent divorces will cease.

The fact that a significant number of women and men chose to end their marriages voluntarily does not imply a rejection of marriage as a desirable state. Since the 1930s, widowed and divorced persons have married more rapidly than single individuals. This combination of divorce and rapid remarriage suggests that, with the exercise of greater individual choice, many husbands and wives are no longer content with one partner for life and may be replacing the old ideal of permanent monogamy with an acceptance of what has been called serial polygamy.

The major cycles in childbearing from 1920 to the present can be quickly outlined. Because virtually all groups of Americans have taken part in these changes within one or two years of each other, no effort will be made to consider differences among regions, races, or economic groups. Levels of childbearing have been higher among black Americans than white, but that is frequently the result of educational, income, and residential differences. The trends have been remarkably similar. Indians, whose childbearing has been consistently high throughout this century, constitute the most notable exception to the general pattern.

The nineteenth-century revolution in fertility continued after 1920 until 1933. Then, in the midst of the worst economic depression in the history of the United States, the birthrate *stopped* falling. In 1933, the birth rate stood at 17.6 per 1,000, about a third as high as in 1800. After several years of minor fluctuations, Americans began to have more babies after 1936. The increase was gradual until the end of World War II. Then, between 1945 and 1947, the number of babies born in a given year jumped from 2.9 to 3.8 million. The birthrate increased from 20.4 to 26.6 over the same three years. Because of peculiarities in the age structure of the population, the birthrate never again went above 25.3 per 1,000 (in 1954), but the total number of births continued to rise, until 4.3 million children were born in 1957. Then, in 1958, American couples reverted to the long-term trend toward lower levels of fertility. By 1975, the number of births dropped to 3.1 million (equal to the number of babies in 1943), and the birthrate stood at 14.8, lower than any time in American history.[29]

These changes in the trends of childbearing were unexpected at the time, and have been difficult to explain in retrospect. The post-World War II baby boom has been explained, at least in part, as the result of relief from war and as a response to increased prosperity that appeared to auger well for the future, especially after the depression of the 1930s.[30] The limits of this explanation appear when we remember that, after more than a century of trying to have fewer children, American couples changed their minds and began to have more babies, not in 1945, but in 1933. The reversion to more frequent childbearing before the war and before the depression was over embarrassed demographers, who were predicting the end of population growth in this country.

Why the baby boom came to an end in 1957 is no clearer than why it began in the first place. No major social or economic upheavals persuaded couples to have fewer rather than more babies. The decline in the birthrate since 1958 is in keeping with the long-term trend toward smaller families, but it is surprising even in view of the extent of fertility control. As the boys and girls of the baby boom years grew up and began to have children of their own, it was expected that an "echo" of the baby boom would appear about 1970. Such has not been the case. Although the number of women between the ages of twenty and twenty-nine increased from 11 million to 16.6 million between 1960 and 1972, the number of babies born declined by more than a million. Thus, in recent years, Americans have limited their childbearing more strictly than ever before. In 1977, the birthrate actually rose slightly; it is uncertain whether this marks a new trend, the appearance of the long-delayed "echo," or merely a short-term fluctuation. Whatever its meaning, it is clear that individual control over childbearing, widely established by the 1930s, has made it extremely difficult to predict how many children American women and men will have in the future.

In spite of the variations in childbearing since 1920, it is important to remember that, even at the peak of the baby boom, American parents behaved more like their counterparts in the 1930s and 1970s than like eighteenth-century husbands and wives. Most of the recent changes occurred because couples decided to have three or four children, rather than none, one, or two. Few returned to the large families common before 1800. Among one group of wives born between 1750 and 1799, fully 71 percent had five or more children. In contrast, only 15.6 percent of wives born in the first five years of the twentieth century had that many children. Wives born between 1931 and 1935 were among those who contributed the most to the baby boom, yet only 21.6 percent of them had at least five children. Between the late eighteenth and early twentieth centuries, the proportion of wives who had no children rose from 1.9 to 20.4 percent. At least part of the baby boom resulted from the fact that only 7.2 percent of wives who were in their prime childbearing years in the 1950s remained childless. In addition, 38.4 percent of the baby boom mothers had three or four children, up from 22.4 percent of the wives born at the start of the century. This shift occurred because only 32.8 percent of the mothers who contributed to the baby boom had one or two children, a decline from the 41.5 percent of the early twentieth century wives who had such small families. Nevertheless, the basic similarity of childbearing in the twentieth century is made clear by the fact that only 11 percent of eighteenth-century wives had one or two children; an additional 16.1 percent had three or four.[31]

A sharp increase in illegitimacy constitutes one of the few really new patterns of childbearing to emerge since 1920. Between 1955 and 1975, the percentage of all births accounted for by children born to unwed mothers more than tripled, from 4.5 to 14.3 percent. This is particularly surprising since, in the nineteenth century, fertility control among married women and men was paralleled by a decline in illegitimacy. Yet, between 1960 and 1975, the number of illegitimate births rose by almost 265,000, in spite of the fact that total births were declining sharply.[32] At this point, it is difficult to determine what this trend means, or even how long it will continue, though considering the present relatively easy access to contraceptives and abortion compared to earlier decades, it would appear at least partly voluntary.

The attitudes twentieth-century Americans have had toward childbearing are as interesting as their biological behavior. Conscious efforts by wives and husbands to improve their future well-being continue to have a major effect on their personal decisions regarding childbearing. Although private organizations like Planned Parenthood, and various governmental policies, have made public discussion of birth control more acceptable than ever before, there is little evidence that this has had any great influence on the decisions of individual Americans. Margaret Sanger's successes in getting official endorsement of the birth control movement from such "influential" groups as clergy, lawyers, and doctors came in the late 1930s, just after Americans decided to have more children.

Surveys of Americans' opinions on ideal family sizes since the mid-1930s indicate that preferences and performance have been in close accord over the last forty years. The example of white women demonstrates this clearly. In 1936, white women thought that three to four children would be ideal 57 percent of the time; by 1957, at the peak of the baby boom, 73 percent preferred families of that size; the proportion wanting such "large" families had fallen to 41 percent by 1972. Many of the remaining women thought 1 or 2 children would be ideal. Through this entire period, no more than 14 percent (in 1945) thought five or more children desirable. In preference, as in practice, Americans have become remarkably devoted to smaller families.[33]

There is one notable difference between actual and preferred childbearing. It is a rare American, male or female, who sees (or at least admits to seeing) childlessness as the ideal married state. Most surveys show no more than 1 percent of adults as preferring no children, even though the actual proportions without children have varied from 7 to 20 percent. Marriage still implies the goal of children, even though biological and economic difficulties may force other decisions.

Control over childbearing was well established by 1920, but the means by which it has been practiced have continued to evolve. During the last fifty years, more and more Americans have become family "planners," who control *when* as well as *how many* children they will have; fewer are simply family "limiters," for whom size alone is the only matter of consequence. In view of the unpleasant and unreliable techniques available to earlier generations, it is easy to see why technological improvements in birth control have been enthusiastically welcomed. The years immediately after World War I saw the widespread adoption of male condoms as contraceptive devices. In the 1930s, over 300 million condoms were manufactured in the United States each year. By 1933-1934, they were the first choice of about one fourth of all couples practicing birth control.[34] Since 1960, the birth control pill, intrauterine devices, and sterilization have all been widely adopted. Abortion has become more public in recent years, but whether it is more common is another question.[35]

New forms of birth control had little to do with the actual revolution in fertility; nevertheless, they have been important.[36] They have significantly reduced anxieties over possible contraceptive failure for many people. They have also offered many women a chance to control their own bodies in relatively pleasant ways. The appeal of the condom was that it was both safer and more pleasant to use than many late nineteenth-century tech-

niques; but it also depended upon male cooperation. Technological improvements of the past two decades have returned birth
control to women in much improved forms. Finally, by making
birth control convenient and comfortable, more Americans have
been freed to explore the full range of their sexuality without
concern for reproduction. Previous techniques and strong
motives allowed earlier Americans to establish control over the
biology of sex. New devices enabled recent generations to
explore the emotional and psychological side of sex.

Curiously, Americans have been much more comfortable with
private decisions to limit births than with some of the public
aspects of those choices. Obvious inconsistencies between private practice and public policy have only recently been eliminated. Until the 1966 Supreme Court decision of *Griswold* v.
Connecticut ruled the practice unconstitutional, various states offi-
cially prohibited the sale of contraceptives. The Comstock Act of
1873, which made dissemination of information on contraception a federal offense, was amended only in 1970. Two years
later, the Supreme Court declared that unmarried individuals
could have equal access to birth control advice and devices as
married people. Public ambiguity toward birth control is also
evident from the fact that it has been advocated as the solution to
many social problems, and opposed as a form of imperialism or
genocide. Birth control is almost universally accepted as a means
to improve one's future, and the future of one's children. But
when it is used to free the young from the consequences of
sexual activity, or to lessen the control of parents over children,
or husbands over wives, birth control can still generate opposition from those who fear overt sexuality, and who equate certain
types of sex with sin. And sin, for many, requires punishment,
rather than understanding. For birth control, the ends continue
to condemn or justify the means.

It is difficult to envision future generations of Americans
willingly abandoning any of the control over childbearing and
mortality they have so recently attained. Nor is it likely they will
give up the right to move where and when they want. But it is
equally difficult to anticipate how twentieth-century men and
women will exercise the control they have over their own lives,
and what the sum of all their decisions will mean for society. It is

possible, however, to examine what the choices made since 1920 have meant to American families.

Notes

1. Chart 7 continues the information presented earlier in Charts 2 and 3, pp. 101 and 105.

2. In addition to specific census volumes, there are three valuable sources of data for twentieth-century American population patterns: U.S. Bureau of the Census, *Historical Statistics of the United States, Colonial Times to 1957* (Washington, 1960); U.S. Bureau of the Census, *Statistical Abstract of the United States* (Washington, annual); Irene B. Taeuber and Conrad Taeuber, *People of the United States in the 20th Century* (Washington, 1971). I have used the *Statistical Abstract* for 1977 here. Readers should be aware that serial data are occasionally revised from one volume to another.

3. Richard Irwin, "Changing Patterns of American Immigration," *International Migration Review* 6 (1972): 18–31.

4. Donald Fleming and Bernard Bailyn, eds., *The Intellectual Migration: Europe and America, 1930–1960* (Cambridge, Mass., 1969); Judith Fortney, "International Migration of Professionals," *Population Studies* 24 (1970): 217–32.

5. John Higham, *Strangers in the Land: Patterns of American Nativism 1860–1925* (New York, 1965); Maldwyn A. Jones, *American Immigration* (Chicago, 1960), pp. 247–307.

6. Charles B. Keely, "Effects of the Immigration Act of 1965 on Selected Population Characteristics of Immigrants to the United States," *Demography* 8 (1971): 157–69.

7. Ellen P. Kraly, "Limits in the Land of the Free," *American Demographics* 2 (March, 1980): pp. 14–21 offer a brief history and comments on revisions to the law passed in 1978.

8. In addition to data in the 1970 census volumes, *see* Irene B. Taeuber, "The Changing Distribution of the Population of the United States in the Twentieth Century," in Commission on Population Growth and the American Future, *Population, Distribution, and Policy* (Washington, 1972), pp. 29–107.

9. Reynolds Farley, "The Urbanization of Negroes in the United States," *Journal of Social History* 1 (1967): 241–58; Florette Henri, *Black Migration: Movement North, 1900–1920* (Garden City, N.Y. 1976).

10. Ruth P. Vickers, "Japanese-American Relocation," *Alabama Historical Quarterly* 10 (1951): 168–76.

11. Neil Betten and Raymond A. Mohl, "From Discrimination to Repatriation: Mexican Life in Gary, Indiana During the Great Depression," *Pacific Historical Review* 42 (1973): 370–88.

12. Jane R. Wilkie, "The United States Population by Race and Urban-Rural Residence 1790–1860: Reference Tables," *Demography* 13 (1976): 139–48.

13. Taeuber, "Changing Distribution," pp. 60–94; Warren S. Thompson and P. K. Whelpton, *Population Trends in the United States* (New York, 1933), pp. 24–26.

14. Herbert J. Gans, *The Levittowners: Ways of Life and Politics in a New Suburban Community* (New York, 1967); A. Speare, Jr., "Home Ownership, Life Cycle Stage, and Residential Mobility," *Demography* 7 (1970): 449–58.

15. Reynolds Farley, "Residential Segregation in Urbanized Areas of the United States in 1970: An Analysis of Social Class and Racial Differences," *Demography* 14 (1977): 497–518.

16. Louis H. Masotti and Jeffrey K. Hadden, eds., *Suburbia in Transition* (New York, 1974).

17. S.L.N. Rao, "On Long-Term Mortality Trends in the United States, 1850–1968," *Demography* 10 (1973): 405–20. The most recent figures are always printed in the current edition of the *Statistical Abstract of the United States.*

18. Taeuber and Taeuber, *People of the United States*, p. 504; Population Reference Bureau, "Major Causes of Death in the United States, 1900–1975," factsheet, April, 1977.

19. Merrill K. Bennett and Rosamond H. Pierce, "Change in the American National Diet, 1879–1959," *Food Research Institute Studies* 2 (1961): 95–119; Milton I. Roemer and Barbara Faulkner, "The Development of Public Health Services in a Rural County: 1838–1949," *Journal of the History of Medicine and Allied Sciences* 6 (1951): 22–43.

20. James H. Young, *The Medical Messiahs: A Social History of Health Quackery in Twentieth-Century America* (Princeton, N.J., 1967).

21. William Dusenberry, "Foot and Mouth Disease in Mexico, 1946–1951," *Agricultural History* 29 (1955): 82–90.

22. *Statistical Abstract, 1977*, p. 94.

23. Young, *Medical Messiahs.*

24. Elisabeth Kubler-Ross, *On Death and Dying* (New York, 1969); Thomas Powers, "Learning to Die," *Harper's Magazine* 242 (June, 1971): 72–80; Jessica Mitford, *The American Way of Death* (New York, 1978).

25. James H. Jones, *Bad Blood: The Tuskegee Syphilis Experiment* (New York, 1981).

26. *Ms.* 4 (November, 1975):26–35.

27. Kingsley Davis, "The American Family in Relation to Demographic Change," in Commission on Population Growth and the American Future, *Demographic and Social Aspects of Population Growth* (Washington, 1972), pp. 242–46; Paul C. Glick and A. J. Norton, "Marrying, Divorcing, and Living Together in the U.S. Today," *Population Bulletin* 32, no. 5 (1977); C. Hirschman and J. Matra, "A New Look at the Marriage Market and Nuptiality Rates, 1915–1958," *Demography* 8 (1971): 549–69.

28. Davis, "American Family," p. 256.

29. Ansley J. Coale and Melvin Zelnik, *New Estimates of Fertility and Population in the United States* (Princeton, N.J., 1963), pp. 21–24; *Statistical Abstract, 1977,* p. 56.

30. Richard Easterlin, *The American Baby Boom in Historical Perspective* (New York, 1962); Peter H. Lindert, *Fertility and Scarcity in America* (Princeton, N.J., 1978).

31. U.S. Bureau of the Census, *1970 Census of Population,* Subject Report PC (2)-3A, "Women By Number of Children Ever Born," p. 8; Frederick S. Crum, "The Decadence of the Native American Stock: A Statistical Study of Genealogical Records," *American Statistical Association Journal* 14 (1916–1917): 215–22.

32. *Statistical Abstract, 1977,* p. 61.

33. Judith Blake, "Can We Believe Recent Data on Birth Expectations in the United States?" *Demography* 11 (1974): 25–44.

34. Norman E. Himes, *Medical Historical of Contraception* (New York, 1936), pp. 186, 337.

35. Leslie A. Westoff and Charles Westoff, *From Now to Zero: Fertility, Contraception and Abortion in America* (Boston, 1968); Charles Westoff and Norman B. Ryder, *The Contraceptive Revolution* (Princeton, N.J., 1977).

36. Linda Gordon, *Woman's Body, Woman's Right: A Social History of Birth Control in America* (New York, 1976); James Reed, *From Private Vice to Public Virtue: The Birth Control Movement and American Society since 1830* (New York, 1977).

9

THE MAKING OF MODERN
FAMILIES

Families of the mid-twentieth century are in the process of adjusting to demographic realities unique in human history. It is much too soon to tell whether they will eventually meet the needs of their members and their society better, worse, or much the same as families of the past. Families of the past were far from perfect, and many arrangements that made sense in 1800 would be ill-suited to current needs. Thus, to perceive major alterations in the rhythms of family life is accurate; to interpret those changes as decline is not.

In spite of anxieties generated by new and unfamiliar patterns, families have proved to be flexible and adaptable in the face of some of the most remarkable revolutions in human history. This capacity to adapt reflects more an enduring strength in families than any weakness that threatens the well-being of individuals or society. New demographic realities require new family arrangements, and those who wish to maintain families as they existed (or were thought to exist) in the past are guilty of intervening to create a world as artificial as that prescribed by reformers certain of what is necessary to perfect the families of the future.

It is necessary to have a full understanding of current patterns of birth, death, marriage, and migration before predicting what forms of family life will be most appropriate for future generations. However, given the duration of the debate on the family, and the variety of options that have been tried, new standards will probably emerge from practices already in existence. Likewise, family life, in one form or another, will survive as a central part of most individuals' existence, if only because those who have a preference to mate produce the next generations.

Although what people expect of their families is still far from certain, it is clear that the demographic revolutions of the nineteenth century have enhanced the similarity of individuals' actual experiences within their families in the twentieth century. Thus, by first exploring various aspects of family structures, it is possible to place in context the ongoing experiments and debates through which the meaning of contemporary family life adjusts to the underlying demographic realities.

The full extent of the revolution in childbearing that occurred after 1800 is evident in Table 5. This table demonstrates the maximum impact of the establishment of fertility control by contrasting a group of wives married before 1700, whose families were among the largest observed in early America, to white wives born between 1906 and 1910. The latter women have had the fewest children over the *entire* span of their childbearing years of any group in American history. Quaker wives of the eighteenth and early nineteenth centuries have been included since they were among the first women to show signs of deliberately limiting births.

From the perspective of parents, the importance of birth control lies in the dramatic shift in the proportions of wives who had five or less, or ten or more, children. About one of every four wives of the seventeenth and early eighteenth centuries had at least ten children; a similar proportion had five or less. In contrast, less than two of every hundred white wives born between 1906 and 1910 had ten or more children; over nine out of ten had five or fewer babies. The proportion of wives who bore and raised more than three children fell from about nine out of ten, to about two out of ten. The experience of most American wives and their husbands falls somewhere in between these extremes. But that does not alter the fact that twentieth-century couples in general have significantly fewer children to care for than their eighteenth-century counterparts. Whether this has reduced the overall burden of child care, or has merely altered the time and effort devoted to any one child, is not certain.

Table 5 Comparisons of Family Size as Experienced by Adults and
   Children (Whites only)

Number of Children	Crum's Study of 17th- and 18th- Century Wives		18th- and 19th- Century Quaker Wives		Wives Born 1906-1910	
	% Wives Having	% Children Living in Families of	% Wives Having	% Children Living in Families of	% Wives Having	% Children Living in Families of
3 or less	10.9	2.6	29.9	8.5	78.7	48.8
5 or less	25.4	11.9	48.3	23.8	92.0	73.7
8 or less	64.1	49.3	77.4	59.6	97.4	90.5
10 or more	24.3	36.5	14.8	28.1	1.8	6.6
12 or more	6.9	11.9	4.9	10.0	0.5	2.6
Median borne by wives	8	—	6	—	2	—
Median number of siblings	—	9	—	8	—	4

SOURCES: U.S. Bureau of the Census, *1970 Census of Population*, Subject Report PC(2)-3A, "Women By Number of Children Ever Born," p. 8; Frederick S. Crum, "The Decadence of the Native American Stock: A Statistical Study of Genealogical Records," *American Statistical Association Journal* 14 (1916–1917): 215–22; Robert V. Wells, "Family Size and Fertility Control in Eighteenth-Century America: A Study of Quaker Families," *Population Studies* 25 (1971): 75.

Children were also affected by their parents' decisions to have fewer offspring, but in a somewhat different fashion. As Table 5 shows, only 11.9 percent of the children of the first group of wives grew up in families of five or fewer children, including themselves. Three times as many boys and girls were raised by parents who had to manage ten or more children. Children of the twentieth-century wives frequently had quite different experiences. Almost half lived in families with no more than three children. Only 6.6 percent shared a home with nine other sisters and brothers.

Precisely what this change has meant for children is uncertain; at least one possibility deserves mention. In the twentieth century, children whose mothers have relatively few pregnancies frequently are both healthier than boys and girls from large families, and perform better in school and on the job. If this was true in the past, then children have grown into healthier and more capable adults over the past two centuries, at least partly because their parents altered the physical and psychological burdens of childrearing by having fewer babies.

The demographic revolutions eventually produced impressive changes in the day-to-day living arrangement Americans now experience. Surprisingly, the demographic revolutions of the nineteenth century had relatively little effect on average household size at the time—it declined by less than one person between 1790 and 1900. The most important statistical and social change during this period came with the end of slavery, as black families emerged from the control of white-dominated households. Since 1900, however, the average number of persons per household has decreased noticeably, from 4.8 in 1900 to 2.9 in 1976 (see Table 4, p. 151). The latter figure is about half that of an average household in 1790. One of the most obvious reasons for today's smaller households is that more Americans live alone than ever before. As recently as 1900, single individuals accounted for only 5.1 percent of all households, only slightly more than in 1790. In 1976, the proportion of households of only one person is four times greater (20.6 percent) than at the start of the century. Conversely, large households, with five or more individuals, have dropped from 62.9 to 15.9 percent of the total. Once again, the major change occurred after 1900. Much of this decline can be traced to longer life and smaller families, but some of it undoubtedly reflects preferences related to the emphasis on individual autonomy associated with the modern personality, and affluence, which allows the expression of those preferences. As a result, adults who once boarded with a family or lived in rooming houses now prefer and are able to live alone.

The meaning of this change for individual Americans must not be overstated. One household with five people contains as many individuals as five households with only one resident each. Thus, although households with only one person are more common than those with five or more people, the proportion of all Americans who live alone is only 7.1 percent, whereas 32.3 percent of people share their home with at least four others. Since several smaller housholds often emerge from one larger unit, either by death, divorce, or the maturing of children, it is fair to say that most Americans, at some time in their lives, still live in relatively large households. However, today "large" would mean five or more persons; two centuries ago it meant almost twice that size, since 15.6 percent of the households in 1790 had nine or more members.

An increase in the proportion of households headed by women marks another common characteristic of daily living arrangements that has emerged in this century. Changes in divorce, remarriage, the sex ratio, the differences between male and female life expectancy, and the willingness of young women to leave home, have recently produced a sharp increase in the proportion of households headed by women, from 14.9 percent in 1950, to 24.2 percent in 1976. Both black and white American women share this tendency, though the pattern is still more common among the former than the latter.

The quantity and quality of available housing may be as important as household size in determining how the daily cycle of life affects any individual. As a result of rising standards of living, better construction techniques, and domestic technology, homes today are warmer, cleaner, and safer places in which to live than those of the past. In addition, there is much more space available to each member of the family. Recall that in Germantown, Pennsylvania, in the later eighteenth century, an average household of five people shared five hundred square feet of floor space. By the 1970s, household size had been cut in half, and the space available had at least doubled.[1] In two hundred years, Americans went from a situation in which there were often two persons per room, to living arrangements in which there are two rooms per person. Americans now often carry on the various aspects of daily life in separate rooms specifically designed for only one or two activities. They also have greater privacy and personal independence available within the home.[2] Smaller families may have increased the amount of potential contact between any two members, but larger homes have made it possible for individuals to control the extent of that contact to some degree, by the simple act of withdrawing to a different part of the home.

Changes in the life cycles of American families produced by the demographic revolutions of the past two centuries have further altered the meaning of family life. Although there is remarkable similarity between the ages at which young women and men formed families and had their first child in the eighteenth and twentieth centuries, reduced childbearing has dramatically altered much of the rest of the family cycle. Before 1800, a couple could expect to spend the better part of twenty years having children. By the middle of the twentieth century, it was rare for a woman and her husband to add new members to their family for more than nine or ten years. Because childbearing ended earlier in a marriage, so too did childrearing. In early America, forty years might pass between the birth of the first child and the marriage of the last; today the amount of time spent raising a family is closer to thirty years.[3]

Higher life expectancy also had its effect on the meaning of family living. In eighteenth-century America, couples living in the most favorable environments might expect thirty years of marriage, at best. Most unions were broken by death almost ten years before the last children were gone. Today, marriages last over forty years on average (unless ended voluntarily by divorce). A husband and wife can expect to live together more than a dozen years after their children leave home. Equally important, life expectancy has increased so much that the death of a spouse and a prolonged period of old age alone is now a reality for many Americans, especially women. Adult companionship has joined reproduction as a central part of family life. Quite possibly, this is why divorce and remarriage have become so prominent a part of contemporary American family life.

In practice, variations in family size and mortality meant that many early-American couples never experienced the family patterns that the average life cycle would have led them to expect. Today, more and more couples can follow the complete cycle if they choose, because of the convergence in patterns of childbearing and life expectancy that has occurred since 1920. Among native-born Massachusetts women, about half those born in 1830 never even formed a family, primarily because they died before marrying; eight out of every ten women born in 1920 could expect to marry. Of the women born in 1830, only one-fifth could expect to complete the family cycle with their husbands still alive; for the women born ninety years later, the corresponding figure was almost three-fifths. Of course, rising divorce rates have meant that many of these women will not live through the complete family cycle, but by choice rather than chance.[4]

More predictable life cycles, arising from less frequent births and deaths, mean fewer adjustments to new living arrangements for both parents and children. Ties between parents and children, or brothers and sisters, last longer, and because there are fewer competing relationships, may be stronger as well. Whether this is better or worse than in the past obviously depends on whether love or hostility dominates. But unless the modern concern for individual development and personal dignity has failed miserably in practice, American families may be pleasanter to live in now than in the past.

Obviously, all family members have been affected by new patterns in the life cycle, but women have probably felt the changes more than their husbands or children. Clearly, they benefit most from fewer pregnancies and fewer children for whom to care. Since 1920, women have entered the public work force in increasing numbers.[5] Frequently a woman's decision to work is closely related to the family cycle, especially the presence or absence of small children. But women often take jobs when a "life cycle squeeze" occurs, during which expenses associated with different stages of the family cycle do not match the ebb and flow of their husbands' earnings.[6] In this instance, the move from rural, agricultural, to urban, industrial environments has interacted with demographic change to bring new meaning to family life cycles.

Kinship is the aspect of family structure in which it is hardest to trace the impact of the demographic revolutions. On the one hand, kinship has been simplified as smaller families and longer life both reduced the total number of relatives an individual might have, and increased the duration (and probably the intensity) of many of the separate relationships. On the other hand, divorce and remarriage are creating complex networks of kin that may soon rival those found in the early Chesapeake.

As individuals move around the country, direct daily contacts with relatives are hard to maintain. Yet in times of personal crisis, kinship still plays an important role in American life. Births, marriages, and deaths often reunite families, at least temporarily. Furthermore, the time it takes to communicate by telephone or airplane is now so short that it is difficult to compare the impact of physical separation in 1790 and today. Time taken to communicate, rather than distance, is the true measure of separation for families. The telephone makes it possible to seek advice from a parent or sister a continent away faster than one can walk to the next-door neighbors'. It is evident that the demographic revolutions altered the nature of kinship, but what that has meant in the practical sense of whom we consider to be our relatives, and what forms of support we expect from them, has yet to be determined.

Because of the magnitude of change entailed in the demographic transformations in Americans' lives, and the fact that many attitudes regarding families were centuries old when the change began, much of the nineteenth-century debate on the family has continued to the present. Century-old issues such as divorce, abortion, birth control, and women's rights still generate fears about American families and America's future. To these older concerns have been added fears that automobiles, television, movies, sex education in schools, and homosexual rights all undermine the authority of families and society, and provide too much choice for sexual expression for individuals.

As in the nineteenth century, the debate involves individuals ranging from supporters of "the classical family of western nostalgia" to those who wish to overturn the family almost entirely.[7] One of the earliest twentieth-century innovators was Judge Benjamin Lindsey of Colorado, who advocated companionate marriage stressing adult needs rather than children or intergenerational concerns. Lindsey argued that if no children were born to a couple, they should be able to live together as long as they wished, and then separate by mutual consent with a minimum of fuss.[8] The social upheavals of the 1960s and early 1970s produced experiments in communal families and complex living arrangements similar to some of the utopian approaches of the nineteenth century, although virtually no one recently has argued that celibacy and human perfection are closely linked.

The harshest critics of family life are part of the current women's movement; a few of the most radical feminists have suggested that marriage and families ought to be abolished as oppressive carryovers from a patriarchal past.[9]

Many supporters of more traditional forms of family life recognize that improvements can be made in relations between husbands and wives, or parents and children. Churches sponsor advertisements on radio and television in favor of loving, caring families; Planned Parenthood and Right-to-Life chapters are both committed to strong families, no matter how much they may differ over how to attain their goal; public schools include courses on how to achieve a good family life; and on the private level, many women and men are attempting to work out new relationships regarding domestic and public responsibilities within the context of their families.

As the debate has continued, more and more experts have emerged to study and diagnose family ills, and advocate household remedies. Specialists on the family first appeared in the late nineteenth century, with regard to care for dependent children. Since that time, the numbers of social workers, marriage counselors, and academics who have established careers and professional reputations as students of families have increased greatly. These people offer guidance on everything from how to manage a budget to how to manage in bed.

The professionalization of the debate on the family has eliminated (or at least reduced) some of the worst excesses of earlier arguments by providing information upon which to build opinions. But facts have often confused as much as clarified. Anthropologists such as Margaret Mead have demonstrated that family arrangements are primarily the result of cultural preferences.[10] They are not ordained by God or genetics, or made holy by Saint Paul or Saint Sigmund. Similarly, Alfred Kinsey's famous reports on sexual behavior documented the striking inconsistencies between Americans' actions regarding masturbation, virginity, and marital fidelity, and their publicly expressed attitudes.[11]

Often these studies have been far more radical attacks on the ideal family than any utopian recommendations. Because there is neither reputation nor money to be made in studying well-organized, smoothly functioning families, most professionals have focused on families that in one way or another can be defined as in trouble, in the process encouraging fears that Americans' family life needs help if it is to be saved. Equally important, professionals have made it clear that, within the limits defined by the demographic realities of the day, we have only our own preferences to guide us in the way we organize our families. The search for *the* ideal or normal family is as futile as the quest for the Holy Grail or El Dorado. As twentieth-century Americans realize this, and accept the fact that only *families*, not *the* family exist, individual choice and control may enhance variety, unless a limited range of family forms clearly demonstrate their superiority for their individual members and society.

Although ardent defenders of the perfect families of the past are fewer in number now than in the nineteenth century, they still exist. Until recently, women's magazines frequently took the conservative side of the debate. For example, in the 1950s, both the *Ladies Home Journal* and *Good Housekeeping* put a strong emphasis on family, togetherness, and the maintenance of clear age and sex roles.

Curiously, some of today's most conservative participants have adapted radical remedies to their own ends. Advocates of "fascinating womanhood" desire to keep women and men in their proper places, but they consciously exploit sexuality to achieve their goal in ways that would have shocked nineteenth-century conservatives, who feared civilization would collapse if women did not maintain an asexual purity in the face of their husbands' animal lusts.[12] To encourage such behavior would have been unthinkable to previous generations. On the other hand, advocates of parents' rights to decide on the proper form of medical care for their children are defending traditions of parental authority and free choice of health care options that would have been acceptable to many mid nineteenth-century Americans. Similarly, the feminine mystique identified by Betty Friedan had extensive roots in the nineteenth century.[13]

The debate on the future of American families in the twentieth century has resolved a few issues. It is apparent from the fact that the vast majority of Americans will marry and have children, that Americans are still strongly committed to family life. Their families might seen unfamiliar and even shocking to nineteenth-

century men and women, but they are still far from a society
based on unattached individuals. We may need reassurance from
newspaper columns like "Dear Abby" or "Ann Landers," or from
family professionals, that divorce, living together without marrying, enjoying sex, and any number of other choices regarding
family life are both normal and normally perplexing, but family
life as an ideal remains strong. In addition, Americans almost
universally perceive of birth control as acceptable practice. Since
the 1930s, they have limited both preferred and actual family
sizes to a remarkably narrow range.

Concensus regarding stages by which children become adults
seems also to have appeared in recent decades. Both lower fertility and longer life made it possible, but not necessary, for more
individuals to share a similar life cycle. Hence, it is interesting
that *choices* involved in becoming an adult have been more standard. Between 1880 and 1970, an increasing proportion of all
young men *and women* entered and left school, took jobs, left
home, married, and established their own households. Not only
have more youth shared all these transitions into adulthood and
family life, but they have done so over a shorter span of their
lives. In 1880, many of these transitions occurred in sequence;
today they frequently overlap, suggesting that children are
expected to become adults within a fairly narrow age range.[14]

The compression of the transition to adulthood, and the rapid
assumption of family responsibilities require remarkable read-
justments to complex new living patterns in a short span of time.
Interestingly, the children who must make these adjustments are
the same ones whose family experience has been the most stable
as they grew up, because of low levels of childbearing and death.
Eighteenth-century individuals faced an uncertain life as children until they married and began the dominant task of rearing
the next generation; today it is the children whose lives are most
predictable, and adults who face the uncertainties, although in
this century uncertainties are the product of choice and individual expression rather than social and biological forces.

A few of the issues in the twentieth-century debate on American families are either new, or have evolved significantly from
the way they were first posed in the nineteenth century. Child-

rearing is one area where important new ideas have emerged. A careful reading of the manuals and guides used by contemporary American parents in raising their children shows some subtle but important change from the start of the century. In 1920, guides advocated individual development for children, but in the context of self-discipline and control, to meet the demands of a competitive world. These themes are still present, but to them has been added a recognition that each child can and ought to express her or his individuality. The idea that children should "find" themselves would have struck earlier participants in the debate as dangerously permissive. They were more interested that children "place" themselves in society, preferably as high up the ladder as possible.

Defenders of a family style that is clearer in recall than in reality have often accused Dr. Benjamin Spock of being the man most responsible for distorting the widespread goal of individual achievement into the more divisive aim of individual expression. As anyone who has read Spock carefully knows, such blame is unfair, for much of his advice is in the older tradition. It is merely tempered by a recognition that children develop at different speeds, and so he seeks to reassure parents that they are not failures if their daughters and sons progress more slowly than their neighbors' children.[15] Much more typical of the new emphasis on individuality is A. S. Neill's *Summerhill*, a British book on childrearing and education that has received widespread, and occasionally hostile, attention in this country.[16]

As in the nineteenth century, general attitudes about society and child care have influenced institutional arrangements for care for dependent children. The growth of private and public agencies with the power to intervene in the life of separate families to protect the interest and well-being of children marks one of the most significant changes. Their actions range from providing financial aid to parents, to keep their families together, to the removal of children from the control of parents whose actions threaten their sons' and daughters' safety and even survival. Recent interest in child (and spouse) abuse in America reflects more the recognition that individuals must occasionally be protected from their families than any widespread increase in violence within homes.

Even foster care and adoption have been affected by the increased concern for children's needs. First, social service agencies recognized that private homes were better places for children to grow in than orphanages. Then, as the needs of children became more central, agencies gave up trying to find appropriate children for prospective parents and began to look for appropriate parents for children in need of families. This latter shift has resulted in a greater willingness to allow adoptions across racial and religious lines, and by single persons.[17] Prospective parents must go through a detailed scrutiny before they can adopt a child, which indicates the state is far more demanding of parents than is Mother Nature. The state is concerned with the future of the individual; nature is only interested in the survival of the species.

Between 1770 and 1920, the focus of family life changed from an emphasis on adult needs and responsibilities, to stressing the development of children. With smaller families and more stable arrangements since 1920, families have become both adult and child centered. The needs of all members of a family are recognized, in keeping with the modern emphasis on individual development.

The return to family patterns that give greater recognition to adult needs is apparent in several recent trends. One of the most interesting is the tendency of adults to view children as part of the total package of products that grown-ups purchase for their pleasure. So far, most Americans have continued to feel that the benefits of childrearing are worth the high cost, estimated to exceed $64,000 per child in 1977.[18] But, it would be easy for such attitudes to change quickly, and children could eventually become deferrable, and eventually expendable, in favor of other consumer goods. Such overtly rational and subjective choices are not conducive to the prediction of general social patterns.

As companionship within marriage became an important part of family life, the enjoyment of sexual relations between adults became of greater concern. Birth control techniques that are both pleasant and reliable, and the almost universal acceptance of the ethos of family planning, have encouraged sexual activity quite apart from reproduction. Occasionally adults have intercourse to conceive, but more often it is for pleasure, companionship, and individual fulfillment. Books such as *The Joy of Sex* or *The Hite Report*, and professionals like Masters and Johnson, offer advice to American adults on how to get the most out of their sex life.[19] Only a few of the most radical participants of the debate in the nineteenth century would have viewed this with approval.

Sexuality is only one part of adult development that has received attention in recent years. Both academic and popular psychologists have demonstrated that the development of personality does not stop at age twenty-one. They argue adults can and ought to continue to grow and expand as human beings. Some of this growth will occur within the family, but some of it can best happen outside that context. Women especially have profited by this new emphasis, for it provides them with both the expectation and justification of establishing their identities as persons who are more than parents. This is particularly beneficial as declining fertility and longer life expectancy have reduced the proportion of adult life devoted to parenting.[20]

It is likely that the psychology of adult development emerged in response to new demographic realities that have created new meanings and opportunities for the adult years of life. In the eighteenth century, adults' futures could easily be anticipated within the uncertainties of birth and death; today, control over the basic rhythms of life offers options to adults about what to do with their lives for which there are few precedents. The mid-life crisis which has received considerable attention in recent years is a luxury available only in a world in which men and women can reflect on what they want to be, rather than concentrating on what they must do to survive.

Concern over the role of old men and women in the family is so recent an addition to the debate that specialists have dominated discussion almost from the first realization that geriatrics was a subject needing study.[21] As with so many other parts of the debate, basic demographic shifts made the topic important. In 1880, only 3.4 percent of all Americans had reached the age of sixty-five. By 1920, the proportion of older Americans had risen slightly, to 4.7 percent of the total. In 1970, the census recorded 9.9 percent of all men and women as at least sixty-five years old. Since the population grew fourfold during those ninety years, the actual number of older Americans increased from 1.7 to 20.1 million between 1880 and 1970.[22]

Until the end of the nineteenth century, it was rare for three generations to live in the same household for more than a brief span of years. High death rates, large numbers of brothers and sisters, and frequent migration meant that many children never had to be concerned with the well-being of aging parents. However, when the need did arise, elderly men and women were generally cared for by their families. But as the demographic revolutions had their effects, more and more parents and children could anticipate that they would at some time in their lives find the early relationship of dependency reversed. As this occurred, the place of older persons in the family became a matter of general concern.

As a result, after 1920 several questions that had never before been raised entered the debate on the family. The most basic of these are simple: What does it mean to be old? Is "old" an age, like fifty or seventy-five or eighty? Is it a physical or psychological state? Is it a stage in the life cycle with appropriate transitions and roles? The answers have been far from clear. In practice, the ill health that accompanied lower levels of life expectancy in the past combined with pension plans and mandatory retirement ages to define people as old once they reached somewhere between sixty and seventy years of age. Americans in the mid twentieth century became eligible for old-age assistance at sixty-five, only five years above the age at which men in the eighteenth century were relieved of militia duty, and sometimes taxes. With better health and longer lives this working definition of old age has come under attack. The grandparent role has proved ill-defined and unsatisfactory for many adults who preferred to go on working. Similarly, dependency on one's children has had little appeal. As a result of attacks on the accepted definition from those who have reached sixty-five but do not feel themselves to be different people, the meaning of "old" is perhaps less certain now than it has been in the past half century.

A major source of confusion is that the onset of physical infirmity is no longer clearly linked to a relatively narrow range of ages. Although families are most vitally concerned with problems originating in infirmity, the debate is often phrased in terms of the increasingly irrelevant concept of age. Virtually everyone recognizes that most people of advanced age eventually reach a point when they need physical assistance. In the past, this stage was often brief, and most families could meet the needs of the infirm from within. Today, medical care can prolong infirmity (sometimes at considerable cost); children and parents have often been living apart for a number of years when a crisis strikes; and the emphasis on individual autonomy has sharply reduced the sense of family obligations. Thus, the second major question raised by the emergence of the "old age" problem is: Who is responsible for the care of the infirm in our society? Is it families? The state? Or, the individuals themselves? The answers so far are ambiguous; all three solutions have been tried, but none has achieved almost universal acceptance. Whether Americans will continue to see the needs of the infirm as a family matter, or of concern only to individuals and the state, is at present unclear. It will, however, be a central part of the debate on the family for the foreseeable future.

Relationships within families and between families and other parts of twentieth-century society are best understood by reference to changes that have occurred since the eighteenth century. In early America, roles within the family were determined primarily by age, sex, and servitude. Since servitude has all but disappeared from twentieth-century family life, the master-servant relationship is of no concern here. Age and sex continue to influence an individual's experiences with family life, but in ways that differ from those of two centuries ago. Many of these changes have been made possible, and occasionally necessary, by the demographic revolutions.

In early America, age roles were clearly defined and involved a high degree of subordination on the part of the young. Between 1800 and the present, age roles have blurred somewhat, and the degree of subordination expected has been reduced. The blurring of age roles occurred as Americans distinguished more stages in the life cycle. In early America, individuals were divided into young children (under seven), adults, and, occasionally, "superannuated" persons. Anyone who did not fit easily into one of these categories was in the uncomfortable position of not knowing his or her responsibilities and rights. Today we distinguish, or at least think we can, infants, preschoolers, children, adolescents, young adults, the middle aged, "golden" agers, and the senile. As a result, the contrasts between one stage in the life cycle and those immediately before and after have become less striking. In the past, many children died before they could exercise the authority that came with being an adult, but today most Americans will survive long enough to experience most of the family roles attained by advancing years.

Although age is still closely related to the division of power within the family, the concern for individual rights has altered obligations between various family members. In the course of two hundred years, the difference in privileges of the most and least powerful persons in a family has been significantly reduced. Power based on age has been circumscribed but not eliminated. It is difficult to envision parents today adopting the practice of some early Americans, of placing their children in the homes of relatives or friends out of fear that they might love their own children too much to discipline them effectively.

Roles based on sex have also been redefined since the end of the eighteenth century, as is apparent in the treatment of sons and daughters. In the middle of the twentieth century, both sons and daughters receive formal education outside the home, and both frequently leave home and take jobs before marrying. Some families still offer more encouragement to their sons to pursue their education and get a high status job. But the contrast between current opportunities families provide daughters, and the restrictions imposed in the seventeenth and eighteenth centuries makes it clear that privileges which came from being a male child are disappearing, though the rate of change may displease some as being too slow or too fast.

The appropriate sex roles of adults has also received considerable attention in recent years.[23] Part of the debate has considered whether men and women should have equal access to all the roles in our society. Part of it has been concerned with who exercises power within the family, and for what ends. In general, the trend has been toward greater equality between husbands and wives, both in making decisions and sharing various family tasks. The idea of a woman's sphere and a man's sphere within the family is disappearing. Nonetheless, the remaining advantages still accrue to the men, and conservative thinkers oppose further elimination of sex roles. The uncertainties of the present continue to produce anxieties about the future that call forth a reverence of the past. Age and sex roles are important primarily because they determine who shall exercise power within families. In the past, adult males were almost unchallenged in their authority. Today the privileges and responsibilities that once belonged to adult males are more and more often shared.

The question of *who* exercises power is important, but it is only one dimension of how power is used within families. It is also important to consider *how* power is exercised (that is, both the quantity and quality of control), and, *for what purposes*. From earlier comments it is clear that the purposes for which power is exercised within families have shifted from subordinating individuals to the immediate needs of the family and society, to the enhancement of personal dignity and happiness for the individual members of a family, even at the cost of social stability.

But what about how power is exercised? Has the quantity and quality of control changed as dramatically over two centuries as the other dimensions of family power? What little evidence exists on this subject suggests a positive answer. A shift in the emphasis in family life from controlling individuals to enhancing individuality obviously reduces the potential for conflict and fosters encouragement rather than restrictions. In the eighteenth century, parents used an imposing array of physical, economic, religious, and psychological weapons to elicit obedient responses from their children. Contemporary parents make use of various techniques such as transactional analysis or parent effectiveness training that stress love and reason rather than force to persuade rather than coerce. In practice, earlier families may have been more loving than our discussion suggests; force is still present in family life. Nevertheless, the quality of life within families appears to have changed for the better as a result of new attitudes and practices in the exercise of domestic power.

The place of families within society as a whole has also changed significantly during the age of the demographic revolutions. In particular, modern families are much more limited and specialized in what is expected of them than those of the eighteenth century. Many of these changes are less obviously related to the demographic revolutions than were the shifts in structure and relationships within the family. However, they are connected, if only as separate manifestations of modern attitudes that stress specialization of institutions along with individual development.

At first glance, the tremendous growth of formal education from kindergarten through trade schools and postgraduate degree programs suggests that families have lost much of their responsibility for training the next generation. Adult education programs offer courses ranging from formal academic subjects to organic gardening, home buying, automobile repairs, and various ways to perfect one's personality. On close examination, however, it is apparent that families continue to play an important, and perhaps dominant, role in the education of children. Children are still acquainted with the basic form of their culture at home as parents transmit attitudes toward politics, economics, work, religion, other people, sex, death, honesty, and a wide range of other matters to the next generation. The abilities of children to use words and numbers quickly and easily, skills schools are designed to teach, are closely tied to how well their parents manage language and arithmetic. Public education has presented parents with an institution that can share the blame when their children fail, thus relieving them of some of the burden that the emphasis on individual development first placed on the shoulders of mothers and fathers in the early nineteenth century. On the other hand, most parents are willing to take full credit for the successes of their children, indicating that many Americans still understand the importance of families in educating the next generation.

The economic activities of families have also changed dramatically over two hundred years. In the eighteenth century, most production occurred in and around the home. Men, women, and children had different tasks, but they often worked within eyesight of other members of the family. As industrial and service occupations became more important in the nineteenth century, men at work were physically separated from their families. In the twentieth century, women have increasingly followed men out of the home and into public employment. Children, on the other hand, have found their needs and opportunities for work restricted by mandatory schooling laws, child-labor legislation, better wages for adults, and the fact that most residential neighborhoods today offer few tasks for small hands.

Consumption, also, has moved out of the home to some extent. Two of the fastest growing parts of the contemporary American economy are restaurants and recreation, both of which have strong family orientations as whole families dine out, go on vacations, ski, or see movies together. Airlines and railroads offer special fares for families travelling together. It is possible, however, to overstate the removal of consumption from the home, for households rather than individuals are the major consumers of large appliances, furniture, and similar forms of goods. Likewise, most Americans continue to expect parents to provide their children with a start in life. This may mean buying them a degree from a professional or trade school rather than a farm, but the purpose is basically the same.

The needs and wants of a family are often critical in determining who works outside the home. Most women who work today do so in order to supplement their husband's income, or because they are the head of the household. Personal development through a career is a very minor motive, at least in part because truly creative jobs for either women or men are relatively rare. Adult wages have risen enough since the late nineteenth and early twentieth centuries that children no longer must contribute income to ensure most families' economic survival, but household rather than individual income continues to be the principal factor shaping most people's standard of living.

Relations between families and the state have also undergone some significant transformations. The modern emphasis on individuals has resulted in the state interacting directly with all adults with regard to voting, and responsibilities before the law. In the eighteenth century, most Americans were content if suffrage extended to the heads of most households, a condition that was replaced by the expectation that all adults ought to vote. Before 1800, household heads exercised much of the police power of the state, controlling the members of their families with only occasional public support. In addition, households provided manpower for militia units or police patrols in times of crisis. Since about 1870, the state has shown an increased willingness to interpose itself between household heads and subordinates, sometimes to reinforce the power of the former, but often to protect the latter (be they women or children) from the overzealous exercise of authority. As part of this change, governments began to hire full-time police in order to enforce a wide range of laws directly on individual offenders.

The ability of powerful families to control access to public office has also eroded in the past two centuries. Families such as the Byrds, Kennedys, Goldwaters, Longs, and Rockefellers may have undue political influence, but compared to their eighteenth-century counterparts, their capacity to shape public policy has been diluted in a vast flood of individuals of modest background. Of course, the great increase in public positions, combined with smaller families, has contributed as much to the democratization of power as any deliberate assault on family influence.

The relationships between families and churches have shown the greatest continuity between the eighteenth century and the present. Churches continue to provide public support for family life, as religious groups sponsor advertisements on television and radio, and in newspapers and magazines, in support of close family ties. Recording births, marriages, or deaths in civil registers is insufficient to mark one of the major transitions in life, so many Americans continue to celebrate those events in religious ceremonies. Religious teachings continue to emphasize family order and responsibilities. Many of the most conservative participants in the debate on the family are members of religious groups such as Missouri Synod Lutherans, Mormons, Roman Catholics, Hasidic Jews, Southern Baptists, and Seventh-Day Adventists. Churches continue to draw their strength from the children of members, much as they did in earlier periods.

Obviously, some changes have occurred. Many Americans have only a tenuous relationship with a church. Nonreligious marriage chapels and funeral homes provide alternative places in which to mark a change in a basic rhythm of life.[24] Curiously, nonsectarian equivalents of baptism, confirmation, or circumcision to mark the birth of children have yet to emerge. Many churchgoers are willing to challenge the teachings of their sect regarding birth control and divorce—many churches have altered their positions on these and other matters in accord with the practices of their members. Nonetheless, contacts between families and churches have probably been less affected by the demographic revolutions, the debates on the family, and other related changes than any other relationships between families and other parts of society.

By and large, the roles families performed in the past have been either altered or eliminated with time. However, at least one important new burden has been added to the responsibilities of families. It was sufficient, in the eighteenth century, for families to work for the survival of their members and the incorporation of the next generation into society. Over the course of the nineteenth century, many Americans came to expect that families would provide a measure of "progress" for their members, although what exactly that meant was not clear. In the twentieth century, expectations of progress have evolved into the anticipation of present and future happiness to be derived from parents, children, or spouses.

Because happiness or even contentment are difficult to achieve and maintain over any prolonged period, many families "fail" to achieve what is expected of them. The addition of this new and unrealistic burden, combined with numerous other changes in what families do for their members, has led many to express unwarranted concern for the "decline" of American families. Certainly modern families are different from those of the past, but so are the demographic realities underlying basic family and social forms.

Notes

1. U.S. Bureau of the Census, *Statistical Abstract of the United States, 1976* (Washington, 1976), pp. 739, 744; U.S. Department of Housing and Urban Development, *Statistical Yearbook, 1975* (Washington, 1975), p. 174; Stephanie G. Wolf, *Urban Village: Population, Community, and Family Structure in Germantown, Pennsylvania, 1683–1800* (Princeton, N.J., 1976), p. 35.

2. For the lack of privacy in earlier times, *see* David Flaherty, *Privacy in Colonial New England* (Charlottesville, Va., 1972).

3. Robert V. Wells, "Demographic Change and the Life Cycle of American Families," *Journal of Interdisciplinary History* 2 (1971): 273–82.

4. Peter R. Uhlenberg, "A Study of Cohort Life Cycles: Cohorts of Native Born Massachusetts Women, 1830–1920," *Population Studies* 23 (1969): 407–20.

5. William H. Chafe, *The American Woman: Her Changing Social, Economic, and Political Role, 1920–1970* (New York, 1972), pp. 48–111, 151–254.

6. Valerie K. Oppenheimer, "The Life Cycle Squeeze: The Interaction of Men's Occupational and Family Life Cycles," *Demography* 11 (1974): 227–46.

7. This phrase appears in a discussion of ideal family types in William J. Goode, *World Revolution and Family Patterns* (New York, 1970), p. 6.

8. Charles Larsen, *The Good Flight: The Life and Times of Ben B. Lindsey* (Chicago, 1972).

9. Carl N. Degler, *At Odds: Women and the Family in America from the Revolution to the Present* (New York, 1980), pp. 418–73; Peter G. Filene, *Him/Her/Self: Sex Roles in Modern America* (New York, 1974), pp. 131–240; Edward Shorter, *The Making of the Modern Family* (New York, 1975); Laurence Veysey, "Communal Sex and Communal Survival: Individualism Busts the Commune Boom," *Psychology Today* 8 (December, 1974): 73–78.

10. Margaret Mead, *Male and Female: A Study of the Sexes in a Changing World* (New York, 1949).

11. Alfred Kinsey, et al., *Sexual Behavior in the Human Male* (Philadelphia, 1948); Alfred Kinsey, et al., *Sexual Behavior in the Human Female* (Philadelphia, 1953).

12. Marabel Morgan, *The Total Woman* (Old Tappan, N.J., 1973).

13. Betty Friedan, *The Feminine Mystique* (New York, 1963).

14. Howard P. Chudacoff, "The Life Course of Women: Age and Age Consciousness, 1865–1915," *Journal of Family History* 5 (1980): 274–92; John Modell, et al., "Social Change and Transitions to Adulthood in Historical Perspective," *Journal of Family History* 1 (1976): 7–32.

15. Benjamin Spock, *Baby and Childcare* (New York, first published in 1946). For comment on Spock, *see* William Graebner, "The Unstable World of Benjamin Spock: Social Engineering in a Democratic Culture, 1917–1950," *Journal of American History* 67 (1980): 612–29; Michael Zuckerman, "Dr. Spock: The Confidence Man," in *The Family in History*, ed. Charles Rosenberg (Philadelphia, 1975), pp. 179–207.

16. A. S. Neill, *Summerhill: A Radical Approach to Child Rearing* (New York, 1960).

17. Olivette Simmons, "The Care of America's Dependent Children" (Senior Thesis, Union College, 1976).

18. Thomas J. Espenshade, "The Value and Cost of Children," *Population Bulletin* 32 (April, 1977).

19. Alex Comfort, *The Joy of Sex: A Cordon Bleu Guide to Lovemaking* (New York, 1972); Shere Hite, *The Hite Report: A Nationwide Study on Female Sexuality* (New York, 1976); William H. Masters, et al., *The Pleasure Bond: A New Look at Sexuality and Commitment* (Boston, 1975).

20. Gail Sheehy, *Passages: Predictable Crises of Adult Life* (New York, 1976).

21. W. Andrew Achenbaum, *Old Age in the New Land: The American Experience since 1790* (Baltimore, 1978); David H. Fischer, *Growing Old in America* (New York, 1977).

22. Beth J. Soldo, "America's Elderly in the 1980s," *Population Bulletin* 35 (November, 1980); Irene B. Taeuber and Conrad Taeuber, *People of the United States in the 20th Century* (Washington, 1971), pp. 133–74.

23. Filene, *Him/Her/Self,* is an excellent place to begin a study of this topic.

24. Jessica Mitford, *The American Way of Death* (New York, 1978); Marcia Seligson, *The Eternal Bliss Machine: America's Way of Wedding* (New York, 1973).

10

PLENTY OF PEOPLE?

A curious paradox emerges regarding the effects of the demographic revolutions when we shift our focus from individuals and their families to the aggregate. More and more control over the basic rhythms of our lives has brought considerable uncertainty about the future, as individual and legislative whim have replaced biological and sociological regularities as determining influences. Prior to 1800, individuals' experiences with birth, death, marriage, and migration were unpredictable, but many of the demographic characteristics of the total population were remarkably stable. After 1920, individuals gained greater control over their lives, and variations in experience began to disappear. But the increased ability of men and women to determine their own future, and their willingness to pursue individual interests in place of the needs of their families or communities, have often produced dislocations for society as a whole, as collective patterns of childbearing, marrying, moving, and even dying have changed abruptly and for reasons that often remain obscure. Although the problems facing society as a whole which result from the revolutions in Americans' lives may not be any more serious than those confronting modern families (and often they are closely related), they certainly merit consideration in order to complete this study.

In spite of extraordinary limits on childbearing, the increase in number of the American people continues to be a matter of considerable importance to the shape of their society. Between 1920 and 1970, the number of Americans grew from about 106 million to 208 million people. Surprisingly, the rate of increase has been slower since 1920 than at any time since the early

seventeenth century, for if the growth rates of the late eighteenth and early nineteenth centuries had prevailed after 1920,
the 1970 census would have counted about 425 million Americans. Nonetheless, in absolute terms, more than 100 million
more Americans needed food, clothing, houses, jobs, schools, and
other goods and services in 1970 than in 1920. Fortunately, the
physical size of the United States and the tremendous strength of
the American economy have enabled the overall growth of the
population to occur with surprising ease.

Although the rate of growth has been relatively low since
1920, interest in the subject has been intense. In the 1920s and
early 1930s, growth itself attracted less attention than did the
cause of the increase. Fearing the influence of certain groups of
immigrants, many commentators opposed growth on the
grounds that the "wrong" kind of people accounted for most of
the increase. Even after immigration restriction and the Great
Depression slowed the influx of foreigners, some Americans
continued to fear for the future of their society on the grounds
that the poorest and least educated people (often immigrants and
black Americans) had larger families than the "better" elements
in society, and hence would eventually replace them.

In the 1930s, the concern over growth shifted away from who
would make up the population to how many people there would
be. The initial fear was that soon growth might disappear and
that the number of Americans might actually begin to shrink.
Record low levels of fertility and an excess of emigration over
immigration combined to produce predictions that the population might soon reach a maximum of about 150 million and then
begin declining.[1] This was an alarming possibility to a nation
accustomed from the days of Benjamin Franklin to consider
growth to be good, so long as it involved the right kinds of people.
Furthermore, Keynesian economics, popular at the time, explained
the depression in terms of underconsumption of goods and services, a problem compounded by a slow rate of population
growth (that is, new consumers). As a result, when it became
clear that American couples were having more babies in the
1940s and 1950s, the general response was enthusiastic. News
magazines and business periodicals hailed the millions of new
consumers who would spur the economy on to new heights.[2]

As the baby boom came to an end, so did public approval of rapid growth. It is unlikely that articles in *Time, Saturday Review,* or *U.S. News and World Report* ever persuaded many couples to have fewer children, but by 1960 the popular press was expressing in public what many couples decided in private—that larger families were mixed blessings. Recently, concern for sheer numbers has been replaced by anxieties about the quality of life, as growth has become the symbol of a complex set of threats to current styles of life. The ability of individuals to pursue an independent existence, and to achieve and maintain high standards of living appear endangered not only by increasing numbers of competitors for jobs, homes, and recreation but also by crowding, pollution, and the cost of running a large and complex society.[3]

Whether the heritage of seeing growth as good has been permanently replaced by visions of increased numbers as mixed blessings or positively bad is uncertain. Rapid changes in attitudes over the past half century suggest that further shifts could occur. If population growth falls so low as to portent decline, and if economic growth becomes very low, it is possible that advocates of larger families or large-scale immigration as the engine of economic advancement will once again become prominent. Whether or not anyone will pay attention is an entirely different matter.

Where people choose to live affects how they earn a living, what kinds of social arrangements they make, and who they argue with and what they argue about in the political arena. Thus, the geographic distribution of the population has had an effect on American society that equals, and perhaps exceeds, the influence of any increase in numbers. In spite of recent migration patterns that have helped reduce regional differences which were pronounced in the nineteenth century, the residential preferences of Americans continue to have a strong impact on the shape of their society.

Decisions by millions of Americans to move off farms and into towns and cities have had a cumulative effect since 1840 which can only be outlined here. The influence on the economy is perhaps most obvious. Greater concentrations of people combined with increased numbers to allow more complex patterns of economic specialization and exchange to develop. As more and more people have shifted their homes from rural to urban settings, industrial, commerical, and service occupations have emerged as the primary ways by which Americans earn their livings.

Many of the most pressing political issues of the twentieth century are directly connected to the need to adjust a political system once oriented to the rural majority of the nineteenth century to the interests of the 70 percent of the people who now live in urban areas. As urbanization has eroded regional differences and contributed to the growth of a complex, national society, the federal government has assumed an ever-larger role in the political affairs of the country. In the twentieth century, a variety of new cabinet posts have been added to the executive branch of the government; all are involved in one way or another with urban problems. In 1903, the Department of Commerce and Labor was created to handle the problems of an urban-based economy. A decade later, matters of commerce and labor both became so important that each was granted a separate department. Forty years later, in 1953, the Department of Health, Education, and Welfare was created, with major responsibilities for programs affecting urban life.[4] In 1966, two additional departments were added (Transportation, and Housing and Urban Development) to better manage urban problems. Finally, in 1977, the demands of an industrial society with a highly mobile population forced the creation of the Department of Energy.

The major domestic political issues of the past half century reflect the new demographic and economic realities as fully as any new governmental structures. One of the most perplexing problems for the federal government has been to develop policies that balance the needs of rural and urban residents. The most basic issue has often been the relationship between prices of goods produced in one area and consumed in the other. Farmers wish to sell food for high prices and buy machinery and other manufactured goods for low; urban residents generally prefer the opposite. Similarly, programs for rural electrification, postal service, and highway building raise the question of how many of the benefits of urban life can be delivered to rural Americans without placing undue tax burdens on city dwellers. The flow of federal money for public works such as highway building or river control has been a matter of some contention, especially when the discrepancy between where taxes come from and where they go to gets too large.

The opposite side of this issue is, of course, the physical deterioration of the urban centers, a matter of some concern in recent years. Virtually everyone admits that cities are necessary to our nation's well-being; debate is vigorous over who should bear the costs of keeping them in repair. Welfare costs also generate rural and urban hostilities. Whatever the financial improprieties of New York City, at least part of that city's budgetary problems can be traced to the fact that poor Americans cross state boundaries more easily than do tax dollars. The reluctance of more rural states to help out hard-pressed cities with large welfare rolls may in part be the heritage of an old suspicion of the city as an immoral place, but it may also reflect a selfish attempt on the part of rural Americans to advocate local solutions for problems with national origins.

The political problems faced by twentieth-century Americans would be complicated enough if the basic division had remained city versus country. But over the last half century, the two-way struggle has turned into a triangular tug-of-war as many Americans moved to suburbs. Because suburban populations are often heavily weighted toward families in the childbearing stage of life, they obviously need different services and public works than do rural areas and cities. That alone would produce some friction. But suburbs have also perpetuated, and even enhanced, racial, cultural, and class separation within American society, confusing the issues at stake and making their solution more difficult. The busing of schoolchildren, one of the touchiest topics of the 1970s, is a clear example of how a simple action (and an old practice in rural areas), is complicated when it becomes a symbol for racial antagonisms, concerns over the quality of education, and the conflict between local and national governments over issues with local impact but whose origins are regional or national in scope.

Americans' residential preferences will continue to produce political problems over the next several decades.[5] The high mobility associated throughout our history with the search for a better place to live culminated in recent years in an ideal, expressed on a local level by the single-family home on a small plot of land. On the national scene, Americans' search for residential perfection has seen climate replace economics, reinforcing the centuries-old tradition of westward migration, especially into the Southwest. As a result, many Americans now live in places that put severe demands on supplies of energy and water. The energy needed to heat (or cool) detached private homes, and to provide transportation to and from places of work, study, and play will be in increasingly short supply over the next decades. It is already apparent that producing equitable policies for our society will be a difficult task. Dependence on foreign supplies of oil will become the central influence on our international relations, if it is not already.

An issue less obvious at the present, but no less important for the future, is water supply.[6] Nineteenth-century Americans were reminded on many occasions of the importance of water, but those lessons seem to have been forgotten in recent decades. With a casual disregard for climatic realities, Americans have moved into regions where water is scarce. So long as the numbers of people in drier regions remained small, the rest of the population could be persuaded to subsidize their choices by building dams and aqueducts. Recently, however, resistance has developed over the extent to which such disregard for climate should be supported. Colorado River waters, important to several southwestern states and Mexico, are the subject of ongoing domestic and international disputes.[7] In the 1960s, the whole of California was taxed to provide northern waters to southern inhabitants. Whether this could be done again on a national level is an open question. The map on page 271, which predicts the regions of the United States that will be short of water in the next fifty years, suggests that much of the western half of the country will soon be affected. Elsewhere, in theory there is enough water to meet the needs of the people, although in practice it has been and will be necessary to institute extensive pollution controls on human, agricultural, and industrial wastes to keep supplies usable.

To the extent that it fostered residential patterns that have and will produce excessive demands for water and energy, the federal Interstate Highway Act of 1956 is among the single most

YEAR OF PROBABLE WATER SHORTAGE BY REGION

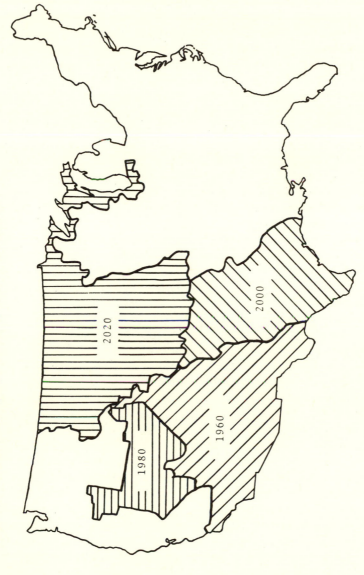

SOURCE: Commission on Population Growth and the American Future, *Report* (Washington, 1972), p. 46.

significant pieces of social legislation of the twentieth century. Only civil rights and social security legislation can match it in importance.

Continued growth and movement into urban areas has produced anxiety over what crowding might do to individual personalities, and hence, to society as a whole. Stimulated by the official closing of the frontier after the census of 1890, Frederick Jackson Turner was among the first to explore the possible negative effects of crowding. Among other things, he feared that Americans would become less free and less innovative. Although not as widely known to historians as Turner's writings, experiments by John Calhoun in the 1950s on the response of rats to crowding renewed nineteenth-century fears that American cities posed real and potential threats to the people who lived in them.[8] Calhoun found that when his rats were too crowded, normal relationships broke down and all sorts of deviant and hostile actions occurred, even with ample food and water. These experiments seemed to offer a scientific explanation for the odd behavior many critics of urban life saw in American cities, and to suggest serious threats to city dwellers and their families.

In fact, the results of urban crowding and a general increase in population density through growth are uncertain. With most metropolitan growth occurring in suburban rings, many urban cores have not had a significant increase in numbers for several decades. Even more important, more spacious housing means that private crowding within families is probably at an all-time low, even though the number of persons per acre or square mile is higher than ever before. Thus, fears of dramatic changes in American personality as the result of congested living conditions seem unwarranted at present.

The composition of the population is as important to American social, economic, and political development as growth and distribution. In the twentieth century, cultural pluralism continues to have important effects, as do new patterns in the age and sex structure of the population. The decline after 1920 of some of the most obvious regional differences which occurred as blacks moved out of the South, foreign born became less common and more evenly distributed, and city life became more standard, could easily be interpreted to mean that the cultural pluralism that has so long been an important part of American history is finally coming to an end. Such a view would be consistent with an emphasis on individual development over group needs. However, upon careful examination of the evidence, it is apparent that Americans continue to identify strongly with other individuals of the same heritage.

Geographers and anthropologists have traced the interaction of ethnic identity with national influences in twentieth-century American communities as diverse as Kalamazoo, Michigan, Cullman County, Alabama, western Wisconsin, Houma, Louisiana, Westchester County, New York, and El Cerrito and "Rimrock," New Mexico. On the one hand, it is clear that national media, and a national system for product distribution have homogenized styles and tastes around the country. In El Cerrito, New Mexico, migration to cities, television, and automobiles fostered the adoption of some aspects of the more widespread Anglo culture by the predominantly Hispano-Indian community.[9] Similarly, blacks and Cajuns in Houma, Louisiana, began to blend national values and behavior with their own distinctive local culture when white oil-field workers moved into their neighborhood.[10] In Kalamazoo, Michigan, Dutch residents who had been segregated both residentially and economically throughout much of the nineteenth century had, by 1965, become well integrated with many of the other groups in town.[11]

On the other hand, in many communities cultural groups still maintain definite preferences about how they organize their lives. In Westchester County, New York, differences in ethnic background are manifested through membership in churches, volunteer organizations like garden clubs or the volunteer fire company, attendance at public or private schools, and even style of mailbox.[12] In Cullman County, Alabama, German and non-German farmers distinguished themselves not only by the size and quality of their farms, but also by the crops they planted. Germans more often raised potatoes, strawberries, and grapes than did their cotton-conscious neighbors.[13] Similarly, the farmers who dominate the tobacco industry of western Wisconsin are either Norwegian or have Norwegian wives.[14] The five cultural groups living in the part of western New Mexico known to scholars as "Rimrock" differ not only in how they use their land, but also regarding basic attitudes toward nature, time, work, family, property, and community.[15] General regional differences that were once an important part of American history may be on the wane, but cultural heritage is still an important factor in individual lives on the most local level.

Ethnic groups on the local, state, and federal levels have continued to have important political influence since 1920.[16] Parties balance tickets, and presidents appoint Supreme Court members to appeal to and appease contending ethnic and regional interest groups. Cultural hostilities still generate friction, and occasionally violence, within American society. The Ku Klux Klan, which played an important role in politics in the 1920s as a prowhite, pro-Protestant group, still exists, though with considerably less influence. Black, Hispanic, and Indian Americans have exercised increased political power since the middle of the 1950s, when the Supreme Court decision of *Brown* v. *Topeka Board of Education*, in 1954, and the black boycott of buses in Montgomery, Alabama, in 1956, marked new efforts by all Americans to attain full access to the "goods" as well as "bads" of our society. By and large, the political system has contained, and occasionally even resolved, issues with strong ethnic overtones such as voting, education (and busing), welfare, housing, and fair employment practices. But violence still does occur over these issues. Riots expressing the frustrations and anger of various ethnic groups peaked in the 1940s and 1960s, but they have been present in every decade, if not every year, since 1920.

The nature of American society has had a strong influence on foreign as well as domestic policy. In general, American diplomacy has concentrated on Europe and Asia; the former was the source of many immigrants, and the latter was a place of confrontation among rapidly expanding nations. Both Japan and Russia (and, later, the Soviet Union, a country demographically similar to ours) met our westward movement with expansion of their own in the opposite direction. In contrast, Latin America, India, and Africa, all regions with large populations, have received relatively little attention from the public until recent years. The willingness of Americans to ignore Latin America and India is understandable, for until recently few immigrants came from either region. The lack of a tradition of public interest in Africa is significant, for it demonstrates not only the inability of black Americans to make their place of origin as important to the government as persons of European descent have been able to do, but also an insidious form of racism that considers white minority rule in Africa appropriate, even though tyranny and oppression might be opposed in Spain, Greece, Hungary, Germany, and Russia.

On a more specific level, strong American interest in conflicts in Ireland and Israel in the twentieth century is explained more by the presence of large numbers of Irish and Jewish Americans with political influence, than by the scale of conflict or any factor making these struggles inherently more important than strife in Indonesia, Pakistan, or Paraguay. Support for Israel is becoming more complicated, for decisions made several decades ago have produced a society based on separate, single-family residences, which in turn has increased American dependence upon foreign sources of energy, much of which comes from nations hostile to Israel. Similarly, greater awareness of Africa and Latin America in recent decades results, in part, from the fact that our particular pattern of life can be maintained only by access to the resources those areas have to offer. Of course, the growth of population in those regions has contributed to Americans' recognition of their existence as important elements in the political and economic structure of the world.

In view of the long-term importance of pluralism to American society, it is worth asking what will happen if the trends toward individualism and a more homogeneous society succeed in eliminating significant cultural differences. One possibility is that as one source of conflict subsides, others will emerge. James Madison's argument that human beings always find reasons to disagree leads to the conclusion that the elimination of ethnic differences from American society will only enhance the importance of divisions based on class, education, sex, age, marital status, or some other factor. A second possibility is that cultural pluralism will not disappear altogether; instead small groups will consolidate into larger blocs. Scholars have already seen this happening in American religious life.[17] The 1968 report of the Commission on Civil Disorders expressed the fear that in the future American society would be more sharply polarized between black and white.[18] In either case, distinctions among Americans might become *more*, rather than *less*, sharply drawn. A potentially dangerous outcome of such a trend could be the creation of a permanent political majority both able and willing to tyrannize the remaining minorities. It would be especially ironic if an emphasis on individual rather than group identity eventually produced a society in which individual peculiarities could easily be eliminated by majority action.

Changes in the age pyramid of the American population (if it can be called such at present), brought about by millions of private decisions regarding childbearing, offer the most striking examples of how extensive individual control has led to unstable social patterns. Chart 1, page 81, presents the age and sex composition of the population in 1770, 1900, and 1970.

As fertility has fallen, older Americans have become an increasingly prominent part of our society both in absolute numbers and as a percentage of the total population. As late as 1920, only 4.7 percent of the people had reached their sixty-fifth birthday, scarcely more than in the late eighteenth century. Without large numbers of immigrants between the ages of fifteen and forty-five, the proportion of older Americans would have been higher in 1920 than it was, since fertility, the major determinant of the age pyramid in the absence of migration, had been falling for over a century. With the continuation of low levels of childbearing and the curtailment of immigration, the proportion of Americans sixty-five and older began to rise, until they accounted for 6.8 percent of the population in 1940. By 1960, the corresponding figure stood at 9.2 percent; it reached 10.7 percent in 1976.[19]

In the absence of well-defined family or social roles for large numbers of older women and men, Americans have been relatively free to experiment with how best to adjust social arrangements to meet their needs. The initial response, fostered by high unemployment and other economic problems of the 1930s, was to treat older Americans as people who required pensions and health care, but who should retire from any productive role in society. Social security legislation was passed as the proportion

of older Americans became an important element in the population, a development that repeated the experience of many European countries whose populations had aged earlier, at least partly
because many young adults moved to America.[20] As it became
apparent that the trend to an older population would continue,
and that, unlike children, older "dependents" voted, both major
political parties made efforts to provide the goods and services
needed and wanted by this new political force. In the 1970s, when
one in ten Americans was at least sixty-five, the same group
accounted for one of every six potential voters. This group's
influence is apparent not only in regular increments in old age
assistance payments and medical insurance, but also in recent
legislation severely restricting mandatory retirement of older
workers, and tax reforms designed to protect the ability of older
Americans to maintain their own homes. Americans over sixty-
five increasingly have sought productive places in our society,
arguing that with better medical care, the automatic association
of age and infirmity is no longer as valid as it may have been in the
past.

Because fertility is the dominant influence on the age composition of a population, the millions of personal decisions by husbands and wives that resulted in the long-term decline in
fertility, followed by the baby boom, and a return to lower levels
of childbearing, have created a rather peculiar age "pyramid" in
this century. In a normal age pyramid, younger people are more
numerous than older people; in the contemporary American
population, relatively small age groups are surrounded by more
numerous groups, and vice versa. As these groups grow older,
distinct cycles of pressure and ease on various institutions have
occurred, and will continue to do so.

The results of the baby boom are a good example.[21] The need
for new schools and more teachers in the 1950s and early 1960s
was one of the first demands placed on society as a consequence
of larger families and higher birthrates in the late 1940s and early
1950s. In recent years, contracting school-age populations have
led to cutbacks, rather than increases. Both processes have
occurred with considerable public debate and discord. As the
children of the baby boom years grew older, new pressures
emerged. The youth culture of the late 1960s reflected the fact

that the boom babies were old enough to have economic and political influence independent of their parents. Since 1970, as large numbers of young Americans have sought their own homes and work, the amount of available housing and jobs has had to increase rapidly. Once the economy has incorporated this influx of new producers and consumers, it is possible that the peculiar economic patterns of the 1970s, including high inflation, high unemployment, and record numbers of Americans working, all at the same time, may disappear. Similarly, the rapid increase in housing costs may subside as the number of new families decreases. Because young males between the ages of fifteen and twenty-five are particularly prone to crime, police forces found themselves faced with crime waves which were, at least in part, the result of decisions on childbearing made by couples two decades earlier. Recently it has occurred to many Americans that similar pressures will eventually come to bear on the social security system; the result has been an uncharacteristic effort within the political system to anticipate the long-term consequences of past demographic actions. Curiously, Americans have granted both credit and blame to politicians, especially presidents, for the good and bad outcomes of basic demographic changes over which they had no control.

Changes in the age composition can have beneficial as well as detrimental effects on society. In certain periods, for example, productivity can be very high as the result of an unusually large number of workers. In 1770, only 47.4 percent of the people were between the ages of sixteen and sixty, years when they were presumably most productive.[22] Two centuries later, in 1970, the corresponding figure was 57.2 percent. Because of the baby boom, and the immigration of more children after 1940, this latter figure was below the 64.6 percent of the people who were prime workers in 1940. Over the next several decades, the most productive age groups should once again become more prominent in the total population, before declining early in the next century as the children of the 1940s and 1950s begin to retire in significant numbers.

For many individuals, their place in the age pyramid has had a significant effect on their economic and social opportunities.[23] Individuals born between 1930 and 1945 will, in general, always have relatively good opportunities, since they have relatively few peers with which to compete, and the large number of Americans younger than they create demands that provide excellent employment opportunities. In contrast, those born from 1945 to 1960 will live out their lives in the midst of large numbers of competitors for the same jobs, houses, and other opportunities. In addition, the fewer babies born after 1960 has already meant fewer openings for teachers, baby-food makers, and others whose jobs involve caring for the needs of children. The effects of the age pyramid on society have probably been greater in the twentieth century than they would have been earlier, because of a recent tendency for all members of a generation to experience major transitions in life at increasingly standard ages, and because the life cycles of men and women have become more similar. The future of the social security system, when people born between 1945 and 1960 reach retirement age, is a matter of some concern, for the current system is based on funding provisions that assume there will always be more persons paying in revenues than there will be pensioners.

In 1950, American women outnumbered men for the first time since the resettlement of the continent began in the early seventeenth century. In 1950, there were 986 men for every 1,000 women, a decrease from the 1,041 men for every 1,000 women present in 1940. Partly because of differences in life chances, and partly because females now make up the majority of immigrants, the trend has continued, until, in 1976, there were only 948 men per 1,000 women. The imbalance is particularly pronounced among older Americans, for in 1976 there were only 690 men sixty-five or older for each 1,000 women. As recently as 1930, men still outnumbered women in those ages by a slight margin.

It is tempting to see this change as one of major consequence for American society, but on reflection it is hard to discern any significant result from the new balance between the sexes, unless one wishes to count that part of the increase, in small or female-headed households, that can be attributed to widows living alone. New roles for twentieth-century women can be more readily explained as products of declines in childbearing and the debate over the family, than as changes in social relations brought about by having more women than men.[24] The entrance of mothers into the labor market has been of far greater economic consequence than any new supply of single women who, in the early part of this century, were most likely to work outside their home. Hopes that a majority of the "guardians of civilization" might redirect the nature of American society have been weakened by the lack of substantial change in the political system since women began to vote, and by the apparent continuity of American economic goals, even though women now own over half of all property. Furthermore, as roles assigned to each sex converge, shifts in the sex ratio will have even less potential consequence than they do at present. To the extent that changes in the sex ratio have any important influence on society, it will be through their effects on marriage, childbearing, life expectancy, and migration rather than by direct impact.

A full understanding of our history is possible only if we grasp the significance of the revolutions in Americans' lives that have occurred over the past two centuries. Our world is both strikingly different from that of our ancestors, and unique in human experience. More and more, we control our own lives, even to the point of freeing ourselves from the most rigorous aspects of natural selection, and the oldest of social customs. Whether or not such extensive control is, in the long run, desirable may be open to question, for as individuals have acquired a greater capacity to determine their future, basic demographic patterns have become less predictable, and social arrangements built on those patterns have broken down.

The process of adjusting to new demographic realities is still in progress, partly because the revolutions are not yet completed, and partly because social arrangements that were in accord with past population patterns have a resistance to change which comes from hundreds, if not thousands, of years of practice. Given the uniqueness of the modern world, and its short duration in the context of human history, it is not yet certain what current demographic patterns will remain in the future. No doubt the twin processes of demographic change and social adjustment will continue in the future, accompanied, as in the past, by tensions and anxieties. A better understanding of what has happened to our lives, our families, and our society may make the process of adjustment easier; but we must resist the claims of those ready to prescribe rigid solutions (whether founded in theory, a reverence of the past, or professional arrogance) for problems arising from changes that are still underway.

The fact that many other peoples have shared in some, though not all, of the revolutions that have altered Americans' lives, affects the way we interpret our own past. For centuries, Americans have seen themselves as a people set apart, with a special mission in the world. The Puritans went on their "errand into the wilderness" to preserve true religion for the rest of humanity. The founding fathers fought Great Britain, both in 1775 and 1812, at least in part to save republican government for the world. By the middle of the nineteenth century, Americans felt their manifest destiny was to bring the virtues of "civilization," first to North America, and then to the rest of the world. In this century, Americans have fought wars to make the world safe for democracy, and have destroyed people and villages in order to save them from "erroneous" sets of values.

From the perspective of demographic history, this behavior is both curious and cruel. In the most basic aspects of their lives, that is, in their experiences with and expectations about birth, death, marriage, and migration, Americans are remarkably similar to any number of other peoples. English, Russians, Japanese, Germans, and groups of Chinese are among those whose lives have been transformed in similar fashions to Americans'. In many ways, our lives have more in common with contemporary Japanese and Russians than with eighteenth-century Americans.

If this is so, is it possible to sustain a view of American history that sees our past as unique? The answer is both "no," and "yes." On the one hand, many of the central trends in American history have occurred elsewhere. Urbanization, lower fertility, and longer, healthier lives are part of the history of a number of other peoples. On the other hand, the vast majority of men, women, and children alive today, and in the past, have not experienced the fundamental changes in the basic rhythms of life that Americans today share with about one-quarter of the world's inhabitants. It is possible that the revolutions in Americans' lives will never be repeated in the future. In addition, considering immigration, westward migration, and the timing of changes in fertility, mortality, and marriage, it is clear that the revolutions that transformed Americans' lives were similar but not identical to those experienced by other peoples. Perhaps the most fundamental difference distinguishing the United States from other countries that have undergone similar changes is the extraordinary diversity of its people. Other countries, such as Argentina, received large numbers of immigrants; other countries, such as the Soviet Union, are continental nations with a history of rapid growth and cultural pluralism. But no other nation received as many people of as many different backgrounds for as long a period as did the United States.

Since demographic patterns have been so important in shaping our past, it is appropriate to ask what influence they will have in the future. In addition to the extensive comments made earlier on the prospects for continuing the demographic revolutions within Americans' lives, and the need for further adjustments in families and more general social structures, two brief observations remain to be made.

The future course of American history will be significantly altered if the homogenization of the people that has been visible in this century continues to the point where even cultural pluralism on a local level disappears. If that should happen, then both the violence and concern for individual freedoms which have long been a part of American life may be replaced by a more peaceful and more oppressive majority. If American society ever does become a "melting pot," the resulting alloy could be a danger to other institutions, for reasons quite different from those feared by the racists and social Darwinists of the late nineteenth and early twentieth centuries.

The rapid increase in world population in recent decades is also of great importance to our future. Many Americans currently alive can anticipate living in a world they will share with 10 to 15 billion other people, numbers that stagger the imagination. In such a world, we and our descendents will be deeply influenced, not only by our own decisions regarding birth, death, marriage, and migration, but by the decisions of billions of people who live beyond the borders of the United States. Thus, worldwide demographic patterns are of vital importance to us, if only because the

future development of the American economy, and our international influence, both will be restricted severely by extensive
growth abroad. In foreign affairs, as in domestic matters, demographic realities will continue to challenge and perplex not only
America's leaders, but also her people.

The importance of basic demographic behavior in determining
the rhythms of people's lives, and hence their history, is fundamental to any demographic perspective on history. However, the
significance of birth, death, marriage, and migration extends well
beyond individual experiences, into family patterns, political
structures and issues, economic relations, and social arrangements. Demographic history, which appears simple on the surface, is extraordinarily complex when pursued through all its
relationships. But, however complicated the story may become,
as we work out from basic patterns to more subtle relationships,
we can keep the fundamentals in mind by remembering the
passage from T. S. Eliot's poem, *Sweeney Agonistes,*

> Birth, and copulation, and death.
> That's all the facts when you come to brass tacks:
> Birth, and copulation, and death.[25]

Notes

1. Harold F. Dorn, "Pitfalls in Population Forecasts and Projections,"
in *Demographic Analysis: Selected Readings,* eds. Joseph J. Spengler and Otis D.
Duncan (Glencoe, Ill., 1956), pp. 69–90.

2. Marti Berthold, "The Interrelationship of History and Demography as Reflected in Periodical Literature from 1920 to 1970,"(Paper,
Union College, 1971).

3. *See* the special issue, "The No-Growth Society," *Daedalus* 102 (Fall,
1973).

4. The creation of a separate Department of Education under Carter
was seen by many as a political payoff. Its future under the Reagan
administration is, at present, uncertain.

5. Jeanne C. Biggar, "The Sunning of America: Migration to the
Sunbelt," *Population Bulletin* 34 (March, 1979); U.S. Commission on Popu-
lation Growth and the American Future, *Population, Distribution, and Policy*
(Washington, 1972).

6. Norris Hundley, *Dividing the Waters* (Berkeley, 1966); Ronald G. Ridker, "Future Water Needs and Supplies, with a Note on Land Use," Commission on Population Growth and the American Future, *Population, Resources, and the Environment* (Washington, 1972), pp. 215-28.

7. Norris Hundley, "The Politics of Water and Geography: California and the Mexican-American Treaty of 1944," *Pacific Historical Review* 36 (1967): 209-26.

8. John B. Calhoun, "Population Density and Social Pathology," *Scientific American* 206 (February 1962): 139-48; Harvey M. Choldin and Michael J. McGinty, "Bibliography: Population Density, Crowding, and Social Relations," *Man-Environment Systems* 2 (1972): 131-58.

9. Charles P. Loomis, "El Cerrito, New Mexico: A Changing Village," *New Mexico Historical Review* 33 (1958): 53-75.

10. John Western, "Social Groups and Activity Patterns in Houma, Louisiana," *Geographical Review* 63 (1973): 301-21.

11. John A. Jakle and James O. Wheeler, "The Changing Residential Structure of the Dutch Population in Kalamazoo, Michigan," *Annals of the Association of American Geographers* 59 (1969): 441-60.

12. James S. Duncan, Jr., "Landscape Taste as a Symbol of Group Identity: A Westchester County Village," *Geographical Review* 63 (1973): 334-55.

13. J. Allen Tower and Walter Wolf, "Ethnic Groups in Cullman County, Alabama," *Geographical Review* 34 (1944): 276-85.

14. Karl B. Raitz and Cotton Mather, "Norwegians and Tobacco in Western Wisconsin," *Annals of the Association of American Geographers* 61 (1971): 684-96.

15. Evon Z. Vogt and Ethel M. Albert, *People of Rimrock: A Study of Values in Five Cultures* (Cambridge, Mass., 1966).

16. Mark R. Levy and Michael S. Kramer, *The Ethnic Factor: How America's Minorities Decide Elections* (New York, 1973). For an interesting series of articles on one state, *see* Roger Daniels and Spencer C. Olin, Jr., eds., *Racism in California: A Reader in the History of Oppression* (New York, 1972).

17. Will Herberg, *Protestant, Catholic, Jew: An Essay in American Religious Sociology* (Garden City, N.Y., 1955).

18. U.S. National Advisory Commission on Civil Disorders, *Report* (Washington, 1968).

19. Irene B. Taeuber and Conrad Taeuber, *People of the United States in the 20th Century* (Washington, 1971), pp. 133-74.

20. Roy Lubove, *The Struggle for Social Security 1900-1935* (Cambridge, Mass., 1968).

21. Leon F. Bouvier, "America's Baby Boom Generation: The Fateful Bulge," *Population Bulletin* 35 (April 1980).

22. *See* Chart 1, p. 81.

23. Richard A. Easterlin, *Birth and Fortune: The Impact of Numbers on Personal Welfare* (New York, 1980); P.M.B. Harris, "The Social Origins of American Leaders: The Demographic Foundations," *Perspectives in American History* 3 (1969): 159-344.

24. Suzanne Keller, "The Future Status of Women in America," in Commission on Population Growth and the American Future, *Demographic and Social Aspects of Population Growth* (Washington, 1972), pp. 267-87; Jeanne C. Ridley, "On the Consequences of Demographic Change for the Roles and Status of Women," ibid., pp. 290-304.

25. T. S. Eliot, *Collected Poems 1909-1962* (New York and London, 1963), p. 119. The author wishes to thank Faber and Faber, Ltd., of London, and Harcourt Brace Jovanovich, Inc., of New York, for granting permission to quote this passage.

SELECTED BIBLIOGRAPHY

Since I first became interested in demographic history fifteen years ago, I have consumed a wide range of materials that have contributed to this book. My first draft included a bibliography of 190 pages, listing about 1,500 items. Rather than publish that here, a separate guide to the literature of American demographic history is in preparation. Nevertheless, a short bibliography is in order, both to give additional recognition beyond the notes to those scholars whose work has been especially important to me, and to provide readers with some brief suggestions of where they might begin to explore some of the main topics considered in the text. This is, however, no more than the tip of the iceberg, and many scholars, in a number of different disciplines, will have to wait until the guide is published to receive full recognition. I extend my deepest appreciation and thanks to them now.

On the assumption that many of the readers of this work are not trained in demography, it is appropriate to begin by mentioning several useful textbooks on the subject. Ralph Thomlinson, *Population Dynamics*, 2d ed. (New York, Random House, 1976) is one of the clearest and most readable texts. Another helpful text which includes a great deal of data for the American population up to 1960 is Donald Bogue, *Principles of Demography* (New York, John Wiley and Sons, 1969). Two more technically oriented works are George W. Barclay, *Techniques of Population Analysis* (New York, John Wiley and Sons, 1958), and Henry S. Shryock, Jacob S. Siegel and Associates, *The Methods and Materials of Demography*, 2 vols. (Washington, D.C., G.P.O., 1971).

Aside from several works published in French by Louis Henri, and E. A. Wrigley, ed., *An Introduction to English Historical Demography* (New York, Basic Books, 1966), there are no general texts on how to do demographic history. T. H. Hollingworth, *Historical Demography* (Ithaca, N.Y., Cornell University Press, 1969) does provide some discussion of techniques in what is now a quite dated bibliography. Almost no American works are mentioned in that volume. Readers can find helpful examples of particular kinds of studies, and get some sense of some of the main issues of historical demography, in the following three collections: D. V. Glass and D.E.C. Eversley, eds., *Population in History* (Chicago, Aldine, 1965); D. V. Glass and Roger Revelle, eds., *Population and Social Change* (New York, Crane, Russak, 1972); and Maris Vinovskis, ed., *Studies in American Historical Demography* (New York, Academic Press, 1979). E. A. Wrigley, *Population and History* (New York, McGraw-Hill, 1969) is important, but more for issues than techniques.

It is difficult to isolate all the various influences, both personal and intellectual, that have helped convince me of the fundamental importance of birth, death, marriage, and migration in people's lives. The following have helped to focus my thoughts, if not necessarily to generate them: Jessie Bernard, *The Sex Game: Communication Between the Sexes* (New York, Atheneum, 1968); Elliot Chapple, *Culture and Biological Man: Explorations in Behavioral Anthropology* (New York, Holt, Rinehart and Winston, 1970); James T. Fawcett, ed., *Psychological Perspectives on Population* (New York, Basic Books, 1973); C. S. Ford and F. A. Beach, *Patterns of Sexual Behavior* (New York, Harper and Row, 1951); Clifford Geertz, *The Interpretation of Cultures: Selected Essays* (New York, Basic Books, 1973); Paul C. Glick, *American Families* (New York, John Wiley and Sons, 1957); Edward T. Hall, *The Hidden Dimension* (Garden City, N.Y., Doubleday, 1966); Weston LaBarre, *The Human Animal* (Chicago, University of Chicago Press, 1954); and John B. Lansing and Leslie Kish, "Family Life Cycles as an Independent Variable," *American Sociological Review* 22 (1957): 512-19. In addition, *see* the special issue of the *Journal of Social Issues* 30 (1974), on "Population Policy and the Person: Congruence or Conflict?"

The importance of the family is a major concern of my study, and a number of the studies just listed relate to family life. However, there are several other works that deserve mention here. Journal literature is extremely important, not only in the *Journal of Family History* (1976 to present), but also in the special issues of *Daedalus* 106 (Spring, 1977); the *Journal of Interdisciplinary History* 2 (Autumn, 1971), 5 (Spring, 1975), and 6 (Autumn, 1975); and the *Journal of Marriage and the Family* 35 (August, 1973). John Demos and Sarane S. Boocock, eds., *Turning Points: Historical and Sociological Essays on the Family* (Chicago, University of Chicago Press, 1978) is a supplement to the *American Journal of Sociology* 84 (1978). In addition, many important articles have been collected in Michael Gordon, ed., *The American Family in Social-Historical Perspectives*, 2d ed. (New York, St. Martin's Press, 1978). Gordon's book, *The American Family: Past, Present, and Future* (New York, Random House, 1978) is one of the few texts to take a consciously historical approach.

Studies of European families in the past have had a major influence on me and other specialists in family and demographic history. Two French scholars must be given recognition. It is difficult to envision the field today without the influence of Philippe Aries, *Centuries of Childhood: A Social History of Family Life* (New York, Random House, 1962), translated by Robert Baldick, on attitudes and values, or the technical contributions of Louis Henri in *Anciennes Familles Genevoises* (Paris, Presses Universitaires de Frances, 1956), and his study with Etienne Gautier of *La Population de Crulai Paroisse Normande* (Paris, Presses Universitaires de Frances, 1958). Although they do not rank with Aries's and Henri's efforts, Peter Laslett, ed., *Household and Family in Past Time* (Cambridge, England, Cambridge University Press, 1972), and Edward Shorter, *The Making of the Modern Family* (New York, Basic Books, 1975) deserve attention.

An important early effort to study American families was Edmund S. Morgan, *The Puritan Family: Religious and Domestic Relations in Seventeenth-Century New England* (Boston, Public Library, 1944; rev. and enl., New York, Harper and Row, 1966). However, probably the studies with the greatest impact were John Demos, *A Little Commonwealth: Family Life in Plymouth Colony* (New York, Oxford University Press, 1970), and Philip J. Greven, Jr., *Four Generations: Population, Land, and Family in Colonial Andover, Massachusetts* (Ithaca, N.Y., Cornell University Press, 1970). These books were outgrowths of earlier articles, and reflected the influence of Bernard Bailyn, *Education in the Forming of American Society* (Chapel Hill, University of North Carolina Press, 1960).

At a critical point in the evolution of this study, I was significantly influenced by the work of geographers who had a historical perspective. The work of Donald Meinig was especially important, not only through his brilliant essay, "The Mormon Culture Region: Strategies and Patterns in the Geography of the American West, 1847-1964," in *Annals of the Association of American Geographers* 55 (1965): 191-220, but also his books, *The Great Columbian Plain* (Seattle, University of Washington Press, 1968); *Imperial Texas: An Interpretive Essay in Cultural Geography* (Austin, University of Texas Press, 1969); and *Southwest: Three Peoples in Geographical Change 1600-1970* (New York, Oxford University Press, 1970). Terry G. Jordan has produced several interesting local studies, including "The Imprint of the Upper and Lower South on Mid-Nineteenth Century Texas," *Annals of the Association of American Geographers* 57 (1967): 667-90, and "Between the Forest and the Prairie," *Agricultural History* 38 (1964): 205-16. Wilbur Zelinsky, *The Cultural Geography of the United States* (Englewood Cliffs, N.J., Prentice-Hall, 1973) is packed with both information and insight.

On a much different scale, but still related to issues of geography and environment, I want to mention Alfred W. Crosby, Jr., *The Columbian Exchange: Biological and Cultural Consequences of 1492* (Westport, Conn.,

Greenwood Press, 1972); Reid Bryson and Thomas J. Murray, *Climates of Hunger: Mankind and the World's Changing Weather* (Madison, University of Wisconsin Press, 1977); and Fernand Braudel, *The Mediterranean and the Mediterranean World in the Age of Phillip II*, 2 vols. (New York, Harper and Row, 1972–1974), translated by Sian Reynolds. These works act as important reminders of the fact that a human life and human affairs are often rather small when compared to the scale of ecological and geographic events. Although not always on the same scale, Carl Sauer, *Land and Life* (Berkeley, University of California Press, 1963) offers insights into the many ways humans interact with their surroundings.

By and large, most of this study is based on my reading and synthesis of secondary sources. There are several exceptions, however. Obviously, comments that draw on previous studies I have done ultimately reflect my use of primary sources such as censuses; records of births, deaths, and marriages; and nineteenth-century books for or against birth control. In consulting approximately 100 periodicals it was only natural that I should read some articles that are both about demographic history and are a part of that history by now. For example, Frederick S. Crum, "The Decadence of the Native American Stock. A Statistical Study of Genealogical Records," *American Statistical Association Journal* 14 (1916–1917): 215–22, not only provides data on family size and marriage patterns in early America, but also reflects an anxiety of some in the first decades of this century that older groups of immigrants were committing "race suicide" in the face of large numbers of new arrivals. Finally, the federal censuses which have been taken every ten years since 1790 provide an immense store of information; they have been utilized throughout.

Although the censuses are the major government source of demographic data, there are several other works that readers might wish to consult. The *Statistical Abstract of the United States* has been an annual publication of the Census Bureau since 1880. Special volumes by the Census Bureau such as *A Century of Population Growth* (Washington, D.C., G.P.O., 1909), and *Historical Statistics of the United States, Colonial Times to 1957* (Washington, D.C., G.P.O., 1960) provide data for long periods of American history. In addition, the Census Bureau has sponsored special studies on American demographic patterns, including such important works as the *Statistical Atlas of the United States, 1900* (Washington, D.C., G.P.O., 1903); Irene B. Taeuber and Conrad Taeuber, *People of the United States in the 20th Century* (Washington, D.C., G.P.O., 1971); and Warren S. Thompson and P. K. Whelpton, *Population Trends in the United States* (New York, McGraw-Hill, 1933). Many of these studies provide extensive data, but limit their analysis to the narrowest of demographic questions. One notable exception is the final *Report* and six volumes of research papers published by the President's Commission on Population Growth and the American Future (Washington, D.C., G.P.O., 1972). These are invaluable for recent American demographic history.

One hesitates to begin listing works on birth, death, marriage, or migration because there are so many important studies on each of these topics that to take a "first step" is like venturing onto quicksand. Nonetheless, readers can get some idea of where to *begin* to explore the subjects if they consult the following.

International migration is the easiest to deal with because there are two outstanding synthetic works that offer excellent bibliographies. They are, Maldwyn A. Jones, *American Immigration* (Chicago, University of Chicago Press, 1960), and Philip Taylor, *The Distant Magnet: European Emigration to the U.S.A.* (New York, Harper and Row, 1971). In recognition of the influence of both the man and the work, Oscar Handlin's, *Boston's Immigrants, 1790–1880: A Study in Acculturation,* rev. ed. (New York, Atheneum, 1969) requires mention. Stephen Thernstrom, ed., *Harvard Encyclopedia of American Ethnic Groups* (Cambridge, Mass., Harvard University Press, 1980) offers abundant information.

Movement within the United States has long been the object of study, resulting in numerous state and local studies. One important nationwide survey is Simon Kuznets and Dorothy S. Thomas, eds., *Population Redistribution and Economic Growth, United States, 1870–1950,* 3 vols. (Philadelphia, American Philosophical Society, 1957–1964). The turnover of population within communities has received much attention. One such work which draws together many similar studies and is important in its own right is Stephen Thernstrom, *The Other Bostonians: Poverty and Progress in the American Metropolis, 1800–1970* (Cambridge, Mass., Harvard University Press, 1973). The first study to examine turnover in a precise fashion was James C. Malin, "The Turnover of Farm Population in Kansas," *Kansas Historical Quarterly* 4 (1935): 339–72. Two studies that have made use of census data on place of birth to trace migration flows are Barnes F. Lathrop, "Migration into East Texas, 1835–1860," *Southwestern Historical Quarterly* 52 (1948): 1–31, 184–208, 325–48; and William A. Bowen, *The Willamette Valley: Migration and Settlement on the Oregon Frontier* (Seattle, University of Washington Press, 1978).

Unlike migration, there are surprisingly few historical studies on marriage. George E. Howard, *A History of Matrimonial Institutions,* 3 vols. (Chicago, University of Chicago Press, 1904) is wide ranging but dated. Thomas P. Monahan, *The Pattern of Age at Marriage in the United States,* 2 vols. (Philadelphia, Stephenson Brothers, 1951) provides a good deal of data, although the coverage is uneven. A study of mine on early American marriage patterns that is useful, not only for the information and conclusions, but also because of the numerous additional references in the notes, is Robert V. Wells, "Quaker Marriage Patterns in a Colonial Perspective," *William and Mary Quarterly* 29 (1972): 415-42.

Divorce has received only a little attention from the historical perspective, but two extremely important studies are: Kingsley Davis, "The American Family in Relation to Demographic Change," in Commission on Population Growth and the American Future, *Demographic and Social Aspects of Population Growth* (Washington, D.C., G.P.O., 1972): 239-65; and William L. O'Neill, *Divorce in the Progressive Era* (New Haven, Yale University Press, 1967).

Childbearing and the decline in fertility have received wide attention since the start of this century. Many early works on this topic can be found by reference to my article, cited above, in the section on marriage patterns. Perhaps the most important recent study in terms of both conclusions and techniques is Yasukichi Yasuba, *Birth Rates of the White Population in the United States, 1800-1860: An Economic Study* (Baltimore, Johns Hopkins University Press, 1962). The best place to find long-run data is Ansley J. Coale and Melvin Zelnik, *New Estimates of Fertility and Population in the United States* (Princeton, N.J., Princeton University Press, 1963). Both these works make use of censuses. One of the first studies to make use of family reconstitution to explore fertility patterns in some detail, albeit for a small part of the population, is Robert V. Wells, "Family Size and Fertility Control in Eighteenth-Century America: A Study of Quaker Families," *Population Studies* 25 (1971): 73-82. A recent work that examines trends in the American population since World War II, and summarizes a number of important studies is Leslie A. Westoff and Charles F. Westoff, *From Now to Zero: Fertility, Contraception and Abortion in America* (Boston, Little, Brown and Co., 1971).

Since the control of fertility is an important part of the story, readers may wish to consult the classic work by Norman E. Himes, *Medical History of Contraception*, rev. ed. (New York, Schocken, 1970), or the more recent studies by Linda Gordon, *Woman's Body, Woman's Right: A Social History of Birth Control in America* (New York, Grossman, 1976), and James Reed, *From Private Vice to Public Virtue: The Birth Control Movement and American Society Since 1830* (New York, Basic Books, 1977).

The study of health and death has produced a large and very uneven literature. Readers should begin to explore this topic by references to the texts cited at the start of this essay, and in Louis I. Dublin, A. J. Lotka, and Mortimer Spiegelman, *Length of Life: A Study of the Life Table*, rev. ed. (New York, Ronald Press, 1949). Two works that provide useful data on life expectancy over long periods include S.L.N. Rao, "On Long-Term Mortality Trends in the United States, 1850-1968," *Demography* 10 (1973): 405-20; and Maris A. Vinovskis, "Mortality Rates and Trends in

Massachusetts before 1860," *Journal of Economic History* 32 (1972): 184–213.

The history of medicine and health has been well served by two outstanding journals, the *Bulletin of the History of Medicine*, and the *Journal of the History of Medicine and Allied Sciences*. I have found the books and articles by John Duffy and Richard H. Shryock uniformly helpful. But special note should go to John Duffy's *Epidemics in Colonial America* (Baton Rouge, Louisiana State University Press, 1953), and *Sword of Pestilence: The New Orleans Yellow Fever Epidemic of 1853* (Baton Rouge, Louisiana State University Press, 1966). Of Shryock's works, readers should begin with *Medicine and Society in America 1660–1860* (New York, New York University Press, 1960), and *Medicine in America* (Baltimore, Johns Hopkins University Press, 1966). Two additional studies that influenced my thought, both through their quality and because of when I read them, are Charles E. Rosenberg, *The Cholera Years: The United States in 1832, 1849 and 1866* (Chicago, University of Chicago Press, 1966); and James H. Young, *The Toadstool Millionaires: A Social History of Patent Medicine in America before Federal Regulation* (Princeton, N.J., Princeton University Press, 1961). The works mentioned here are often more important for what they tell us about how people looked at health and death, than they are for describing what people actually experienced.

INDEX

About the Author

ROBERT V. WELLS is Professor of History at Union College in Schenectady, New York. He is the author of *The Population of the British Colonies in America before 1776.*

COMMUNITY COLLEGE
CHARLESTOWN, MASS.